DELAWARE

By William Henry Williams

Photo Research by Carolyn Stallings
Partners in Progress by Ann Frazier-Hedberg

Produced in cooperation with the Delaware State
Chamber of Commerce

Windsor Publications, Inc.
Northridge, California

A Delaware Heritage Commission book,
commemorating the ratification of the
United States Constitution.

The First State

AN ILLUSTRATED HISTORY OF

DELAWARE

By William Henry Williams

Credits/Copyright/Library of Congress

Windsor Publications, Inc.
History Book Division

Publisher: John M. Phillips
Editorial Director: Teri Davis Greenberg
Design Director: Alexander D'Anca

Staff for *The First State: An Illustrated History of Delaware*
Senior Editor: Lynn Kronzek
Production Editor: Lane Powell
Editorial Development: Jill Charboneau, Laurel Paley
Director, Corporate Biographies: Karen Story
Assistant Director, Corporate Biographies: Phyllis Gray
Editor, Corporate Biographies: Judith Hunter
Layout Artist, Corporate Biographies: Mari Catherine Preimesberger
Editorial Assistants: Kathy Brown, Patricia Cobb, Laura Cordora,
  Marilyn Horn, Lonnie Pham, Pat Pittman, Deena Tucker, Sharon
  Volz
Design & Layout: Christina McKibbin

First Edition

Library of Congress Cataloging in Publication Data:

Williams, William Henry, 1936-
  The first state.

  "Produced in cooperation with the Delaware State Chamber of Commerce."

  Bibliography: p. 219
  Includes index.
  1. Delaware—History. 2. Delaware—Description and travel. 3. Delaware—Industries. I. Delaware State Chamber of Commerce. II. Title
F164.W55   1985   975.1   85-22474
ISBN 0-89781-158-5

CONTENTS

*To Dawn Esther Williams and Mark Thomas Williams,
natives of the First State.*

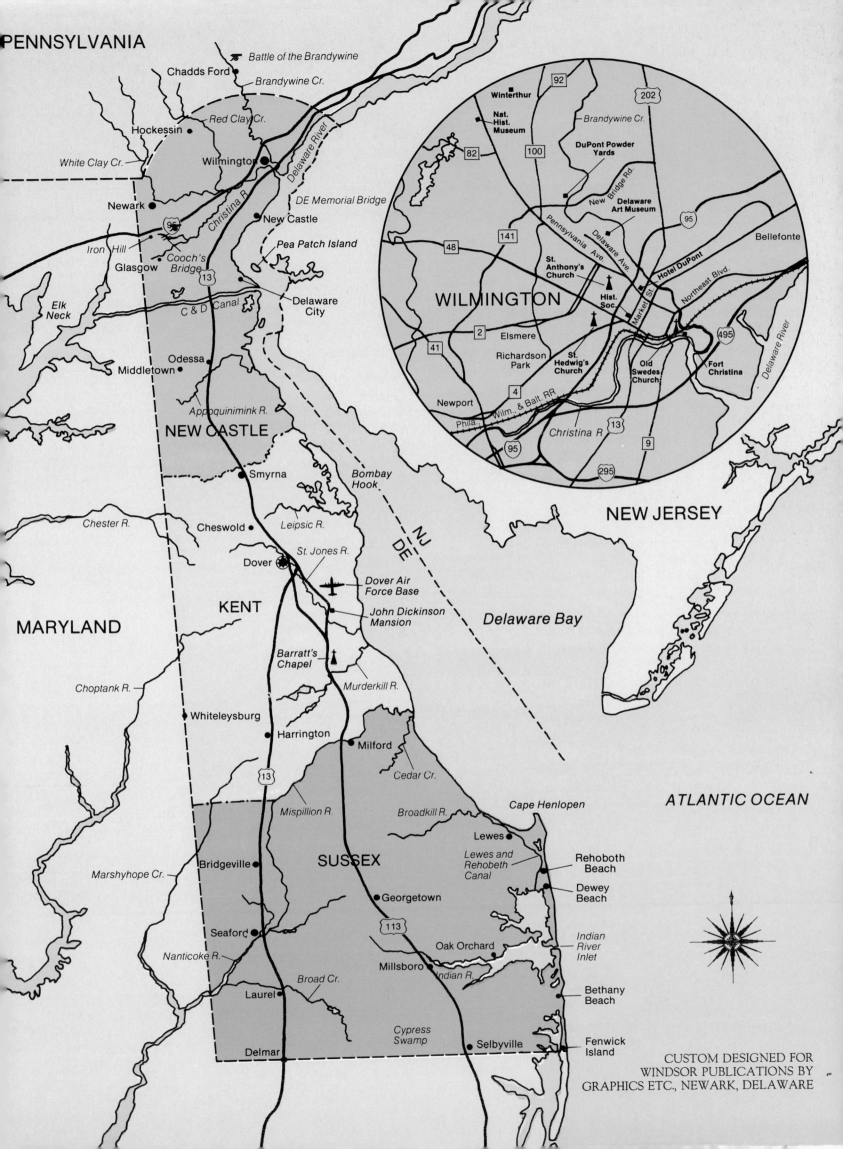

PENNSYLVANIA

Battle of the Brandywine

Chadds Ford

Brandywine Cr.

Red Clay Cr.

Hockessin

White Clay Cr.

Wilmington

Delaware River

Newark

Christina R.

DE Memorial Bridge

Iron Hill

New Castle

Cooch's Bridge

Glasgow

Pea Patch Island

Elk Neck

C & D Canal

Delaware City

Odessa

Middletown

Appoquinimink R.

NEW CASTLE

Smyrna

Bombay Hook

Chester R.

Cheswold

Leipsic R.

St. Jones R.

Dover

Dover Air Force Base

John Dickinson Mansion

MARYLAND

KENT

Barratt's Chapel

Murderkill R.

Delaware Bay

Choptank R.

Whiteleysburg

Harrington

Milford

Cedar Cr.

Mispillion R.

Broadkill R.

Cape Henlopen

Marshyhope Cr.

Bridgeville

SUSSEX

Lewes

Lewes and Rehobeth Canal

Rehoboth Beach

Dewey Beach

Georgetown

Seaford

Indian River Inlet

Nanticoke R.

Oak Orchard

Millsboro

Indian R.

Broad Cr.

Laurel

Bethany Beach

Cypress Swamp

Selbyville

Fenwick Island

Delmar

NJ
DE

NEW JERSEY

ATLANTIC OCEAN

Wilmington Inset

Winterthur

92

202

Nat. Hist. Museum

82

100

Brandywine Cr.

DuPont Powder Yards

New Bridge Rd.

Delaware Art Museum

141

95

48

Pennsylvania Ave.

Delaware Ave.

Bellefonte

St. Anthony's Church

Hotel DuPont

WILMINGTON

Hist. Soc.

Market St.

Northeast Blvd.

2

Elsmere

495

41

Richardson Park

St. Hedwig's Church

Old Swedes Church

Fort Christina

Delaware River

Newport

4

Wilm. & Balt. RR

Phila.,

Christina R.

13

9

95

295

CUSTOM DESIGNED FOR
WINDSOR PUBLICATIONS BY
GRAPHICS ETC, NEWARK, DELAWARE

PREFACE

Throughout most of its history, Delaware has been tagged with a number of labels including: The Diamond State; The First State; and, more recently, The Small Wonder. Because each captures something of the unique flavor of Delaware, each is appropriate. And yet the Delaware story is far too complex to be captured by a clever label or epigram.

Part of the Delaware story supports Voltaire's observation that "history is little else than a picture of human misfortunes." For most of the First State's past, its Indians, blacks, and even its white women were exploited. Indeed, the Delaware story is often about ruthless ambition, greed, and prejudice. The figures who move across its stage include the corrupt, the shortsighted, and the inordinately selfish. But Delaware's history is also about altruistic sacrifice, empathy for the less fortunate, and hope for the future. It embraces visionaries, public servants, and many others who concern themselves with the public good. Above all it is a history of a state that, despite its small size, is really a microcosm of the United States.

Extending only 110 miles from north to south and only thirty-five miles at its widest from east to west, America's second smallest state incorporates in its past most of the major themes of American history. The clash between native Americans and Europeans, the development and exploitation of the land, the struggle for political independence, the rise of political parties, the popularity of religious revivals, the agony of slavery and the staying power of racism, the problems and possibilities created by industrialization and urban growth, the impact of immigration and the implications of suburbanization, have all been central to the development of both the First State and the United States. And yet, for those with an appreciation of the unique, Delaware's past also offers a fascinating array of singular personalities, events, and developments.

By its very nature, this short history must omit many of the important people and events that helped shape the First State. For this reason it is my hope that the reader will next turn to the books and articles of John A. Munroe, Harold Hancock, Carol E. Hoffecker, Clinton Weslager, Bill Frank, Richard Carter, Roger Martin, and others for a more detailed treatment of Delaware's past. Indeed, this history of Delaware draws extensively from their seminal works.

I am grateful to Dr. Munroe, Dr. Hoffecker, Dr. Barbara Benson, Richard Carter, and Helen Williams for reading the manuscript. I am also indebted to numerous other Delawareans for providing information on their state's history, to Brenda Baker for typing the manuscript, to Lynn Kronzek for editorial encouragement and advice, and to the Library of Delaware Technical and Community College, Georgetown, for the use of a writing room.

William Henry Williams
University Parallel Program
Georgetown, Delaware
1985

In "Return Day—Georgetown, Delaware, 1796," artist Robert E. Goodier captures a historic tradition which lives on to the present time. Until the early 1800s, Sussex County voters had to travel to the county seat to cast their ballots. Since the trip was an arduous one, they remained in Georgetown to await the electoral results. Booths, food stalls, and the gathering of candidates all added color to the scene. Courtesy, Bank of Delaware

The Lenni Lenape, whose name roughly translated to "common people," inhabited Delaware, Pennsylvania, and New Jersey until the late seventeenth century. Tribal wars, European settlement, and disease reduced their numbers, and the survivors migrated westward. Courtesy, Historical Society of Delaware

CHAPTER I

RED AND WHITE ON THE DELAWARE

On December 2, 1632, two Dutch-owned ships commanded by David de Vries beat their way northwest towards Cape Henlopen and the Delaware Bay. While still too far away to see land, northwesterly winds carried the fragrance of burning herbs and sassafras to the two Dutch ships. De Vries had been told that this sweet aroma filled the air at the beginning of every winter, when Indians set fire to thickets and underbrush to make hunting easier.

On December 5, Indians were still much on De Vries' mind as he sailed the smaller of his two vessels along the south shore of Delaware Bay. Dropping anchor at one point, the Dutch commander spotted a whale near his ship and commented on the pleasing prospects of the region with "the whales so numerous—and the land so fine for cultivation." The next morning, De Vries' small force, heavily armed and anticipating an Indian ambush, moved up Lewes Creek. There the terrible news, which had reached the Netherlands ten months before, was confirmed. On the west bank lay the burnt remains of a fort, and scattered about were the bleached bones of thirty-two Dutchmen, as well as the skeletal remains of their horses and cattle. The first act in the drama of white-Indian relations in the present state of Delaware had ended in a decisive victory for the native Americans. But there were other acts to follow and they would have a different ending.

❦

Native Americans have lived in Delaware for at least 10,000 years. When Europeans first sailed into Delaware Bay and up the Delaware River, the Indians they encountered called themselves Lenni Lenape which, loosely translated, meant "common people." The English called them the Delawares because they lived along the bay and river named for Lord De La Warr (Thomas West), who had been appointed Governor of Virginia in 1610. Ironically, Lord De La Warr never did see the bay, river, Indians, and state that would perpetuate his name.

The Lenni Lenape occupied the land on both sides of Delaware Bay and on both sides of the Delaware River as far north as its headwaters. They lived in small, self-governing villages that seemed independent of any central authority. What unity existed among the Lenape seemed to rest on a shared language and the sense of being a separate people.

The largest concentration of Lenape villages was north of Delaware in what is now southeastern Pennsylvania. Evidently, northern Delaware was primarily used as a hunting and fishing ground by Lenape warriors and for temporary campsites by their accompanying families. Further south, Lenape settlements seemed more permanent. The land from Bombay Hook south to Cape Henlopen was claimed by a branch of the Lenape called Sickoneysincks, described by a Swedish observer in 1654 as a "powerful nation rich in maize plantations."

Lenape men hunted and fished while their women cultivated corn, beans, squash, pumpkins, and tobacco. They lived in one-room bark huts or wigwams and dug silo-shaped pits in the ground in front of their dwellings to store the bounty from their fields. On fishing and hunting expeditions they paddled dug-out canoes rather than the birch bark variety popular further north. Probably monogamous, the Lenape nevertheless seemed willing to offer the sexual favors of their wives and daughters to European visitors as a hospitable gesture. Indeed, it was the warm hospitality of the Sickoneysincks that caused the Dutch to name present day Lewes Creek, Hoerenkill or Whorekill (Whore's Creek).

The Lenape were about the same physical size as contemporary Europeans with Lenape men averaging

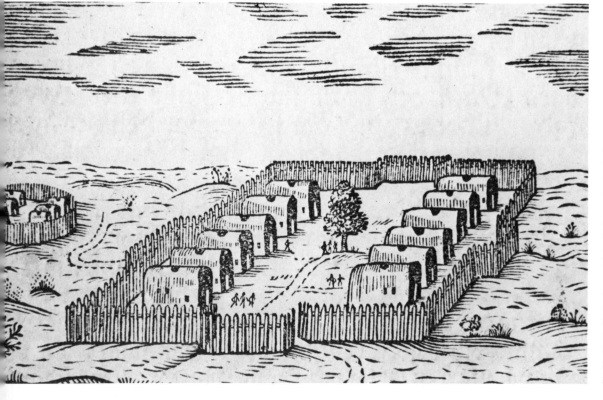

Left
A peaceful, sedentary tribe who practiced agriculture, hunting, and fishing, the Lenni Lenape lived in autonomous villages near freshwater streams. Each village of several hundred people was led by a chief, but no central government united the Lenni Lenape tribes. Courtesy, Historical Society of Delaware

Facing page
Delaware Indians constructed canoes of hollowed-out logs and used these vessels for fishing, trading, and transportation to neighboring villages. Courtesy, Historical Society of Delaware

between 5'7" and 5'10" in height. Ranging in color from light to dark brown, Lenape faces rarely exhibited beards. When facial hair did appear, it was pulled out by the roots with hinged clam shells. (Smooth faces were easier to paint for special occasions.) Older men allowed their hair to grow long, but young males shaved their scalps, leaving only a small lock on top. Bear grease was used by both sexes for hair dressing and for insect repellent.

Because the Lenape lacked a unified central government and were generally peaceful prior to the arrival of Europeans, they were often victimized by more aggressive Indian neighbors to the north and west. The Susquehannocks, or Minquas as the Lenape called them, often left their villages in the Susquehanna Valley to invade Lenape lands. When Dutch fur traders appeared on the Delaware in the early seventeenth century, the Minquas increased military pressure on the Lenape because the latter were seen as commercial rivals who occupied the key geographic location. To cross into the Delaware Valley to get at the Lenape, the warlike Minquas used the Christina and Appoquinimink rivers so often that the Dutch called both water-

ways Minquakill. Later in the seventeenth century, after English fur traders made their way into the northern Chesapeake, the Minquas lost interest in attacking the Lenape. But by that time, however, the Lenape were facing a much more serious threat.

When Europeans first sailed along the Delaware coast, they noted that the land was abundant with such wildlife as black bears, wolves, elk, and deer, and that the streams teemed with fish and beaver. In the past, a natural balance in the wildlife population had been maintained because the Lenape killed only what they needed for food and clothing. The European fur trader changed all of this by cleverly creating insatiable appetites among the Lenape for such imported products as guns, metal utensils, cloth, beads, and liquor. Driven by their newly developed thirst for European goods, the Lenape soon exhausted the beaver and deer population of Delaware in order to meet the fur trader's bartering price.

But even more significant to the Lenape than the change in hunting habits and the deplorable resulting impact on Delaware's wildlife, was the real possibility of cultural suicide caused by an increasing dependence on

Highly regarded for his knowledge of the Delaware Bay and River, Henry Fisher of Lewes (1735-1792) was called upon to choose the site of the first Cape Henlopen lighthouse in 1765. The lighthouse stood at this location until 1926 when it fell into the sea, the victim of a spring storm and shifting sands. Painting by Robert E. Goodier. Courtesy, Bank of Delaware

When Europeans first explored what was to become the First State, they encountered Lenni Lenape villages adjacent to freshwater streams on both sides of the Delaware River. The land boasted an abundance of wildlife which settlers hoped to turn into a profitable fur trade. Courtesy, Historical Society of Delaware

A small group of Nanticoke Indians preserves its heritage through membership in the Nanticoke Indian Association. Most members of the original tribe left Delaware in the 1750s, but a few remained. This unidentified Nanticoke from Millsboro was photographed in Indian dress about 1920. Courtesy, Delaware State Archives

products made in Europe. Along with their brothers in the Delaware Valley to the north, Delaware's Lenape had to make a traumatic choice: they might be allowed to remain in Delaware if they were willing to surrender their native American lifestyle for that of the white man, or they could leave Delaware and move west beyond the white frontier where they might live again like their ancestors. Decimated by the white man's diseases and bewildered by his concept of private property, Delaware's Lenape joined the Indian migration to central Pennsylvania and then to the Ohio country. By the last quarter of the seventeenth century, there were only a few Lenape remaining in Delaware.

South of the Lenape region, a small number of other Indian people spilled over into Delaware from their tribal homelands on Maryland's Eastern Shore. Among these were the Nanticokes whose villages extended up the Nanticoke River as far as a site on Broad Creek

just west of Laurel, Delaware. Despite the ravages of a smallpox epidemic, the Nanticokes seemed to be more successful than the Lenapes in surviving white encroachments. In 1742, however, the increasingly frustrated Nanticokes joined with remnants of a few neighboring tribes in an aborted plot against nearby English settlements. The failure of the uprising caused the discouraged Nanticokes to follow the earlier Lenape example and leave the Delmarva Peninsula. Initially settling in Iroquois country along the upper Susquehanna where they gave their name to Nanticoke, Pennsylvania, the tribe was soon pushed further west and became a scattered people.

In 1705, under pressure from white settlers, a party of Assateague Indians moved north from their home in Worcester County, Maryland to the south bank of Indian River in Sussex County. Some of them joined the ill-fated plot of 1742 and subsequently left Delaware, while other Assateagues remained behind.

Despite the exodus to the West and the heavy toll taken by white man's diseases, a few Indians continued

Henry Hudson sailed his ship, the Half Moon, *into Delaware Bay, and then left to explore the Hudson River, as illustrated here, hoping to find a northwest passage to the Orient. In 1609, he became the first European to view the Delaware. Courtesy, Historical Society of Delaware*

to live in Delaware. Today two "mixed blood" communities, the Moors of Cheswold, northwest of Dover, and the Nanticokes of the Oak Orchard area, on the north bank of the Indian River, are at least partially descended from the remnants of Delaware's native Americans. In the case of the Moors, the Indian ancestors were probably Lenape, while modern-day Nanticokes may actually have as much Assateague, Choptank, or Lenape as Nanticoke blood in their veins. Delaware's Nanticokes are particularly active in claiming their Indian ancestry. To celebrate their heritage, each September they put on a powwow with the

Left
The seal of New Netherland, decorated with a crown and a beaver, reflects the importance of the fur trade to the Dutch colony. Courtesy, Historical Society of Delaware

Right
The Dutch West India Company established trading posts at New Castle and Fort Nassau to strengthen their claim to these lands. Colonists trapped and traded with the Indians for furs to export to Europe. Courtesy, Historical Society of Delaware

proceeds going to the development of the Nanticoke Indian Museum near Oak Orchard.

On August 28, 1609, the *Half Moon,* a Dutch ship commanded by Englishman Henry Hudson, rounded Cape Henlopen to become the first European vessel to enter Delaware Bay. Hudson was searching the eastern coast of North America for a northwest passage to the Pacific and he hoped that Delaware Bay was his route. But Delaware Bay proved to be full of dangerous shoals and, after dropping anchor overnight, a disappointed Hudson was convinced that the sought after passage lay elsewhere. The next day he sailed back into the Atlantic and turned north towards the mouth of the river that would one day bear his name.

On August 17, 1610, Englishman Samuel Argall, an employee of the Virginia Company of London, commanded the second European ship to enter Delaware Bay. While sailing from Virginia to Bermuda, Argall was blown off course and took refuge from the storm in the placid bay behind Cape Henlopen. It was Argall who named the bay in honor of Lord De La Warr, Governor of Virginia.

Despite Argall's visit, over the next three decades the

Dutch, rather than the English, were the most visible Europeans north of Cape Henlopen. By 1616 a Dutch ship had sailed north into the Delaware River, and in subsequent years other Dutch vessels rounded the Cape, bent on commercially exploiting the region beyond. There was, of course, good fishing to be had north of the Cape. A Dutch ship testing Delaware Bay's marine life in 1632 found that one cast of a net brought up enough fish to feed thirty men. But in Europe the beaver hat was the rage, and no matter how fecund the marine life of Delaware Bay and River, it was the presence of that flat-tailed, buck-toothed mammal that really sparked Dutch commercial interest in the region.

Initially, however, the Dutch didn't seem to be all that interested in the new lands claimed for the Netherlands by Henry Hudson. In 1621 the Dutch government granted a charter and monopoly rights on all commerce and colonization in the New World to the Dutch West India Company. Because the Netherlands was at war with Spain to secure its newly won independence, Dutch privateers made fair game of Spanish merchant ships plying the waters between Iberia and

David Peter de Vries, Dutch explorer and trader, was a partner in the Dutch West India Company. He sailed to Delaware in 1632, only to find all the inhabitants of the fledgling colony of Swanendael massacred during an Indian attack. De Vries proved unsuccessful in establishing another colony in Delaware. Courtesy, Historical Society of Delaware

Spanish America. Obsessed with the spoils of war to be found in the Caribbean, the West India Company's efforts to colonize the Hudson and Delaware valleys were only half-hearted. Somehow Dutch trading posts at the present sites of Albany and New York survived. But in the Delaware Valley, the two Dutch settlements established near present day Philadelphia in the 1620s were soon abandoned.

By the end of the 1620s, however, the Dutch West India Company belatedly recognized the profit potential of the fur trade in general and beaver pelts in particular. Fearful of losing its commercial monopoly in the Delaware and Hudson valleys to English interests, the company decided that new, permanent Dutch settlements in both regions must be established. In 1629 the government of the Netherlands enacted a series of measures to entice its citizens to cross the Atlantic and strengthen Dutch claims in the New World. One government measure allowed any West India Company stockholder to purchase an extensive tract of land from the Indians, provided that he would pay the transoceanic passage of fifty adults.

Shortly before the Dutch Government's initiatives

were publicly announced, three stockholders sent seaman Gillis Hossitt to procure Indian land along the Delaware Bay. In exchange for "cloth, axes, adzes, and beads," the Sickoneysincks sold a tract that started in the vicinity of present day Lewes, continued north for thirty-two miles along Delaware Bay, and extended two miles inland. Hossit and his men then exchanged their remaining trade goods for furs trapped by the Indians. The furs proved equal to approximately one-twelfth the value of the annual imports of the Dutch West India Company.

In the spring of 1631, Gillis Hossitt returned with twenty-eight men and, after deciding on a site along Lewes Creek, constructed a brick building with a surrounding palisade. The presence of many swans in the area caused the new colony to be called Swanendael (Valley of the Swans).

Now joined by other Dutch partners including David de Vries, the three stockholders who had commissioned Hossitt's venture addressed the legal obligations mandated by their government in 1629; if they wished to legalize their purchase of Indian land, they would have to transport a sizeable number of new set-

CHAPTER II

EUROPEANS ESTABLISH PERMANENT SETTLEMENTS

t was early October, 1664 and two English ships lay anchored in the Delaware, their restless skeleton crews eyeing Fort Casimir on the West Bank and, next to the citadel, the wooden buildings of the town of New Amstel (New Castle). On a pole towering above the fort, where only yesterday a Dutch flag had been visible, the insignia of England rippled in the breeze.

Ashore English soldiers and sailors, intent on enjoying the spoils of victory, had just looted the fort's storehouse of cloth, shoes, clothing, and liquor. Drunk on Dutch wine and brandy, the enlisted men ignored the commands of their officers as they plundered the homes of New Amstel's Dutch burghers and drove off their livestock. Whatever his riotous troops didn't pillage, the English commander later confiscated for himself and his officers. As for the captured Dutch soldiers, they were summarily packed off to the Chesapeake and sold as indentured servants to English

Left
Queen Christina of Sweden, only seven years of age in 1632 when she inherited the throne, established a Swedish colony in the New World as her father had hoped to do. Courtesy, Historical Society of Delaware

planters.

The sacking of New Amstel marked the beginning of the English phase of Delaware's history, but only after the Swedes, and then the Dutch, enjoyed their day in the sun.

Paradoxically, it was the Dutch drive for commercial profits that brought the Swedes to the New World. Although Sweden was the dominant military power along the Baltic, the Dutch dominated commercial activity in that region. When some Dutch merchants became unhappy with the New World monopoly granted to the Dutch West India Company by their government, they turned to Sweden for a charter that would challenge the Dutch West India Company's dominant position.

In 1637, the New Sweden Company—made up of Dutch and Swedish investors—was chartered with the right to trade from New Foundland to Florida. The *Key of Kalmar* and the *Griffin*, two Swedish-owned vessels commanded by the Dutch former governor of New Netherland, Peter Minuit, set out from Gothenburg, Sweden in the late fall of 1637. Minuit's goal was to establish a Swedish colony in America on territory previously claimed by the Netherlands. Stopping in Holland for repairs, some cargo, and a few passengers, the expedition arrived in Delaware Bay in mid-March, 1638.

Moving up the Bay into the Delaware River, Minuit made contact with five Lenape chiefs. The tribal leaders then sold to the New Sweden Company all of the land on the west bank of the Delaware from Duck Creek in the south to the Schuylkill in the north and stretching westward indefinitely. The Indians, of course, didn't understand the European concept of land ownership and thought that they had merely given the Swedes the right to share in the use of this tract. No wonder there would be future misunderstandings between the Lenape and Europeans!

But at that moment Minuit was more concerned with building a fort and planting crops. He constructed

Left
Settlers set sail from Gothenburg, Sweden, during the fall of 1637 and landed at the confluence of the Christina and Delaware rivers almost six months later. Their arrival marked the beginning of limited and rather short-lived Swedish colonization in the New World. Courtesy, Historical Society of Delaware

Below
Here, a Swedish artist of the late 1600s depicted various aspects of native American life. Three types of dwellings—as well as an Indian burial ceremony and a battle scene of tribal war—are shown. Courtesy, Historical Society of Delaware

Fort Christina on the north bank of the Christina River, approximately two miles from the Delaware on a site presently part of Wilmington's east side. Both the river and fort were named for Queen Christina, the reigning monarch of Sweden, who at the time was only twelve years old.

The future of New Sweden seemed very promising. Subsequent ships brought additional settlers, including Finns living in Sweden and Dutch farmers whose request to come to the New World had been rejected by the Dutch West India Company but accepted by the New Sweden Company. The Indians continued to trade valuable furs, and the first two ships to leave New Sweden for Europe carried a combined total of 1,769 beaver pelts and the skins of 314 otters and 132 bears. Moreover, in 1654, the valley of the Christina was portrayed by the visiting Peter Lindestrom as "suitable for all kinds of agriculture and the cultivation of all kinds of rare fruit-bearing trees." The Christina River, deep and "rich in fish," could "be navigated with sloops and other large vessels a considerable distance." So fertile was countryside along the river, wrote Lindestrom, "that the pen is too weak to describe, praise and extol it." Indeed, "on account of its fertility it may well be called a land flowing with milk and honey."

But even a land "flowing with milk and honey" can be unproductive if mismanaged. By the mid 1640s, intensive trapping had almost exterminated the beaver

population along the lower Delaware, forcing the settlers to turn from the nearby Lenape to the more distant Minquas for pelts. Because New Sweden proved less profitable than anticipated and because certain pressures were brought to bear in the Netherlands, within a few years the Dutch investors sold their shares of the venture, leaving New Sweden as a wholly Swedish undertaking. Since the Swedes had no previous experience in overseas colonization, New Sweden was often badly managed.

In 1643, Lieutenant Colonel Johan Printz, a native of Southern Sweden and the heaviest chief executive in Delaware's history, arrived at Fort Christina to govern New Sweden. A tall man possessing an immense girth (which led the Lenape to call him "Big Belly" and the colonists to dub him "The Tub"), Printz weighed in the neighborhood of 400 pounds. The appointment of this Swedish military officer as governor was significant because it reflected a temporary increase in interest and involvement by the Stockholm government in the struggling colony along the Christina and the Delaware.

For a few years after Printz's arrival, New Sweden took on new vigor, causing those connected with the colony to be optimistic about its future. Through further purchases from the Lenape, the Swedish settlement now claimed the land on both sides of the Delaware Bay and River from Cape Henlopen and Cape May in the south to the falls of the Delaware at present day Trenton on the north. Furs acquired from the Minquas to the west and tobacco purchased from English settlers on Maryland's Eastern Shore were exported to Sweden, while incoming ships brought European-made goods to the Delaware.

Throughout the Swedish occupation of the lower Delaware region, Fort Christina continued to be the chief seaport and commercial center. But Fort Christina's location, two miles from the Delaware, rendered it less valuable in controlling commercial traffic than military posts situated directly on that river. To remedy the problem and strengthen Swedish influence in the entire region, Printz set about building three forts: the first on the east bank of the Delaware just south of the mouth of Salem Creek, the second in the vicinity of the Schuylkill River, and the third on Tinicum Island in the Delaware just south of present day Philadelphia. Printz also made Tinicum Island the capital of New Sweden by constructing his own residence there.

The Swedish colonists adapted well to their New World environment. Their cultivated fields, which dotted the lower Christina Valley and the west bank of the Delaware as far north as the Schuylkill, produced

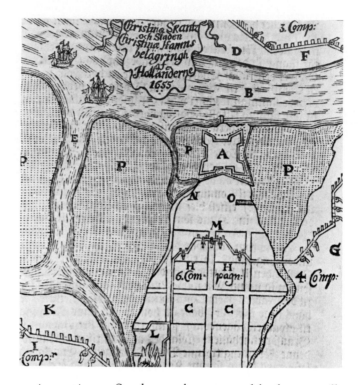

grains native to Sweden, such as rye and barley, as well as the North American Indians' corn and tobacco. Nearby, increasing numbers of livestock grazed. Local Finnish colonists previously had been steeped in the pioneer tradition. While living in Sweden, they had carved out farms from some of that nation's most remote forests. Having built their Swedish homes of logs, they continued to do so in America. The log cabin, first introduced along the Christina and lower Delaware by the Finns, became the standard home of the American pioneer. It was only when the frontier pushed beyond the Mississippi into the treeless Great Plains, that the log cabin gave way to the more practical sod house.

There were also spiritual needs to be met in New Sweden. By 1640, the first Lutheran services in America were being conducted by a Swedish pastor at Fort Christina. The Indians, of course, were regarded as heathens, but settlers always hoped that they could be converted to Christianity. One Lutheran pastor, Johan Campanius Holm, was particularly interested in working with the Lenape and even translated the Lutheran Catechism into the Lenape tongue. Campanius' fascination with the natives' language was partly due to his desire to show its affinity with Hebrew, thereby proving that American Indians were descended from the ancient Israelites.

Despite accomplishments in many areas, New Sweden's existence remained precarious. Increasingly the colony fell under the control of the government in Stockholm where its needs were generally ignored.

From 1648 until 1654, for example, no supply ships or instructions reached New Sweden from the mother country. Without supplies from home, the struggling colony had to make do with goods provided by English and Dutch traders. Yet, the presence of these foreign nationals was an unsettling reminder that both England and the Netherlands regarded the Swedes as trespassers in the Delaware Valley. Despite prior claims to the region, both nations were willing to tolerate the Swedish presence, but only because the three nations were allies during the Thirty Years War in Europe (1618-1648).

A rapidly growing population, fed by shiploads of new immigrants from the Baltic, would have strengthened the Swedish claim to the Delaware Valley. However, the passing of six years without the arrival of one Swedish vessel seriously limited population growth. Indeed, at no time were there more than four or five hundred colonists in all of New Sweden.

Seemingly abandoned by the mother country, surrounded by potentially hostile Indians, and eyed by resentful English and Dutch settlements, New Sweden's survival depended on Governor Printz's ability to maintain good relations with its neighbors. Although he worked hard and was successful at external diplomacy, Printz's authoritarian nature quickly surfaced when faced with internal challenges. In 1653, for example, the leader of a group of twenty-two settlers who were critical of the Governor's rule, was summarily arrested and executed.

While the frustrated Johan Printz grew increasingly apprehensive about the future of New Sweden, only a hundred miles to the northeast on Manhattan Island, an equally authoritarian Peter Stuyvesant waited impatiently for the opportunity to add New Sweden to his domain. The peg-legged governor of the Dutch colony of New Netherland was forbidden by his country to attack New Sweden, but was directed to insist on the maintenance of Dutch rights in the Delaware Valley.

In 1651 Stuyvesant ordered the periodically occupied Dutch base at Fort Nassau to be moved downriver to the site of modern day New Castle. Strategically obstructing the Swedish settlements' access to the Atlantic, the new Dutch post was called Fort Casimir. Although Fort Casimir's garrison was too small to immediately threaten New Sweden, its close proximity to Fort Christina was upsetting to Printz. Realizing that he must raise a relief expedition to reinforce his isolated colony, Printz sailed for Europe in 1653. On his arrival in Sweden, he was pleased to meet an expedition, under the command of Johan Rising, about to set sail for the Delaware.

Rising's fleet arrived on the Delaware River in 1654 and promptly captured the weakly defended Fort Casimir. But that initial Swedish victory gave Stuyvesant the perfect excuse for direct military action against New Sweden. Soon after the capture of Fort Casimir, the Swedish fleet sailed for home, leaving New Sweden unprotected. In late August of 1655, seven Dutch ships—carrying 317 soldiers under Stuyvesant's person-

Facing page
Swedish soldiers and settlers built the garrisoned Fort Christina soon after their arrival. A wall surrounded the small, square fortress ("A" on the map), and the village of Christinaham was laid out in a grid pattern a short distance away. Courtesy, Historical Society of Delaware

Left
Old Swedes Church (1698) served the Lutheran congregation led by Erick Bjork and remained a community center long after Sweden lost its New World claims. English language and customs gradually replaced Scandinavian ones, however, and the Swedes assimilated with the larger population of Wilmington. Courtesy, Historical Society of Delaware

al command—rounded the Delaware capes and beat their way north towards New Sweden. Stuyvesant's superior forces landed between Fort Casimir and Fort Christina, surrounded both Swedish strongholds and then forced each to capitulate.

The victorious Dutch proceeded to integrate the former Swedish colony with New Netherland. The Swedish settlers along the Delaware were offered the choice of returning to the mother country or remaining under the Dutch flag. Only thirty-seven decided to return to their native land. Under Swedish rule the capitol had first been at Fort Christina, then Tinicum Island, and finally, after Printz left, it was moved back to Fort Christina. Under Dutch rule the capitol for the Delaware Valley became Fort Casimir. Alongside Fort

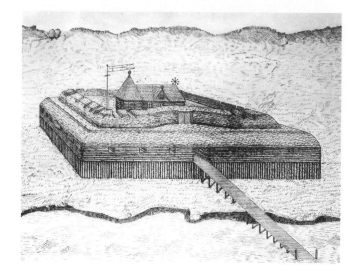

Above
Located on the site of present-day New Castle, Fort Casimir was at the center of a struggle between the Swedish and the Dutch in the New World. In 1651 the Dutch built Fort Casimir a few miles from the Swedish Fort Christina. Minimally protected, the Dutch fort fell to the Swedes before being reclaimed in 1655. Courtesy, Historical Society of Delaware

Left
Dutch settlers laid out the village of New Amstel (now New Castle) near the site of Fort Casimir during the 1650s. The enterprising Dutch traded tobacco, obtained from English colonists, on the world market. Courtesy, Historical Society of Delaware

Casimir, the victorious Dutch laid out streets for the town of New Amstel (present-day New Castle) which, within a few years, contained 110 homes and was the commercial center for the entire Delaware Valley. Despite the fact that the Dutch flag now flew over the region, a new influx of Finns and Swedes joined with immigrants from the Netherlands to swell the population. As labor needs increased, Dutch ships also brought in black slaves, often by way of the Caribbean island of Curaçao.

Initially the settlements along the Delaware were owned and administered by the Dutch West India Company. In 1656, however, the company sold the area south of the Christina River to the Dutch city of Amsterdam. In practice there were now two Dutch colonies on the Delaware, separated by the Christina River.

The Dutch had tolerated the Swedish foothold in America so long as an alliance with Sweden in Europe was necessary. Similarly, the English tolerated the Dutch foothold in North America as long as a European alliance with the Netherlands was useful. With the ending of the Thirty Years War in 1648, English-Dutch relations underwent a remarkable change and the two former military allies became commercial rivals. Indeed, this commercial rivalry became so intense that it led to three Anglo-Dutch wars over the next twenty-five years.

In 1664, James, Duke of York and eventual heir to the English throne, received a grant from his brother, King Charles II, to all lands between the Connecticut and the Delaware rivers. In making this grant, Charles II was obviously claiming for England all of the Dutch

Although Peter Stuyvesant re-
captured Fort Casimir from Swedish commander Johan Rising,
the victory proved costly. It
strained Holland's colonial cof-
fers, and Stuyvesant learned that
the Indians were attacking
Dutch settlements on the Hudson. Courtesy, Historical Society
of Delaware

holdings in North America. And yet, through perverse oversight or inexact knowledge of American geography, the grant didn't include the settlements under Dutch sovereignty on the west bank of the Delaware. But this rather important omission didn't stop the Duke of York from claiming the west bank for himself.

Nor did the fact that Britain and Holland were officially at peace in 1664 deter the future James II from sending a fleet of four ships and 450 soldiers to occupy his new domain. The Duke's fleet struck first at Manhattan Island in late August and then, after the theatrical Peter Stuyvesant was forced to surrender, two British ships headed for the Delaware under the command of Robert Carr. Once in the Delaware River, the English sailed right by New Amstel in order to meet with and win over the upriver Swedes and Finns. After being assured of cooperation, the British moved against New Amstel and the Dutch garrison at Fort Casimir. Outnumbered 130 to 30, Fort Casimir's defenders were quickly overwhelmed by an assault on the rear of the fort which coincided with cannon barrages from the

two English ships stationed in the river. In the brief battle, three Dutch defenders were killed and ten wounded. The English emerged unscathed.

Except for a brief Dutch reoccupation (1673-74), the British ruled the Delaware Valley from 1664 to the American Revolution. New Amstel quickly became New Castle and served as secondary capital to New York City for the Duke's holdings in the Hudson and Delaware valleys. (The Duke gave New Jersey to two of his friends.) For a number of years the Swedes and Finns continued to be the dominant ethnic groups north of the town of New Castle, while the Dutch prevailed in and around it. More importantly, the English element, fed in part by tobacco planters and their slaves pushing east from Maryland, steadily grew. But as British institutions and attitudes were slowly introduced, disputes concerning overlapping land claims contributed to considerable uncertainty among the populace.

To repay a loan, Charles II granted Pennsylvania to William Penn in 1681. It was decided that the southeast-

ern border of Pennsylvania be at least twelve miles from New Castle—a measure initiated to protect the Duke of York's land claims to the south. For the first time Delaware stood as a separate entity from Pennsylvania, and this seventeenth-century decision provided the basis for the present boundary with the Keystone State. Although initially surveyed in 1701 by drawing a circle with a twelve-mile radius centered on the town of New Castle, the precise location of this border was not finalized until 1750.

William Penn was very pleased with the size of his land grant, yet he was greatly concerned about Pennsylvania's lack of direct land access to the Atlantic Ocean. Penn brought his concern to his old friend, the Duke of York. In 1682 the sympathetic Duke turned over to Penn his own claim on all land lying south of Pennsylvania.

This generous gift of the future state of Delaware did not go unchallenged, however. According to the Calverts, the proprietors of Maryland, all of the land south of Pennsylvania belonged to them and, therefore,

was not the Duke of York's to give away. When Charles I granted Maryland to Cecilius Calvert in 1632, the King's charter stated that the eastern boundary of Maryland extended to the Delaware Bay and River, except in those places previously cultivated by Europeans. But a year earlier the doomed Swanendael settlers had plowed and planted fields along Lewes Creek, thus providing legal grounds for denying the Calvert claim to present-day Delaware. Moreover, because the heir apparent to the English throne lay claim—dubious as it might be—to the west bank of the Delaware River and Bay, the Calverts were somewhat cautious about pressing their own territorial ambitions. Between 1670 and 1682, however, Cecil Calvert did make some forty-seven land grants in what is now southern Delaware, causing great confusion.

Despite years of political maneuvering and litigation by the Calverts, William Penn and his descendants successfully held on to Delaware until the American Revolution. In 1685 the English Privy Council ruled that because of the Swanendael settlement, Delaware was not part of Maryland. The Privy Council also ruled that Delaware's southern boundary would run west from Cape Henlopen until it reached a point midway between the Atlantic and the Chesapeake, and then north to intersect with the Pennsylvania line. Unfortunately for Maryland's proprietors, the map used by the Privy Council placed Cape Henlopen at Fenwick Island, almost twenty-five miles south of its present location. As a result, the Calverts were eventually forced to surrender their claim to most of what is now Sussex County.

In spite of the 1685 decision, boundary disputes between Maryland and Delaware continued into the mid-eighteenth century. Finally, the southern border of Delaware was precisely drawn by two Maryland and two Pennsylvania surveyors in 1751. Plotting Delaware's western boundary line, however, proved too difficult for local surveyors, and Englishmen Charles Mason and Jeremiah Dixon were called in to complete the job. In 1765 the two Englishmen finished their Delaware assignment and then turned to marking the boundary between Pennsylvania and Maryland which became the famous Mason-Dixon line.

As soon as they were set off from Pennsylvania in 1681, the west bank settlements comprising the future state of Delaware needed a distinctive geographic label. By late 1682 William Penn was calling them the "Lower Counties." Subsequently, "Lower Counties," "Territories," or even the cumbersome "Counties of New Castle, Kent, and Sussex on the Delaware" were common. Just plain "Delaware" found occasional usage, but it was not until the American Revolution that the name actually stuck.

By contrast, Delaware's three counties officially received their present names at a much earlier date. Initially, under the Duke of York, the only court and public officials in Delaware were stationed at New Castle. But population growth in the southern and central portions of the colony soon created the need for a court and public officials at two other locations.

In 1659 the Dutch established a garrison along Lewes Creek, the first European settlement in the area since Swanendael. Four years later the Lewes settlement—then called Whorekill—was reinforced by forty-one Mennonites from Amsterdam under the leadership of Peter Plockhoy. Despite the sacking of the Dutch fort and Mennonite homes by British soldiers in 1664, population growth continued. The English consequently set up a court in Lewes six years later, with jurisdiction stretching north to include the Saint Jones River Valley. Because "hazards and perils both by land and water" made the trip to this distant court quite difficult, in 1680 farmers along the Saint Jones successfully petitioned for a court in their vicinity.

The jurisdictional areas of these three early courts became the basis of Delaware's three counties. In 1682 Penn gave the two southern counties their modern names of Sussex and Kent, while the town of New Castle lent its name to the northern county. The town that the Dutch had called Whorekill and the English named Deal in 1680, was renamed Lewes (after the county seat of Sussex, England) by Penn two years later. In 1683 Pennsylvania's proprietor directed that a new town named Dover—presumably after Dover in Kent County, England—be built somewhere along the Saint Jones River as the seat of Kent County. Initially, the Kent County court met in a private home at Town Point, near the mouth of the Saint Jones River, before moving seven miles northwest to a tavern located on the future site of Dover. It wasn't until the mid 1690s that a courthouse was completed, however, and it wasn't until well into the eighteenth century that the town of Dover actually appeared.

Penn wished to keep the three "Lower Counties" and Pennsylvania united under one General Assembly, but powerful forces urged their separation. The older town of New Castle, for example, was very jealous of newly-founded, but more rapidly growing, Philadelphia. Furthermore, Anglican leadership, which was dominant in the "Lower Counties," disagreed with the Quaker elite controlling Pennsylvania.

On their part, Pennsylvanians found close political ties with the "Lower Counties" quite objectionable. Al-

though rapidly falling behind in population, the "Lower Counties" had the same number of representatives in the General Assembly as Pennsylvania's three counties and, therefore, could block legislation deemed essential by Pennsylvania.

By 1701 mutual hostility had reached such a point that the representatives of the "Lower Counties" walked out of the General Assembly. Needing American support for his constant struggle in England to maintain his proprietary claims along the west bank of the Delaware, a concerned William Penn persuaded the representatives of the "Lower Counties" to return to the General Assembly. But first he granted them and their Pennsylvania counterparts the right to establish individual assemblies in the future. Consequently, the first separate assembly of the "Lower Counties" met in New Castle during the fall of 1704. Although Delaware would continue to share with Pennsylvania an allegiance to the English crown and would acknowledge the same proprietor and his appointed governor, Delaware was now a separate colony.

Above
Cape Henlopen in Delaware Bay, pictured in this 1780 illustration, formed a safe haven for ships, and the nearby town of Lewes became a home for sailors who regularly maneuvered their vessels up the shallow, rocky waters of the Delaware River to New Castle and Philadelphia. Courtesy, Historical Society of Delaware

Left
Built in about 1722, the New Castle Courthouse served as the seat of government for William Penn's "Three Lower Counties Upon Delaware." It later housed the colonial capitol of Delaware. Courtesy, Historical Society of Delaware

In a scene recreated by Wilmington artist Howard Pyle, members of the Continental Congress leave Independence Hall in Philadelphia to listen to the first public reading of the Declaration of Independence. Only New York's abstention marred a unanimous vote, though Delaware previously had been divided on the issue. The heroic all-night ride of Caesar Rodney ended this deadlock in the Delaware delegation. Courtesy, The American Revolution: A Picture Sourcebook *(New York: Dover, 1975)*

CHAPTER III

FROM DEPENDENCE TO INDEPENDENCE

A curious and excited crowd filed into St. Peter's Anglican Church in Lewes on the afternoon of October 31, 1739. Inside, George Whitefield, a slender, blue-eyed, light-skinned Englishman of twenty-four rose to speak. Despite his relative youth, Whitefield was already a famous evangelist in England and Wales, and his reputation had spread to the American colonies. Although he had arrived by ship from Europe the previous day and had intended to leave directly for Philadelphia, a small delegation of Lewes' leading citizens persuaded him to remain long enough to preach a sermon.

The congregation first noticed the extraordinary force and power in Whitefield's voice—Benjamin Franklin later estimated that it could be heard by as many as 30,000 at a time—and then his crossed eyes, which seemed to mesmerize as they searched the faces of his audience. Finally there was that unmistakable message which warned his listeners that they were "half beast and half devil," and that their only hope for avoiding an eternity in hell was to be reborn in Christ.

William Becket, the Anglican rector at Lewes, was unhappy with Whitefield because he sensed that the great evangelist represented a threat to the Church of England and its staid ways. Whitefield subsequently justified Becket's concern by pointedly criticizing the Anglican Church. In doing so, Whitefield challenged an important English institution and helped set in motion a process that would lead to further suspicion of all English institutions.

The influx of different races and nationalities into Delaware, which had begun in the 1600s, continued throughout the next century. Newcomers so radically altered the ethnic makeup of the population that by the eighteenth century, only a minority of Delawareans could point to a Swedish, Finnish, or Dutch ancestry. According to one estimate, even as early as 1790, descendants of these three ethnic groups together represented less than 6 percent of the state's total population.

The migration of tobacco growers from the played-out fields of Maryland's Eastern Shore to the virgin lands of Sussex, Kent, and lower New Castle counties brought thousands of Anglo-Saxons and their black slaves to Delaware. In 1790 an estimated 50 percent of Delaware's population claimed English descent while, according to the U.S. Census of the same year, 22 percent of the state's population was black.

Although only part English and far wealthier than most, Samuel Dickinson was one example of the Anglo-Saxon immigrants from Maryland's Eastern Shore. Dickinson left his soil-depleted tobacco fields in Talbot County, Maryland to the children of his first marriage in 1740. He then turned to developing approximately 3,000 acres in eastern Kent County, Delaware. In 1741, Samuel, his wife, and two sons by his second marriage—one of whom was John Dickinson, later known as the "penman" of the American Revolution—and his slaves moved into their new plantation on Jones Neck, Southeast of Dover.

Large numbers of Scotch-Irish settled in Delaware during the early and mid-eighteenth century. Primarily descended from lowland Scots who moved to northern Ireland in the 1600s, many came to North America in the next century in search of better economic opportunities. Their primary port of entry was Philadelphia, but thousands disembarked at New Castle. Although the majority eventually moved west in pursuit of cheap land, enough Scotch-Irish remained in Delaware to give New Castle County a decidedly Scotch-Irish flavor by the mid-eighteenth century. Referring to lower New Castle County in 1741, one observer wrote of the "multitudes" arriving "from the North of Ireland." Some Scotch-Irish even formed communities in central and southern Delaware, causing the Reverend William Becket of Lewes to note, as early as 1728, the many Scotch-Irish "families that are settled in Sussex."

Although poor and obliged to finance their Atlantic crossing by agreeing to serve for a time (generally three to seven years) as indentured servants, the Scotch-Irish were usually better educated than other Delawareans. As a result, Scotch-Irish names such as Killen, Tilton, Alison, and McKinly soon became prominant in Delaware's medical, legal, and educational circles. Of considerable significance was the distrust and resentment of English institutions that these newcomers brought with them from Ireland. Anti-English sentiments led Delaware's Scotch-Irish to enthusiastically support the rebel cause during the American Revolution.

Other nationalities settled in Delaware during the eighteenth century, but in far fewer numbers than the

English, Africans, and Scotch-Irish. Thousands of German immigrants poured into the Delaware Valley but, because they were from outside the British Empire, they were denied entry at New Castle and had to disembark at Philadelphia. Intent on finding cheap land and living with other German-speaking people, most Germans moved west and only a few pushed south into Delaware.

More numerous were the Welsh. After spending two years in Pennsylvania, in 1703 fifteen or twenty families moved into the Welsh Tract, a 30,000-acre grant from William Penn which began just below Newark along the Maryland border and extended south for several miles. Subsequently, additional Welsh settled into the Welsh Tract and other parts of Delaware.

Almost all of the newcomers were English-speaking, albeit in some cases with Irish or Welsh accents. This factor made it difficult to distinguish individual ethnic groups from each other and from the older residents of Delaware. But on Sundays, distinct differences did surface as each nationality celebrated its own peculiar religious heritage. Indeed, it seemed that church affiliation more than language kept alive a sense of ethnic identity in eighteenth-century Delaware.

The Dutch, who were never numerous in Delaware, soon intermarried with Swedes, Finns, English, and finally, the Scotch-Irish. Because Delaware had no Dutch Reformed churches during the eighteenth century, some of the Dutch joined the Presbyterian Church in New Castle, a natural occurrence considering that both faiths shared a common theology based on the ideas of John Calvin.

By contrast, many of the Swedes and Finns along the Christina River continued an allegiance to the Lutheran Church which was the official religious institution in both mother countries. Construction on Old Swedes Church began in 1698 in what is now east Wilmington, and Lutheran pastors from Sweden filled the pulpit throughout most of the eighteenth century. By 1767, however, English language services were being

Facing page
The famous English evangelist, George Whitefield, preached to an excited audience in Lewes on October 31, 1739. In the years that followed, Whitefield converted thousands to his enthusiastic brand of religion. Courtesy, Library of Congress

Left
The original Saint Peter's chapel in Lewes, where Whitefield spoke, was replaced in 1858 by this Gothic-style structure. Perhaps the evangelist's greatest achievement was that he truly challenged the beliefs and attitudes of his audience. Courtesy, Historical Society of Delaware

37

The Wilmington Society of Friends built this meetinghouse in 1816 on a site where they had congregated since 1748. Quaker families dominated the state's mercantile, milling, and shipping economy; later, many spoke out for the abolition of slavery. Courtesy, Historical Society of Delaware

conducted on alternate Sundays. The last Swedish pastor departed and Old Swedes Church became Protestant Episcopal in 1791.

Delaware's Anglo-Saxons were drawn to their ancestral church, the Church of England. But Anglicanism in Delaware faced some extraordinary difficulties. Unlike Virginia and Maryland, Delaware's Anglican Church was not tax-supported. This meant that all Anglican pulpits were filled by clergymen sent and partially financed by the Society for the Propagation of the Gospel stationed in London. Furthermore, the Anglican insistence on an educated ministry produced a clergy that had difficulty relating to the concerns of the vast majority of Delawareans.

Most colonial Delawareans lived lives marked by poverty, disease, violence, and early death. Moreover, only a minority could read and write. Sussex Countians, for example, were described as:

a people without learning, which proceeds altogether from their extreme poverty. There is not a grammar school within the county and it is a thing extremely rare to meet with a man who can write a tolerable hand or spell with propriety the most common words in the English language.

Such people found it difficult to respond to a clergy that, in the eighteenth century Anglican manner, read learned sermons on the significance of moral responsibility but did little to address their deepest needs and concerns.

Other hindrances to Anglican success included the lack of a bishop in America and, more particularly, the scattered nature of the population. Delaware was overwhelmingly rural; most of those descended from English stock lived considerable distances from Anglican churches and chapels. Moreover, at no time during the colonial period were there more than five Anglican clergy to serve Delaware's widely dispersed population. As a result, although a large number of Delawareans of English background gave nominal allegiance to the Church of England, only a few took communion, and not many regularly attended services.

A number of English Delawareans continued traditional family connections with the Society of Friends. As the eighteenth century progressed, Quakers increasingly abandoned the emotionalism that marked them in the seventeenth century for a quiet mysticism which reflected their rise in social status. This new Quaker image was not very effective in attracting new members. Despite limited numbers, however, Quakers would dominate the economic and civic life of eighteenth-century Wilmington. Some Anglo-Saxons along the Kent-Sussex border were drawn, in the 1760s, to an emotional variant of Quakerism founded by Kent County native Joseph Nichols. But by the end of the century, only a few Nicholites (as Joseph Nichols followers were called) remained in the state.

Several Roman Catholic families lived in colonial Delaware and they too tended to be of English ancestry. Thanks to the ambiance of religious tolerance established by William Penn, some Catholics felt comfortable in joining other Marylanders in their migration to central and southern Delaware. By 1762 there were five or six Catholic families in Kent County, and priests from the Eastern Shore of Maryland conducted religious services on a regular basis in the Dover and Odessa areas.

Just as most Anglo-Saxons tended to identify with the Church of England, the Scotch-Irish maintained their Old World Presbyterianism. In 1723 one observer noted that almost 200 families had recently arrived in the colony from Northern Ireland and "they are generally Presbyterian." Although Delaware's Presbyterian Church traced its roots back to the 1600s, by the mid-eighteenth century it had taken on an overwhelmingly Scotch-Irish tint and this caused friction between Presbyterians and Anglicans. George Ross, Anglican rector at Immanuel Church in New Castle labelled the Scotch-Irish, "the bitterest railers against the {Anglican} Church that ever trod the American ground." Eventually the animosity between Scotch-Irish Presbyterians, strongest in New Castle County, and Anglo-Saxon Church of England members, most numerous in downstate Delaware, led to the formation of an "Irish party" and a rival "church party" to contest Delaware elections prior to the American Revolution.

Unlike the Scotch-Irish, the Welsh did not have a nationalistic commitment to any one Protestant faith. As a result, their names could be found on the rolls of Anglican, Quaker, and Presbyterian congregations in Delaware. In the Welsh Tract, the Pencader Presbyterian Church and the Welsh Tract Baptist Church, which was the only strong Baptist congregation in Delaware during the colonial period, had almost exclusively Welsh congregations.

But despite the variety of religious choices open to them, most colonial Delawareans remained unchurched. In Kent County, for example, approximately two-thirds of the population had no church attachment in the 1760s and many who did seemed rather passive in their commitment. Although some blacks were baptized and a few might attend church or chapel with their masters, the religious needs of most of them went unattended.

This religious lethargy was briefly challenged by the Great Awakening, a revival that swept through the American colonies in the 1730s and 1740s. From New England to Georgia huge crowds turned out to hear charismatic preachers, such as George Whitefield, who

Religious gatherings, sparked by evangelism, were compelling social events to the overwhelmingly rural population of early Delaware. Probably nine out of ten Delaware families lived on farms during the colonial period. Although holdings varied in size, New Castle County's farms averaged slightly more than 200 acres. Often only a small part of a Delaware farm was actually cleared of trees and brush. This particularly held true in Kent and Sussex where individual land holdings were generally larger than in New Castle.

Soil fertility and, to a greater degree, location dictated the value of these farms. Most New Castle County farm land, for example, was more expensive than land further south because the cash crops produced in northern Delaware had such easy access to the market

urged them to save themselves from the fires of hell by being born again in Christ. While touring Delaware, Whitefield most often visited New Castle County, speaking to thousands at a time. Eight to ten thousand stood in the cold and rain at White Clay Creek, for example, to hear him preach on December 2, 1739.

By the 1750s, however, the enthusiasm created by the Great Awakening had given way to the lethargy of earlier years. And yet, this remarkable outpouring of religious fervor demonstrated beyond doubt that the spiritual needs of many weren't being met by Delaware's churches in general and the Church of England in particular. Indeed, the religious fires may have died down but some hot coals remained to be fanned by itinerant preachers of the future.

towns of New Castle and Philadelphia. In Kent and Sussex, the costliest acres were situated along navigable streams such as Duck Creek, the Broadkill, St. Jones, Nanticoke, and Indian rivers, which afforded a cheap means of transporting produce to distant urban trade centers.

At the beginning of the eighteenth century, tobacco was the chief cash crop in Kent and Sussex. But declining prices and the loss of soil fertility, caused by years of tobacco culture, forced Sussex farmers to turn to corn by mid-century. Both corn and wheat proved a profitable replacement for tobacco among Kent County planters, while in northern Delaware wheat had been the main cash crop almost from the beginning. In fact, the fine quality of New Castle County wheat of-

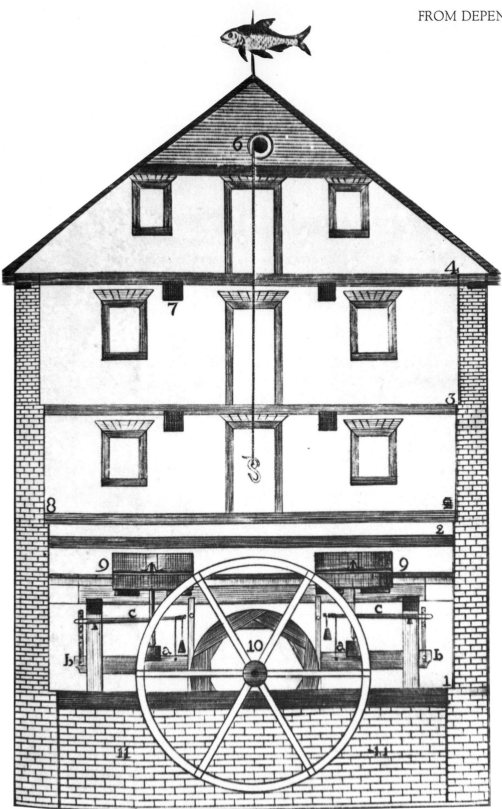

Facing page
Grain mills clustered along the shores of the Brandywine River in Wilmington ground wheat and corn into flour for shipment to Europe and Caribbean cities. Courtesy, Historical Society of Delaware

Left
Oliver Evans, a young inventor from Newport, developed an improved system of flour milling in the 1780s. Although this system was used successfully by Brandywine millers and by George Washington at Mount Vernon, Evans' 1795 book, The Young MillWright and Miller's Guide, *netted only a small profit. Courtesy, Historical Society of Delaware*

ten commanded a higher market price than wheat grown elsewhere.

Beside one or two cash crops, Delaware's farms also produced a large enough variety of vegetables, grains, fruits, and livestock to be virtually self-sufficient. Farm families ate the bounty of their fields and pasture land, and grew flax, sheared sheep, and treated animal hides so that they could manufacture their own clothes. In general, Delaware's farmers were most prosperous in New Castle County and least prosperous in Sussex.

The flourishing agricultural economy created a demand for mills to grind corn, wheat, and barley into flour. The first mills appeared in New Castle County during the Swedish period. By the mid-eighteenth century, they were scattered throughout all three counties, but the most important concentration was along the fast flowing lower Brandywine River. By 1770, for example, eight large, commercial, grain mills were clustered along a quarter mile stretch of the lower Brandywine.

Other economic activities included the tanning of hides and iron production, with one furnace located just south of Newark at Iron Hill and a second at Middleford in Sussex County. Rehoboth Bay was dredged for oysters, and the many streams leading into the Delaware were fished for herring and other species. Wooded lands, particularly in Sussex, produced boards and shingles that often yielded more income for their owners than did cultivated fields. A number of Delawareans also were artisans, especially in the area of a new but rapidly growing town on the Christina.

For decades the small Swedish hamlet built alongside Fort Christina showed little sign of economic vitality or population growth. In the 1730s, about a mile west of the somnolent Swedish settlement, a fledgling community called Willingtown began to rise from the farms and woodland that sloped down to the north bank of the Christina. This location proved ideal for mercantile activity because the Christina served as a commercial highway to and from the rich agricultural regions of western New Castle County and southeastern Pennsylvania. Farmers from the north and west shipped their grain down river to Willingtown where it was ground at the nearby Brandywine mills and shipped via the Christina to Philadelphia or to the West Indies. The farmers then purchased supplies from Willingtown merchants to take back home.

In 1739 Willingtown received its charter of incorporation and was renamed for Spencer Comptom, Earl of Wilmington, who was lord president of the King's Privy Council and perceived as an ally of the Penns in their struggle over proprietary rights with the Lords Baltimore. As Wilmington grew from about six hundred people in 1739 to more than twelve hundred by 1776, it surpassed New Castle as Delaware's largest community.

Despite the growth of Wilmington and the presence of New Castle, Lewes, and a few other towns, the vast majority of colonial Delawareans lived out lives dictated by eighteenth-century rural values. Such mores demanded, among other things, that considerable deference be shown to the gentry, the landed aristocracy. Because it was expected of them, Delaware's gentry quite naturally filled most local and colony-wide political positions. When a political office was hotly contested, it was because the gentry had split into two competing factions rather than because other elements of the population were using the political process to protest aristocratic domination. Obviously, in important decisions concerning Delaware's future—such as what, if any, ties should be maintained with Great Britain—the "middling and lower sorts" would look to such gentry as Caesar Rodney and John Dickinson for guidance.

Politically, the "Lower Counties" enjoyed considerable independence after separating from Pennsylvania in 1704. Delaware's colonial legislature, which met in the town of Newcastle, contained a single body of eighteen assemblymen, six from each county. These officials were elected by white males, twenty-one years of age or older, who owned fifty acres (at least twelve of which were cleared land) or possessed other property worth £40. Probably a majority of Delaware's adult white males met these suffrage requirements.

The Delaware assembly was a very powerful body. Unlike the legislature of Pennsylvania and most of the other thirteen colonies, its enactments were not reviewed

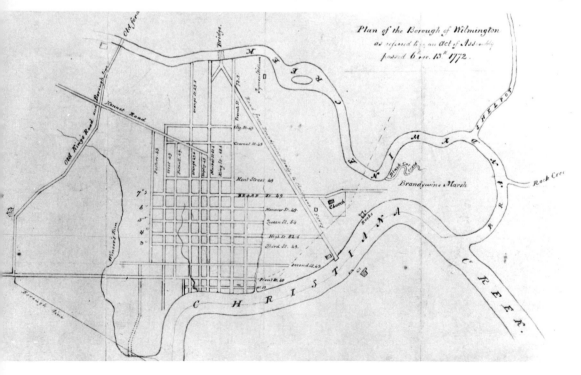

Wilmington's growth was owed to its location at the confluence of three rivers. The swiftly-flowing Brandywine could power dozens of mills; the slow-moving, highly navigable Christina formed a great water highway; and the wide Delaware (not shown) offered commercial and cultural ties to Philadelphia. Courtesy, Historical Society of Delaware

in Great Britain because of confusion over the Penns' proprietary governing rights and the relative obscurity of the "Lower Counties." Only the joint governor of Pennsylvania and the "Lower Counties" (appointed by the Penns) clearly had the power to veto legislation passed by Delaware's colonial assembly; and the governor was usually cooperative because Delaware's assembly annually voted funds for part of his salary. As a result, only Connecticut and Rhode Island enjoyed more self rule than the "Lower Counties" in the mideighteenth century.

The English ancestry of approximately two-thirds of Delaware's white population and the general veneration for English "liberties" caused many to value ties to the British Empire. To those who thought deeply about things political, it was self-evident that the powerful Delaware assembly represented part of the ongoing evolution of representative government which dated back to the Magna Carta.

Just as self-evident was the vulnerability of Delaware

When his term as Governor of Pennsylvania expired in 1785, John Dickinson returned to Wilmington and built the city's largest private house at the corner of Eighth and Market streets. Like other members of the gentry, he provided political and social leadership for the new state. Courtesy, Historical Society of Delaware

to attack by sea and the consequent need for the protective umbrella of the Empire. Pirates ransacked Lewes in 1698 and a French raiding party looted the town a few years later. In 1747 two plantations on Bombay Hook, about ten miles northeast of Dover, were attacked by either French or Spanish raiders. Delawareans recognized that only the might of the British fleet kept such incursions to a minimum.

Delaware also appreciated its tie to proprietary gov-

TO THE
Delaware Pilots.

WE took the Pleasure, some Days since, of kindly admonishing you *to do your Duty*; if perchance you should meet with the *(Tea,)* SHIP POLLY, CAPTAIN AYRES; a THREE DECKER which is hourly expected.

We have now to add, that Matters ripen fast here; and that *much is expected from those Lads who meet with the Tea Ship.*----There is some Talk of A HANDSOME REWARD FOR THE PILOT WHO GIVES THE FIRST GOOD ACCOUNT OF HER.----How that may be, we cannot *for certain* determine: But ALL agree, that TAR and FEATHERS will be his Portion, who pilots her into this Harbour. And we will answer for ourselves, that, whoever is committed to us, as an Offender against the Rights of *America*, will experience the utmost Exertion of our Abilities; as

THE COMMITTEE FOR TARRING AND FEATHERING.

P. S. We expect you will furnish yourselves with Copies of the foregoing and following Letter; which are printed for this Purpose, that the Pilot who meets with Captain *Ayres* may favor him with a Sight of them.

Committee of Taring and Feathering.

TO
Capt. AYRES,

Of the SHIP *POLLY*, on a Voyage from *London* to *Philadelphia.*

SIR,

WE are informed that you have, imprudently, taken Charge of a Quantity of Tea; which has been sent out by the *India* Company, *under the Auspices of the Ministry*, as a Trial of *American* Virtue and Resolution.

Now, as your Cargo, on your Arrival here, will most assuredly bring you into hot water; and as you are perhaps a Stranger *to these Parts*, we have concluded to advise you of the present Situation of Affairs in *Philadelphia*---that, taking Time by the Forelock, you may stop short in your dangerous Errand----secure your Ship against the Rafts of combustible Matter which may be set on Fire, and turned loose against her; and more than all this, that you may preserve your own Person, from the Pitch and Feathers that are prepared for you.

In the first Place, we must tell you, that the *Pennsylvanians* are, *to a Man*, passionately fond of Freedom; the Birthright of *Americans*; and at all Events are determined to enjoy it.

That they sincerely believe, no Power on the Face of the Earth has a Right to tax them without their Consent.

That in their Opinion, the Tea in your Custody is designed by the Ministry to enforce such a Tax, which they will undoubtedly oppose; and in so doing, give you every possible Obstruction.

We are nominated to a very disagreeable, but necessary Service.---- To our Care are committed all Offenders against the Rights of *America*; and hapless is he, whose evil Destiny has doomed him to suffer at our Hands.

You are sent out on a diabolical Service; and if you are so foolish and obstinate as to compleat your Voyage; by bringing your Ship to Anchor in this Port; you may run such a Gauntlet, as will induce you, in your last Moments, most heartily to curse those who have made you the Dupe of their Avarice and Ambition.

What think you Captain, of a Halter around your Neck----ten Gallons of liquid Tar decanted on your Pate----with the Feathers of a dozen wild Geese laid over that to enliven your Appearance?

Only think seriously of this----and fly to the Place from whence you came----fly without Hesitation---- without the Formality of a Protest----and above all, Captain *Ayres* let us advise you to fly without the wild Geese Feathers.

Your Friends *to serve*

Philadelphia, Nov. 27, 1773   THE COMMITTEE *as before subscribed*

A group of Philadelphia patriots calling itself "the committee for Tarring and Feathering" warned Delaware River pilots of the consequences of guiding a British tea ship to port. Following threats of a violent mass meeting, this vessel eventually turned away. Courtesy, Historical Society of Delaware

ernment. The colony's attachment to the Penns provided a necessary legal shield against threatening land claims by the Lords Baltimore, who insisted that parts of the "Lower Counties" belonged to Maryland and made land grants accordingly. No wonder Delaware, at mid-century, seemed quite content to continue as a proprietary colony within the British Empire.

The political contentment of 1750 was not long lasting, however. Twenty-five years later Thomas Rodney, a Kent County planter of English ancestry, laconically summarized an extraordinary change in attitude by writing to his brother Caesar, "Let America be free." Delaware heeded Thomas Rodney's cry and joined with the twelve other colonies in cutting its ties to what had seemed, only a quarter of a century before, a benevolent, protective Empire. Why?

Great Britain's victory in the French and Indian War (1754-1763) drove the French from North America and ended the threat of French sea incursions. Consequently, Delawareans had far less need for the British fleet's

protection. Moreover, the final settlement of the boundary dispute between Maryland and Delaware, just prior to the American Revolution, ended the necessity of Delaware's attachment to the proprietary government of the Penns.

Although the majority of white Delawareans considered themselves Englishmen, by 1775 they were also third and fourth generation Americans who, for the most part, had never seen the mother country. Quite naturally their allegiance to England and its institutions was less intense than that of their ancestors. Of course the Scotch-Irish, from the beginning, felt little loyalty to either the King or Parliament.

While Delawareans began to drift away from some of their British ties, connections with Philadelphia became increasingly important. In addition to serving as a great commercial market for the products of Delaware's fields, woods, and streams, Philadelphia was a magnet for those in search of an education. Caesar Rodney attended Latin school in that city, George Read and

Thomas McKean, a New Castle lawyer, was the first of Delaware's Revolutionary-era statesmen to favor American independence from England. When he voted "for" and George Read "against" the Declaration of Independence, McKean summoned the like-minded Caesar Rodney from Dover to break the tie. Courtesy, Historical Society of Delaware

Conservative lawyer George Read supported independence, but feared popular unwillingness to back the rebellion. At first he voted against separation from England, but later signed the Declaration of Independence. Courtesy, Historical Society of Delaware

John Dickinson read law there, and James Tilton studied medicine at the College of Philadelphia. The Philadelphia connection was further strengthened by the large number of Delawareans who had relatives living in the Quaker city.

Most of the news that reached Delaware concerning the outside world was first filtered through Philadelphia in such a way that many Delawareans perceived Great Britain's relations with her American colonies from the Philadelphia perspective.

After the French and Indian War, Parliament decided to assert its taxing authority over the American colonies with the Stamp Act (1765) and the Townshend Acts (1767). Philadelphians resented the British government's actions, and their growing discontent was soon shared by Delawareans.

Despite living on this side of the Atlantic, most Delawareans joined Philadelphians in regarding themselves as British. Both saw Parliament's new tax programs, adopted without the approval of their respective colonial legislatures, as an open violation of the traditional rights of Englishmen. John Dickinson, who alternately resided in Delaware or Philadelphia, best expressed this shared concern by writing that the issue was "whether Parliament can legally take money out of our pockets without our consent."

Delaware's opposition to British "oppression" generally lacked the zeal that surfaced in many of the other colonies. Nevertheless, like a tiny pilot fish swimming in the wake of a great shark, little Delaware joined her much larger neighbors as they inexorably moved together towards military confrontation with the British Empire.

In 1765 Delaware sent Kent County landowner Caesar Rodney and New Castle County attorney Thomas McKean to the conference held in New York to protest the Stamp Act. From 1767 to 1770, following the passage of the Townshend Acts, Delaware merchants joined with those from other colonies in boycotting English imports. In late 1773, even before the British government turned its wrath on Boston and closed the port because of the Boston Tea Party, Delaware's assembly created a committee of correspondence to maintain contact with the other colonies about this potentially dangerous situation. Then, in 1774, Delaware sent Rodney, McKean, and George Read, another New Castle County attorney, to the meeting of the First Continental Congress in Philadelphia.

After fighting broke out at Lexington and Concord in the spring of 1775, the same three men were again dispatched to Philadelphia for the Second Continental

Congress. There they supported the creation of a continental army but also followed the instructions of the Delaware assembly to seek reconciliation with Great Britain. Indeed, the desire for reconciliation was just one example of the moderation—tempered by the need to keep in step with its powerful neighbors—that characterized Delaware during most of the American Revolution.

On June 7, 1776, the Second Continental Congress accepted a motion from Virginia's Richard Henry Lee for independence, although debate and a final vote were postponed for a few weeks. A week later, Scotch-Irish Thomas McKean presented to the Delaware assembly a recommendation from Congress that all colonies officially suppress "every kind of authority under the crown" and thus place each individual colonial government "under the authority of the people." Delaware's assembly complied with the request on the following day, and the state has subsequently celebrated June 15 as its Separation Day from the British Empire.

The debate in Congress over a collective declaration of American independence began on July 1 without the presence of Caesar Rodney, one of Delaware's three delegates. Rodney had just returned to his home southeast of Dover after leading a militia expedition into Sussex County to nip in the bud a threatened Tory uprising. Back in Philadelphia, the peripatetic John Dickinson, now a delegate from Pennsylvania, spoke out strongly against independence because he feared the effects of a long war and felt that reconciliation with Great Britain was still possible. The vote on independence found the Delaware delegation deadlocked with George Read, an old and trusted friend of John Dickinson, voting against and Thomas McKean voting for independence.

The need for a united front against Great Britain was obvious. Since only nine of the thirteen former colonies cast an affirmative ballot, the delegates decided to put off a final vote until the next day, July 2, so that unanimity might be achieved.

On July 2 only the abstention of New York marred a unanimous vote for independence. South Carolina and Pennsylvania had fallen into line rather easily, but it took an all night ride by Caesar Rodney to end the deadlock in the Delaware delegation. Although some of the details are unclear, an urgent message from Thomas McKean in Philadelphia reached Rodney at his Jones Neck plantation, southeast of Dover, sometime on July 1. Forty-eight years old and suffering from facial cancer and asthma, Rodney ignored a thunderstorm and travelled through the night—it isn't clear whether he rode all the way on horseback or used a

A resident of both Delaware and Pennsylvania, John Dickinson became known as "the penman of the Revolution" for his fervent pamphlets against British colonial policies. Although he always hoped for a reconciliation with England, and, as a delegate from Pennsylvania, refused to sign the Declaration of Independence, he fought bravely for American freedom during the Revolutionary War. Courtesy, Historical Society of Delaware

horse-drawn carriage for part of the trip—to arrive in Philadelphia on the afternoon of July 2. Though tired, dusty, and covered with mud, Rodney was in time to break the deadlock in his own delegation and put Delaware on record as favoring independence. On July 4, the day the delegates formally adopted Jefferson's written explanation of their action, Caesar Rodney laconically wrote of his ride to his brother Thomas: "... I arrived in Congress (tho detained by thunder and rain) time enough to give my voice to the matter of independence."

*An indigenous and initially rev-
olutionary religion, Methodism
perhaps gained its largest following in Delaware, due to the tire-
less efforts of Francis Asbury,
shown here being ordained in
Lovely Lane Methodist Church,
Baltimore. Courtesy, North Carolina Department of Archives
and History*

CHAPTER IV

REVOLUTIONS OF DIFFERENT KINDS

*O*n a hot, humid July morning in 1805 Dr. Jacob Wolf of Lewes, a leading Sussex County Federalist, made ready to leave home for a political meeting in Georgetown. As he mounted his horse, the Lewes physician told his wife that he expected to be murdered by Democrats before the day was out.

Hours later in Georgetown, Dr. Wolf and a number of other Federalists gathered in the jury room on the second floor of the Sussex County Courthouse. While Dr. Wolf was being nominated to chair the meeting, "the most awful flash of lightning and such a peel of thunder as made the whole town tremble" struck the cupola and "slivered the front of the Court House." Dr. Wolf was killed instantly and eleven other Federalists were knocked to the floor and presumed dead, only to be revived "by bleeding and other means."

William Morgan, a devout Methodist who lived

nearby, rushed to the courthouse to find the "most aw-ful scene I ever witnessed." Later, after contemplating what he had seen, Morgan decided that "it was a just judgment from heaven." The victims of the lightning bolt deserved Divine retribution, according to Morgan, because they had abandoned more godly pursuits for the excitement and rewards of the political arena where such sinful practices as impugning the character and motives of opponents were commonplace. Ironically, both the increased interest and emotional commitment by some Delawareans to political parties, and the con-trasting desire of other Delawareans to avoid such in-volvement on religious grounds, can be traced directly or indirectly to the American Revolution and to the resulting destruction of English ties and institutions.

Delaware's declaration of independence from the British Empire created an immediate need for a state constitution. In the late summer of 1776, Delawareans elected delegates to a state constitutional convention which began meeting in New Castle on August 27 and completed its work within a month. The convention created a bicameral assembly and gave it most of the governing power at the expense of the chief executive, who was called the President of Delaware. It was in this first constitution that the title "the Delaware State" was officially adopted. (Delaware's second state constitution, which went into effect in 1792, changed the titles of president to governor and "the Delaware State" to "the State of Delaware.")

During the Revolutionary War, the number of Del-awareans who remained loyal to the British crown was considerable. John Adams wrote in 1780 that more Tories "in proportion" resided in Delaware than in any other state. Often rumors from downstate spoke of armed groups of Loyalists about to start an insurrec-tion. But if there was any substance to the rumors, a quick foray by Delaware militia generally caused the Tories to disband without firing a shot.

Loyalists attracted the greatest support in Kent and Sussex where most of the white population was of En-glish descent. Although such wealthy landowners as Thomas Robinson of Sussex led the downstate Tories, they came from all classes of white society. Poor farm-ers in Sussex, for example, opposed independence be-cause they resented the new state government's taxes, recruitment laws, and ordered seizure of their weapons. But despite opposition to independence, the tendency of Delaware's Loyalists to fade away at the prospect of

William Morgan, shown here at age 67, was a Sussex County farmer and physician whose au-tobiography chronicled Delaware life before the Civil War. His di-ary described political rallies, camp meetings, agricultural trends, and the impact of Meth-odism on everyday existence in Sussex County. Courtesy, Histor-ical Society of Delaware

a military clash with rebel forces demonstrated that most were, at best, only lukewarm Tories.

Perhaps the harsh nature of some of the punish-ments decreed against insurrectionists caused many Loyalists to have second thoughts about participating in uprisings. Eight Tories in Sussex, for instance, were sentenced to be hung "but not till ... dead," at which point their bowels were to be "taken out" and burned in front of them. Finally, the unfortunate Tories were to have their heads cut off and their bodies quartered. But in a gesture that more accurately represented Delaware's treatment of its Loyalists than such draconic decrees, the assembly pardoned all eight. The willing-ness of rebels and Tories to treat each other with more restraint than found in most of the other colonies probably reflected the lack of strong commitment by most Delawareans to either side. Indeed, during the Revolutionary years most Delawareans simply went about the business of making a living and hoping for the best.

Delaware's comparative tranquility was abruptly shattered in early September of 1777 by the invasion of British regulars on their way from Cecil County, Maryland to the rebel capital of Philadelphia. General William Howe, the British commander in New York City, had decided to attack Philadelphia but felt that the direct overland passage through New Jersey or the water route up the Delaware Bay and River were too heavily fortified to augur military success. Instead, he chose to sail around Cape Charles and up the Chesapeake to land his 17,000 soldiers on the Elk Neck Peninsula in Cecil County, Maryland.

After debarking, Howe's army marched eastward into New Castle County where it was confronted by units of rebel light infantry. On September 3, as the British moved north along the road from Glasgow to Newark, the heavily outnumbered Americans held their ground just east of Iron Hill. Near Cooch's Bridge the two sides engaged in a brief fire fight in which forty rebels and an unknown number of British were killed or wounded.

Marching from Head of Elk in Maryland toward Philadelphia, Lord Howe's army encountered a small band of colonial troops at Cooch's Bridge near Newark on September 3, 1777. After skirmishing for several hours with heavy casualties, the Americans withdrew. Lord Cornwallis, the expedition commander, made his headquarters here in the home of Thomas Cooch, a miller. Courtesy, Historical Society of Delaware

The Americans then slipped away to join George Washington's 11,000 soldiers camped at Wilmington, astride the usual route to Philadelphia.

After resting his forces for a few days, Howe surprised the Americans by marching north from Newark to Pennsylvania. Intent on halting the British advance

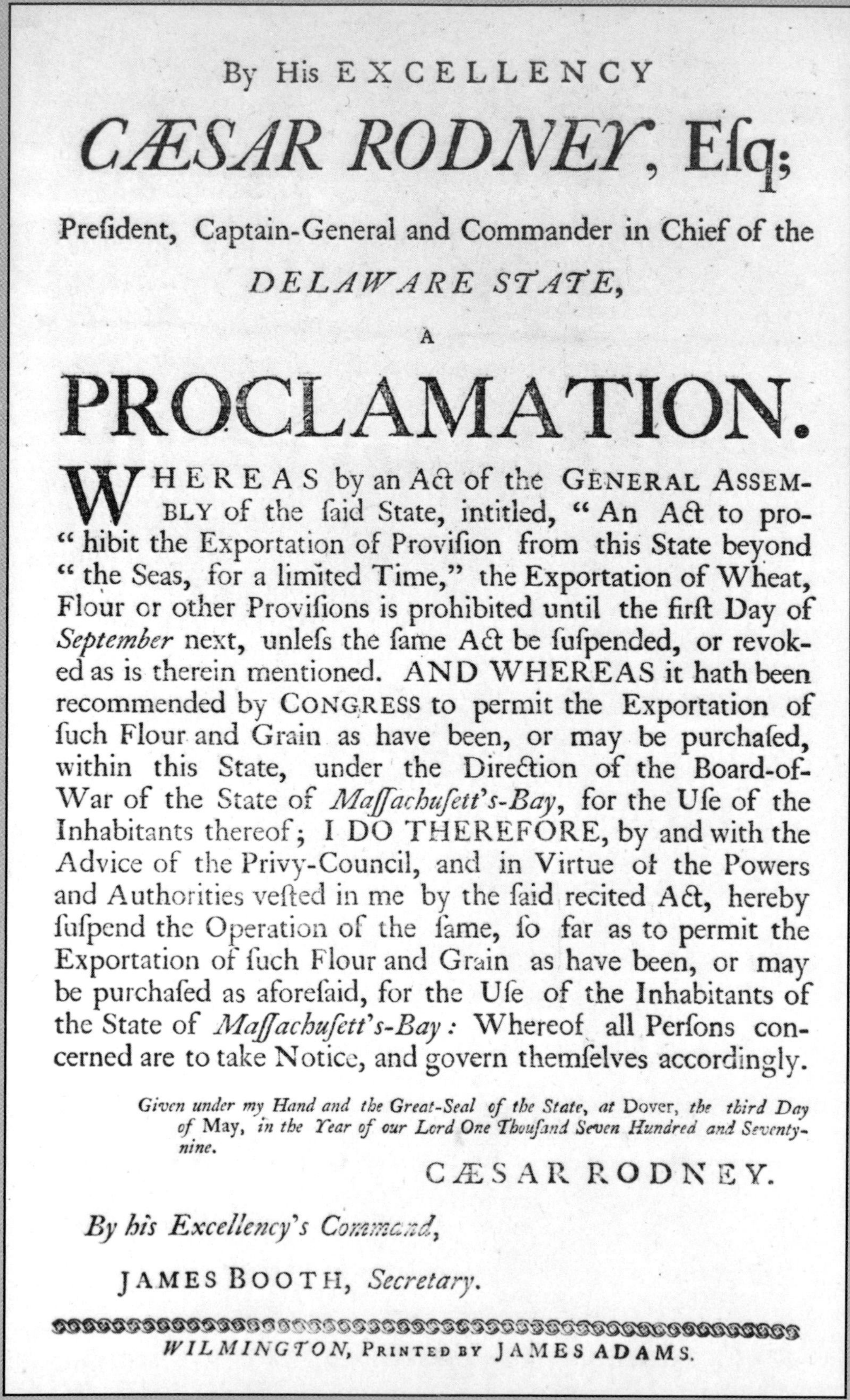

By His EXCELLENCY

CÆSAR RODNEY, Efq;

President, Captain-General and Commander in Chief of the

DELAWARE STATE,

A

PROCLAMATION.

WHEREAS by an Act of the GENERAL ASSEMBLY of the said State, intitled, "An Act to pro-"hibit the Exportation of Provision from this State beyond "the Seas, for a limited Time," the Exportation of Wheat, Flour or other Provisions is prohibited until the first Day of *September* next, unless the same Act be suspended, or revoked as is therein mentioned. AND WHEREAS it hath been recommended by CONGRESS to permit the Exportation of such Flour and Grain as have been, or may be purchased, within this State, under the Direction of the Board-of-War of the State of *Massachusett's-Bay*, for the Use of the Inhabitants thereof; I DO THEREFORE, by and with the Advice of the Privy-Council, and in Virtue of the Powers and Authorities vested in me by the said recited Act, hereby suspend the Operation of the same, so far as to permit the Exportation of such Flour and Grain as have been, or may be purchased as aforesaid, for the Use of the Inhabitants of the State of *Massachusett's-Bay*: Whereof all Persons concerned are to take Notice, and govern themselves accordingly.

Given under my Hand and the Great-Seal of the State, at Dover, the third Day of May, in the Year of our Lord One Thousand Seven Hundred and Seventy-nine.

CÆSAR RODNEY.

By his Excellency's Command,

JAMES BOOTH, Secretary.

WILMINGTON, PRINTED BY JAMES ADAMS.

Left
Supplies of food and grain were low as a result of the British occupation of Delaware from 1777 to 1778. Caesar Rodney, president of the Delaware State, restricted the exportation of wheat and flour as a means of preserving rations. Courtesy, Historical Society of Delaware

Facing page
Fearing that New Castle might come under attack by the British during their march to Philadelphia, Delaware legislators moved the capital from New Castle to Dover in 1777. This photo is of the state capital as it looked in the early twentieth century. Courtesy, Delaware State Archives

on Philadelphia, an alarmed Washington calculated that Howe intended to cross the Brandywine River north of the Delaware line, in the vicinity of Chadds Ford. Washington rushed his forces to the Chadds Ford area only to have Howe unexpectedly cross the river just to the north of the newly established rebel positions. The resulting Battle of the Brandywine ended with the outflanked Americans in retreat and the roads to Philadelphia and Wilmington wide open to Howe's conquering army.

While the main British army pushed on to Philadelphia, a smaller force was dispatched to the Wilmington area where it captured John McKinly, the president of Delaware. After occupying Wilmington for approximately one month, the British marched northeast to join up with Howe's main force in Philadelphia. The state was now free of a conquering army, but His Majesty's fleet still controlled the lower Delaware River and the Delaware Bay, and that caused considerable anxiety.

In June 1778, the British finally evacuated Philadelphia and, except for sporadic forays by small boats, their fleet withdrew from the Delaware River and Bay. Despite occasional raids by small British or Loyalist bands against individual farms along Delaware's coast and creeks, the military phase of the American Revolution had ended in Delaware by the early summer of 1778.

Elsewhere fighting continued and some Delawareans—the number is unclear—volunteered for the Delaware regiment or other units of the Continental Army. The soldiers of the Delaware regiment acquitted themselves so well in the Carolina campaigns that, according to tradition, they were called "Blue Hens Chickens" after some highly prized fighting cocks.

The British presence in and around Delaware during part of 1777 and 1778 interfered with voting procedures. Because of the brief occupation and the subsequent military threats to the town of New Castle by the British fleet, New Castle County's voting site for the fall elections was moved to Newark. But even before the ominous presence of British guns, strong political pressure from Kent and Sussex counties led to the decision to move the state capital from the town of New Castle. From 1777 to 1780 the Delaware assembly met at different sites around the state before finally settling, in 1781, on Dover as its permanent home.

Besides having found a permanent capital, Delaware was ahead of the national government in one other respect: it had a constitution. To remedy this shortcoming, the Second Continental Congress drew up the Articles of Confederation in 1777 and sent them to each of the thirteen states for ratification. The Articles would go into effect only after the approval of every state. Because it was unhappy about the claims of some of the larger states to land west of the Appalachians, Delaware joined Maryland and New Jersey in refusing ratification. The three small states made no claims on the territory beyond the Appalachians and, quite naturally, felt that the unsettled sections of the West should belong to the entire nation. Finally, after making their point, Delaware and New Jersey ratified in 1779. Maryland lent its approval two years later, establishing the Articles as our first written national constitution. Evidently some of the other states got the message and, in subsequent years, surrendered their western land claims to the national government.

The Articles of Confederation provided the United States with a weak central government, unable to either raise money by taxation or control international and interstate commerce. Individual states were even free to impose tariffs on all goods that crossed their boundaries.

Because much of Delaware's import trade with other states and foreign nations was unloaded at the port of Philadelphia, a considerable segment of Delaware's commerce was subject to the taxing whims of the Pennsylvania legislature. Moreover, because the national government could not levy direct taxes, it had to issue increasing amounts of paper money to meet its obligations. The almost worthless national tender produced a disastrous ripple effect, causing a sharp decline in the value of Delaware's state currency.

The chaotic currency situation and growing concern over Pennsylvania's ability to tax—and therefore control—so much of its commerce compelled Delaware to join with other states in supporting amendments to the Articles. But because amendments needed the unanimous approval of all the states, no amendment was ever adopted.

In 1786 Virginia requested that all of the states send delegates to Annapolis, Maryland to address the regulation of interstate commerce. Only Delaware and four other states sent representatives, but their meeting led

New Castle is one of the oldest towns in Delaware. It was first settled by the Swedes in the 1650s and later ruled by the Dutch and English. As the state's colonial capital and an important port, New Castle flourished during the eighteenth century. Courtesy, Historical Society of Delaware

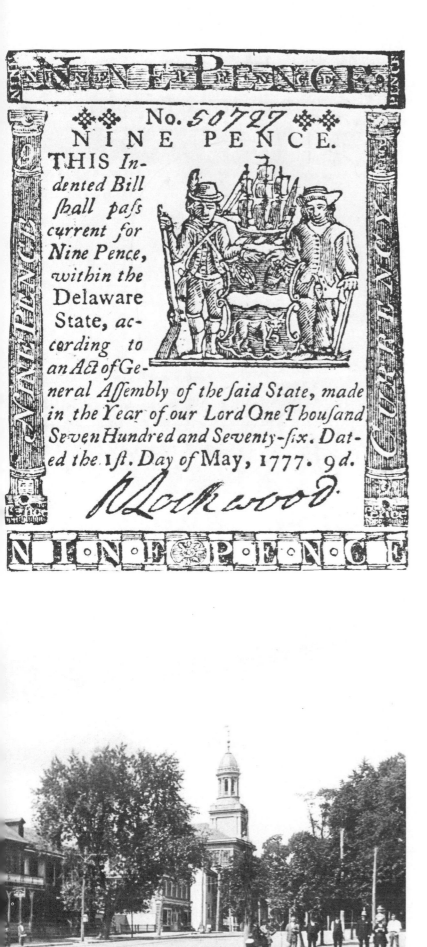

Like other states, Delaware printed its own paper money when British currency was in short supply. Because the federal government issued large amounts of money to finance the revolution, state currencies became almost worthless at war's end. Courtesy, Historical Society of Delaware

to an agreement that a stronger national government was desirable. The Annapolis convention called for delegates from all of the states to meet in Philadelphia in 1787 to explore ways of expanding the national government's role.

The Constitutional Convention, as it has been subsequently called, met in May and continued its proceedings through the hot, sweltering Philadelphia summer of 1787. Only Rhode Island was absent as the delegates quickly decided to scrap the Articles of Confederation and write another constitution. Next, the delegates debated the nature and shape of the new central government. Predictably, Virginia proposed a legislature in which each state was represented according to population.

Delaware's delegation of John Dickinson—who had moved back to Delaware in 1785—George Read, Richard Bassett, Gunning Bedford, Jr., and Jacob Broom had been instructed to be wary of just such a move and to insist that Delaware's representation in the new government be equal to that of the larger states. George Read pointed out to the other delegations that ignoring the idea of equal representation might cause his state to leave the convention. Dickinson bluntly told James Madison of Virginia that Delaware "would sooner submit to a foreign power than be ... under the domination of the large states."

Due, in part, to Delaware's stubborn insistence on the rights of the small states, the "Great Compromise" was reached. It followed Virginia's plan of proportional representation in the House of Representatives while upholding in the Senate the demands of Delaware and the other small states for equal representation. Satisfied with the Great Compromise, the Delaware delegation subsequently supported almost every measure adopted by the Constitutional Convention to strengthen the national government.

The newly drafted U.S. Constitution was to go into effect after ratification by special conventions in two-

thirds (nine) of the states. Considerable political disagreement existed in Delaware about a number of issues, and elections were hotly contested. But on the need to ratify the new national constitution, there was an amazing unanimity. Meeting in Dover on Monday, December 3, 1787, the delegates elected to Delaware's special convention spent only four days in discussion before unanimously approving the new U.S. Constitution on December 7. This speedy response distinguished Delaware as the first state to ratify the U.S. Constitution. Subsequently, it has been called the

"First State" and December 7 is marked by the annual Delaware Day celebration.

Resolution of major political concerns did not put an end to revolution, however. Less than five months after Washington led his forces north out of Delaware to face the British at the Battle of the Brandywine, a second rebel on horseback rode into the First State. He stood a slender 5 feet 9 inches with piercing blue eyes, a prominent forehead, and long, blond hair. His name was Francis Asbury and he seemed to possess inexhaustible energy and a single-mindedness that gave

Above
The Wilmington Whaling Company was a short-lived business venture. One of their ships, the Lucy Ann, is pictured here trying to capture a harpooned whale. The crew of one rowboat is capsized while another comes to their aid. Courtesy, Historical Society of Delaware

Right
John Martin, a sailor on board the whaleship Lucy Ann, kept a journal of a two-year voyage to South America. He recorded the ship's bearings, weather conditions, and the crew's attempts to bring in whales. Courtesy, Historical Society of Delaware

Facing page
Robert E. Goodier depicts eight state convention delegates pondering the contents of the U.S. Constitution. Assembled at Battell's Tavern on December 7, 1787, Delaware delegates unanimously voted for ratification, reaching this decision before the twelve other states. Hence, Delaware became the "First State." The delegates, from left, are: Alan McLane, Gunning Bedford, James Latimer, Richard Bassett, Nicholas Ridgely and Gunning Bedford, Sr. (near fireplace), and James Sikes and Kensey Johns (in foreground). Courtesy, Bank of Delaware

Facing page
Delaware's State House is a
Georgian-style brick structure
facing The Green in Dover.
Erected about 1792 to hold a
court room, legislative chambers,
and Kent County offices, it remains the second oldest government building in continuous use
in the United States. Courtesy,
Delaware State Archives

Right
Colonel John Haslet's regiment
joined the fight for American
independence in 1776. The regiment distinguished itself for
bravery and came to be known
as the "Blue Hens Chickens" after game hens known for their
fighting abilities. The regiment's
motto, later adopted by the state
of Delaware, was "liberty and independence." Courtesy, Historical Society of Delaware

When President Washington
toured the country in 1791, he
stopped in Wilmington to thank
Joseph Tatnall for his Revolutionary War support. Tatnall
had defied British military orders to shut down his mill, and
at great personal risk, continued
to grind flour—food for Washington's armies. Courtesy, Bank
of Delaware

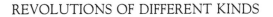

Left
Immanuel Episcopal Church, a New Castle landmark, overlooks the town's green. Founded in 1689, it was the first Anglican parish in the colony of Delaware. The church building, erected in 1703, was severely damaged by a fire in 1980, but has been restored. Courtesy, Historical Society of Delaware

Below
Old Swedes Church, built in 1698, has served the spiritual needs of Wilmington under four national flags—Swedish, Dutch, English, and the United States. Courtesy, Historical Society of Delaware

Left
Rebecca Chalkley worked this sampler of Bible verses in 1734 as a combined theological and needlework lesson. Her father, Reverend Thomas Chalkley, was an itinerant Quaker preacher who landed in Delaware in 1731 when his ship was wrecked on Reedy Island. Courtesy, Historical Society of Delaware

New Castle 3 m.

little thought to anything else but the spread of Methodism. While the American Revolution offered Delawareans freedom from the fetters of the British Empire, Asbury's Methodist revolution promised them liberation from the twin bonds of sin and death.

The first Methodist to actually appear in Delaware was Captain Thomas Webb, a retired British army officer who preached in New Castle County in 1769. Other Methodist itinerants pushed further south in subsequent years, until by 1780 almost all of Delaware had been exposed to the new religious message.

Methodist preachers were unordained laymen who felt moved by the Holy Spirit to saddle up their horses and travel through the countryside, spreading a faith far more evangelical than those found in contemporary houses of worship. Under the direction of Francis Asbury, they particularly criticized the Anglican Church's lack of religious fire, but perceived themselves as merely a reform movement within the Church of England. In fact, Methodist itinerants were careful that their preaching time not conflict with Anglican services, and they encouraged their audiences to attend those services and receive the sacraments from Anglican clergy.

Methodist support of the colonial Anglican Church ended with the collapse of the latter during the American Revolution. Because American rebels viewed the Church of England as just one more institutional example of British imperialism, they suspected Anglican clergy of being Loyalists and often badgered them into returning to Great Britain. Although Delaware seemed less hostile than some states, by 1780 only three Anglican priests remained in the state and at least one, Sydenham Thorne of Milford, was seriously restricted in his clerical duties by the government in Dover. Indeed, four years later a frustrated layman lamented, probably with some exaggeration, that in the entire Delmarva Peninsula there were but two Anglican clergymen, "and one of these is a drunkard."

Although the American Protestant Episcopal Church emerged from the ashes of the colonial Anglican Church, it lacked a clergy either numerous or energetic enough to meet the spiritual needs of most citizens of the First State. Increasingly, a large number of Delawareans and other Americans turned to the unordained Methodist itinerants, demanding that they administer the sacraments. From Britain John Wesley, the Anglican priest who founded Methodism, opposed such an initiative because it would surely cut the umbilical cord that bound the new movement to the Church of England. Wesley's American lieutenant,

Thomas Coke arrived in Delaware in 1784 to advise Methodist preachers on the establishment of an independent church. Courtesy, United Methodist Archives

Francis Asbury, agreed with his mentor.

From February 1778 to April 1780, Asbury lived in the friendly boundaries of Delaware, primarily at Judge Thomas White's home near Whiteleysburg, southwest of Dover. He used the house as a headquarters to evangelize Delaware and to fight against those Methodists who wished to sever the Anglican connection. However, the colonial Anglican Church's obvious demise and increasing pressure from American laymen to receive the sacraments caused Wesley to take further action. He requested that the Anglican bishop of London ordain American-bound Methodist missionaries. His request was refused. Seeing no other choice, Wesley ordained two of his Methodist preachers, Thomas Veasey and Richard Whatcoat, as elders. Anglican cleric Thomas Coke, who was also a Methodist preacher, became superintendent with the power to ordain. The three missionaries sailed for New York in the fall of 1784 with instructions from Wesley to set up an independent Methodist Church in America.

After debarking, the group split up. Coke and Whatcoat stayed together, making their way into the heart of Delaware. On Sunday morning, November 14,

they arrived at Barratt's Chapel, approximately ten miles southeast of Dover, and Coke began to preach. At the end of his sermon, he tells us, "a plain robust man came up to me in the pulpit and kissed me. I thought it could be no other than Mr. Asbury, and I was not deceived." Then, for the historic first time, an ordained Methodist preacher, Richard Whatcoat, joined Thomas Coke in administering bread and wine to about five or six hundred Delawareans—with the approval of Wesley. This symbolic act cut the ties with the colonial Anglican Church and marked Barratt's Chapel as the Independence Hall of American Methodism.

Although the new religion quickly spread into every state, its greatest success during the early years of the Republic was in Delaware and in the rest of the Delmarva Peninsula. In 1778 Francis Asbury expressed the hope that Delaware would "become the Garden of the Lord," and by the end of the American Revolution, Methodists outnumbered the combined totals of all of the state's other faiths. So rapid was the growth of Methodism that in 1808 a euphoric Asbury noted: "In Delaware the millenium has certainly begun."

Methodism was most attractive to residents of Kent and Sussex where it was viewed by the heavily Anglo-Saxon population as the new "English" faith which would fill the void created by the collapse of Anglicanism. In 1810 one out of five adults in the lower two counties was a Methodist, which was extraordinary in view of the low percentage of Americans who officially belonged to any church during this period. By contrast, Scotch-Irish New Castle County had little use for "English" institutions of any nature and remained strongly Presbyterian. It was only after the migration of many Delawareans from Kent and Sussex to Wilmington in the mid-nineteenth century that Methodists became numerous in New Castle County.

The impact of Methodism on the residents of central and southern Delaware was greater than the American Revolution. On becoming Methodists, most slave holders freed their servants; some even joined abolitionist

Barratt's Chapel, a small brick
structure in Kent County, Delaware, is the Independence Hall
of American Methodism. It was
there that Francis Asbury and
Thomas Coke met to plan the
organization of the Methodist
Episcopal Church. Courtesy,
Historical Society of Delaware

societies. Led by Richard Bassett, a Dover Methodist and a future governor of Delaware, the state legislature in 1787 made illegal the sale of Delaware slaves beyond the state's boundaries and, ten years later, came within one vote of outlawing the institution of bondage in Delaware. The Methodist message also encouraged abstinence and hard work. It condemned as self-indulgent, and therefore sinful, such practices as gambling, fox hunting, horse racing, card playing, dancing, unnecessary conversation, "revelings", and all other activity that distracted men and women from the serious business of serving God.

To maintain their Christian purity, Delaware's Methodists often remained aloof from the contaminating world of politics. As William Morgan pointed out after the tragedy in Georgetown's courthouse, political activity could cause men to abandon some of their Methodist principles. And yet other Methodists did turn out to vote and some, such as Richard Bassett, even ran for office, usually on the Federalist ticket.

Elections in Delaware during the colonial era were often contested by loosely organized factions that pitted rival ethnic and religious groups against each other. Independence from Great Britain and the subsequent adoption of the United States Constitution dramatically increased the number and importance of government officials to be directly or indirectly elected. Thanks to the Delaware Constitution of 1792, the property qualification for suffrage was removed, giving all white males over twenty-one who paid taxes the right to vote.

With considerably more at stake than in colonial times, two well organized political parties—the Federalists and the Democratic-Republicans—appeared in Delaware and across most of the rest of the nation during the 1790s to contest state and national elections. In general, the Federalist Party appealed to the conservative-leaning, downstate Delawareans of English ancestry. The Democratic-Republicans, on the other hand, were usually supported by the more radical, Scotch-Irish Presbyterians residing in New Castle County. Questions that divided the two parties tended to focus on national issues: How much power did the Constitution give to the U.S. government? In what manner should the nation react to the French Revolution and to France's arch foe, Great Britain?

Generally speaking, Delaware's Federalists hewed closely to their national party line, favoring a strong central government, restrictions on the constitutional rights of those sympathizing with the French Revolution, and friendly relations with Great Britain. But in other matters Delaware's Federalists demonstrated a

greater ability than Federalists elsewhere to bend with the times and to adopt some of the democratic practices introduced by their Democratic-Republican opponents.

Initially, Delaware's Federalists continued political practices inherited from colonial times, when a few gentry dictated who would run on the party ticket and when all voters were required to travel to their respective county seats to cast a ballot in county and state elections. But as one Democratic-Republican asked: Didn't the former practice assure that political "offices run in the blood of families and descend from father to son?" Moreover, wasn't the latter practice also undemocratic because it restricted voter turnout? Sensing the necessity of change in order to maintain the support of downstate yeoman farmers, Delaware's Federalists switched to the Democratic-Republican practice of a state nominating convention. In 1811 they also joined with their political opponents to enact legislation which set up polling places in each hundred (subdivisions of Delaware's counties).

During the late eighteenth and early nineteenth century, the Federalist Party won most statewide elections. The few Democratic-Republican victories resulted from a strategy of running a downstate candidate who would attract some normally Federalist votes to augment predictable support from New Castle County. David Hall and Joseph Haslet of Sussex, for example, were two Democratic-Republicans elected by this strategy to the governorship in 1801 and in 1810, respectively.

When the United States declared war on Great Britain in 1812, Delaware's Federalist Party faced a particular challenge. Its traditional pro-British stance was well known. Moreover, the national Federalist leadership, now concentrated in New England, made no bones about opposition to the war and in subsequent years, would even talk of secession. Delaware's Federalists also initially resisted what they called "Mr. Madison's war." But unlike their New England brethren, they strongly supported the war effort once hostilities broke out, thus escaping the charge of disloyalty. In fact, at the end of the War of 1812, President Madison chose leading Delaware Federalist and U.S. Senator James A. Bayard as one of the American peace negotiators.

During the war some Delawareans made a name for themselves. Thomas Macdonough directed the key American naval victory on Lake Champlain, while Dr. James Tilton was appointed surgeon general of the U.S. Army. Very little actual fighting occurred on Delaware soil but the presence of English warships in nearby waters, and the constant threat of British landing parties, kept residents in a state of anxiety. Of particular concern were British raids in Cecil County, Maryland in 1813, which brought enemy forces within sixteen miles of the town of New Castle.

The only military event to have taken place in Delaware, however, was the British attack on Lewes. In early 1813 a British squadron appeared at the mouth of the Delaware Bay and bottled up regional shipping. The British commander threatened to destroy Lewes that April if its townspeople didn't supply his ships with provisions. Under the command of native son Colonel Samuel B. Davis, the small Delaware town refused and three British vessels began a twenty-two-hour bombardment. Seeing that the shelling was ineffective, the British experienced further frustration when a landing party of marines was driven off by militia. The British fleet then gave up the attack, leaving the townsmen to survey the results of the bombardment. A few houses were slightly damaged and a few domestic animals had been hit, giving rise to a bit of Lewes doggerel: "The Commodore and all his men, shot a dog and killed a hen."

Above
Commodore Thomas Macdonough, a Delaware native, gained fame as a naval hero when he led the American fleet to victory over the British in Lake Champlain during the War of 1812. Courtesy, Historical Society of Delaware

Right
In April 1813, the village of Lewes was bombarded by British warships demanding provisions. The townspeople held firm, and the English finally gave up their attempt. The cannons used in defense of Lewes remained in place when this photograph was taken sometime during the 1890s. Courtesy, Historical Society of Delaware

The Nanticoke River linked Sea-
ford with the Chesapeake Bay.
During the nineteenth century,
schooners carried oysters to this
town for packing and shipping.
Courtesy, Historical Society of
Delaware

CHAPTER V

DELAWARE IN THE NINETEENTH CENTURY

High on a hill to the west of Wilmington stood the blue granite mansion and farm of Dr. James Tilton, former surgeon general of the United States Army. It was Christmas, 1815, but inside his home the tall, spare, bachelor of seventy-one could be excused for not getting into the festive spirit of the season. Less than three weeks earlier the discovery of a large tumor had led to the amputation of one of his legs.

Confined to his home, Tilton followed from his window the courses of the Brandywine and Christina rivers as they twisted their way to Union just to the east of Wilmington. What a contrast they were and how they complemented each other and the town. The fast flowing Brandywine was ideal for mill sites. Only a decade earlier Tilton had written that the grain mills along the Brandywine, just below the bridge connecting Wilmington with the road to Philadelphia, "were the largest and most perfect [for the] manufacture of flour within a like space of ground in the world." By contrast, the meandering Christina proved unsuitable for mill sites but ideal as a highway for the river traffic which connected Wilmington with the rest of the Delaware Valley and ports beyond. Between the two rivers lay a growing commercial center of approximately 5,000 inhabitants. And yet, despite Wilmington's obvious vitality, the panorama before Dr. Tilton remained fundamentally bucolic. Indeed, most of the mills on the Brandywine, most of the river traffic on the Christina, and much of the commercial activity in Wilmington were tied to the agricultural economy of the surrounding area.

Dr. Tilton died in 1822, too soon to observe from his window the remarkable changes about to occur between the valleys of the Brandywine and the Christina. Perhaps that was for the best because Dr. Tilton believed in the virtues of the agrarian way of life which had characterized Delaware's past. The rapid population growth and industrialization of the Wilmington

Above
Dr. James Tilton, surgeon, abolitionist, and agriculturalist, witnessed many political and economic changes in his native state. He was born during the colonial era, watched Delaware achieve statehood, but died before Wilmington became a manufacturing center. Courtesy, Historical Society of Delaware

Right
The Chesapeake and Delaware Canal became a national waterway in 1919, when purchased by the federal government. Besides being deepened and enlarged, the canal subsequently underwent another major change: its locks were removed to facilitate transoceanic shipping. Courtesy, Delaware State Archives

area during the mid- and late-nineteenth century would have been very difficult to accept.

❦

In 1810 only one of fifteen Delawareans lived in Wilmington; ninety years later it was six of fifteen. By 1900 Wilmington's population had grown to more than 76,000 and had dramatically altered Delaware's traditional population pattern. In 1810 New Castle County had been slightly larger than Kent, but slightly smaller than Sussex. Thanks to Wilmington's remarkable growth, by the turn of the century New Castle County's population was approximately 35,000 larger than the combined total of Kent and Sussex. The key to this extraordinary demographic change was concentrated industrial development along the Christina and, to a lesser extent, the Brandywine.

During the early nineteenth century, the growth and prosperity of an American city was largely dependent on the size and nature of its hinterland. The larger and more bountiful the geographic area serviced by the city, the greater the demand for urban businesses to market the products of the countryside and to provide commercial services and consumer goods for residents of the hinterland.

Philadelphia recognized the importance of expanding its own hinterland—even if it was at the expense of nearby cities—and commenced building canals and railroads into regions economically tied to Wilmington,

Baltimore, and other nearby urban centers. One example was the Chesapeake and Delaware Canal, completed in 1829 and primarily financed by Philadelphia's business community. Crossing the Delmarva Peninsula approximately fifteen miles south of Wilmington, the canal diverted much of the commerce of the Susquehanna Valley from Baltimore to the Quaker City. Although it reduced Baltimore's hinterland, the Chesapeake and Delaware Canal had little impact on Wilmington.

A few years later it was Wilmington's turn to lose much of its hinterland to Philadelphia. The fertile grain lands of southeastern Pennsylvania, which had been economically tied to Wilmington, became part of Philadelphia's economic empire with the completion of a railroad line from the Quaker City to Columbia on the lower Susquehanna in the early 1830s. Toward the end of the decade, the newly constructed Philadelphia, Wilmington and Baltimore Railroad further diminished Wilmington's commercial hinterland and, by 1840, not only New Castle County but most of the rest of Delaware lay under the commercial domination of the Quaker City.

But history is full of ironies. The same transportation innovations that allowed Philadelphia to curtail Wilmington's future as a trading and commercial center, paradoxically made possible the latter's remarkable development as an industrial city. By the mid-nineteenth century a network of railroads and canals was bringing large supplies of coal and iron to Philadelphia which,

The Wilmington and Western Railroad first chugged through the hilly terrain of northern New Castle County in the 1870s. Company directors, local farmers, and industrialists hoped to connect Wilmington to new western markets, but the line only expanded twenty miles to nearby Landenberg, Pennsylvania. Courtesy, Historical Society of Delaware

73

in turn, could be easily transported to Wilmington via rail and barge connections. In addition to the availability of coal and iron, Wilmington already possessed a skilled work force that had built and serviced the Brandywine mills, plus considerable venture capital gained through mill profits and the shipping operations of earlier years. All three of these factors combined to transform the city's economic base. According to historian Carol Hoffecker, so rapid was the industrializing process that "in the thirty years following 1840, Wilmington became the first city in the United States in the manufacture of railroad cars and iron ships."

Most of Wilmington's factories were built on the city's east and south sides, along the narrow corridor of land between the Philadelphia, Wilmington and Balti-

more Railroad and the north bank of the Christina River (see map of Delaware). Besides the availability of transportation facilities, this area attracted manufacturers because the decline in Wilmington's maritime commerce kept real estate prices along the river at reasonable levels.

The once clean air of the lower Christina Valley was now smudged by the plumes of black smoke belching from the factories of railroad equipment producers and iron shipbuilders such as Harlan and Hollingsworth, Pusey and Jones, the Lobdell Car Wheel Company, and Jackson and Sharp. Along the Brandywine a secondary industrial concentration of paper, cotton, and gunpowder mills poured pollutants into the river.

But fouling the air and water seemed a small price to

Facing page
Wilmington's central business district shortly after the turn of the century reached from the banks of the Christina River northward along Market Street. Men in suits and bowler hats jammed the sidewalks making their way to a profusion of stores, offices, and banks. Courtesy, Historical Society of Delaware

Right
By 1900 over one-third of Delaware's people lived in Wilmington. The smokestack city manufactured ships, railroad cars, leather goods, paper, and textiles. Courtesy, Historical Society of Delaware

pay for the new jobs created and the new fortunes amassed. By 1853 railroad car manufacturing employed 675 workers. As 1880 approached, a thousand men labored at Jackson and Sharp's railroad car plant alone and approximately 45 percent of Wilmington's employed residents worked in factories. Employment possibilities in new and expanding plants caused the local population to register enormous gains as shown in the chart on page 126.

Because of rapid industrialization, Wilmington took on many of the social characteristics of a typical American factory town. Recalling his boyhood as a business executive's son during the 1890s, Henry S. Canby remembered the city as a very class conscious society. "There were Negroes, and the working people, the plain people and us."

In the 1700s Wilmington's "Negroes" lived in scattered clusters on the least valuable land, a pattern that continued into the nineteenth century. Although a few black residents owned shops or served as ship's carpenters, trade union discrimination during the nineteenth century seriously diminished opportunities for blacks to become skilled workers.

By the late 1800s, blacks represented between 10 and 15 percent of Wilmington's population. Although a very modest figure by modern urban standards, their presence created tensions that erupted in a race riot in

1880, when seventeen whites and six blacks were injured by flying stones and gunfire. Wilmington's white politicians often took advantage of racial tensions by launching verbal attacks on blacks as a means of diverting attention from controversial local issues.

Henry Canby's "working people" were Wilmington's blue-collar labor force. They and their families lived on the city's crowded east side near the factories and shops where they regularly put in sixty-hour weeks. Their numbers were constantly augmented during the mid- and late-nineteenth century by a steady influx of farm boys from Delaware and nearby Pennsylvania and Maryland, as well as immigrants from Ireland, Germany, and later, southern and eastern Europe. Although 19 percent of Wilmington's population was foreign born by 1860, the immigrant population never reached the proportions found in most other northern American cities. As a result, friction between European immigrant and native born was less in Wilmington than in other urban centers.

Canby's "plain people" represented the city's lower middle class, including clerks, most of the other white-collar business and industrial employees, and owners of small establishments such as grocery and clothing stores. They lived in identical brick houses which covered the lower slopes of Wilmington's hills, overlooking the congested tenements of the factory workers.

Above
Moving pictures and vaudeville shows at theaters like Wilmington's Majestic delighted thousands of city dwellers. Courtesy, Historical Society of Delaware

Right
The Kickapoo Indian Medicine Company, a traveling patent medicine troup, camped at Tower Road and West Nineteenth Street in Wilmington in 1892. Hucksters offered both entertainment and cure-all remedies. Courtesy, Historical Society of Delaware

The growing number of white-collar workers, employed as clerks or managers, kept some distance from the poorer neighborhoods. This unidentified family furnished their home with the "artistic" styles popular after the turn of the century. Courtesy, Historical Society of Delaware

Wilmington's working class and immigrants endured the crowded east side, where public playgrounds and settlement houses provided recreation and educational opportunities. Both children and adults turned out to watch this marbles contest circa 1910. Courtesy, Historical Society of Delaware

Above the "plain people" on the crest of hills that stretched to the west were the spacious homes of Wilmington's wealthy—Canby's "us"—who owned or managed the factories and large business operations. Clearly, by the late nineteenth century, class affiliation dictated where most of Wilmington's citizens resided.

Although the city's housing patterns generally echoed those of other American factory towns, in one significant way Wilmington was different. In many industrial centers such as Lowell and Chicopee, Massachusetts, the owners of local factories often lived elsewhere, and were correspondingly insensitive to the social, educational, and health needs of the community. By contrast, Wilmington's leading entrepreneurs continued to dwell in or near the city, and this made them sensitive to many of the problems created by the city's rapid industrial and population growth. As a result, the factory owners and business executives stood at the forefront of reform movements to improve Wilmington's water supply, sanitation facilities, schools, religious and charitable institutions, and cultural life.

Positive steps to meet Wilmington's specific needs included the establishment, in 1871, of the city's first public high school, complementing thirteen elementary

schools already in service; and municipal sewerage construction and repavement of city streets in the 1890s. By the end of the century, nearly 11,000 students were enrolled in Wilmington's public schools and the city's death rate had significantly declined.

The wives and daughters of Wilmington's upper middle class spearheaded many of these reforms. Freed from the drudgery of domestic labor by house servants, some women found an outlet for their energies and talents in establishing organizations and institutions which would improve the quality of local life. One example was Emalea Pusey Warner, daughter of a Quaker manufacturer and wife of a shipping executive. She founded the city's Associated Charities in 1884 to coordinate the rapidly growing number of private welfare agencies. Martha Gause joined her husband, the railroad car manufacturer J. Taylor Gause, in organizing the Homeopathic Hospital, later Memorial Hospital, which, in 1888, admitted its first patients. The wife of a prominent Wilmington lawyer and politician, Mary H. Harrington played a major role in the founding of the Delaware Hospital which opened in 1890.

The transformation of Wilmington from commercial town to industrial city forced its residents to confront, at an early date, some of the same problems that would one day tax the resourcefulness of the entire state. Because they had already taken positive steps in dealing with health and educational needs, as well as unemployment, Wilmingtonians possessed the necessary experience and insight to lead long overdue state-wide efforts to cope with these and many other issues dur-

Right
Founded by followers of Henry George in 1900, the northern Delaware village of Arden flourished as a haven for artists, writers, and craftsmen who shared utopian ideals. Courtesy, Historical Society of Delaware

Far right
This interesting octagonal structure in Hockessin was one of many schools built after the 1829 passage of the Delaware School Law which first established public education in the state. Courtesy, Delaware State Archives

ing the nineteenth and twentieth centuries.

Education in Delaware was haphazardly organized and questionably effective throughout the late 1700s and early 1800s. Privately run elementary schools and, subsequently, Sunday schools (until the mid-nineteenth century the latter concentrated on basic education rather than religious instruction) could be found in most towns and villages. More advanced education was offered through private academies which first appeared during the 1760s in Newark and Wilmington and later, in many other Delaware communities.

Newark Academy became Newark College in 1833, only to change its name to Delaware College in 1843. It closed within sixteen years because of a financial crisis. The resultant image problem was exacerbated by a murder stemming from a student fracas. In 1870 Delaware College reopened to an assured future as the state land grant institution. It eventually evolved into the University of Delaware.

Despite these private and church related educational efforts, probably a majority of Delawareans were either illiterate or only semi-literate well into the nineteenth century. Moreover, because so few finished high school or had the money to go on, attendance at Delaware College or an out-of-state college was a possibility open to only a tiny minority of young people during the nineteenth century.

In 1803 Willard Hall, a Massachusetts native and Harvard graduate, arrived in Dover to practice law. Accustomed to relatively good schools in New England, he was shocked by the private schools he found in central Delaware and particularly by the teachers, whose primary qualifications seemed to be the "inability to earn anything in any other way," and who were sometimes drunk on the job. After a distinguished political career, Hall was appointed a federal district judge. He moved to Wilmington in 1823 where he viewed first-hand the educational concerns and opportunities facing Delaware's largest community. Convinced that not only Wilmington but the entire state desperately needed a public school system, Hall drew up and then persuaded the legislature to pass the School Law of 1829. This bill divided each of the three counties into a number of school districts, promising state matching funds up to $300 of what the local school distict could raise. Because local districts were free to collect any amount they wished, a considerable disparity developed between them; some districts completely failed to provide public education because they did not wish to levy a local tax. And yet, despite its imperfections, Judge Willard Hall's School Law of 1829 committed Delaware's state government to meet at least part of the expenses of a statewide public school system.

Only two years before the passage of the school law, a special congressional election led to the demise of Delaware's two political parties. In 1827 neither the dominant Federalists nor their Democratic-Republican opponents could unite behind one congressional candidate. Indeed, the election caused so much internal discord that both parties ceased to exist in the state. Louis McLane of Wilmington then led some erstwhile Delaware Federalists and many former Democratic-Republicans into the Democratic party of Andrew Jackson. However, a majority of Federalists and the remaining Democratic-Republicans became anti-Jackson Whigs.

The leader of Delaware's Whigs was John M. Clayton who, according to historian John Munroe, became "the most successful politician in Delaware's history." Clayton was so well known and liked by his fellow Delawareans, that on occasion it would take him an hour just to cross the Dover Green. Dagsboro-born and Milford-raised, he held a number of important state offices, served three terms in the U.S. Senate, and accepted a cabinet seat as U.S. Secretary of State from 1849-1851. The famous Clayton-Bulwer Treaty of 1850, providing for the neutralization of a future canal across Central America, and Buena Vista, Clayton's home, now preserved by the state on the west side of Route 13 in New Castle County, are just part of this remarkable politician's legacy.

One of Delaware's most popular and successful politicians, John M. Clayton, was born in Dagsboro in 1796. He attended Yale, trained in law, and began his long political career in his twenties. Clayton served as U.S. senator, secretary of state, and chief justice of Delaware. Courtesy, Historical Society of Delaware

Like the Federalists before them, the Whigs proved strongest in Kent and Sussex, but also received support from the factory and mill owners of New Castle County who agreed with the Whig program of protective tariffs, internal improvements, and a national bank. This coalition of downstate farmers and upstate manufacturers made the Whigs the dominant political party in the state until 1850. Shortly after mid-century, however, a combination of divisive issues and poor leadership led to the collapse of the Whig Party in Delaware and across the United States.

The most divisive political issue was slavery. Although Delaware never did have the number of slaves found in states to the south, the question of abolition produced heated debates and roiled political waters for decades.

Delaware's slave population declined from a high point of 8,887 in 1790 to 1,798 in 1860. By the latter date, 75 percent of the remaining slaves were concentrated in Sussex County. The anemic condition of slavery in Delaware reflected certain economic realities, plus the early abolitionist efforts of Methodists and Quakers. Another significant inhibiting factor was the absence of one-crop agriculture—such as cotton, sugar, or tobacco—to which slavery seemed particularly well suited. In addition, the profitable Virginia practice of selling slaves to the plantations of the rapidly expanding cotton lands of Alabama, Mississippi, and Texas was difficult to emulate in Delaware because a 1787 law prohibited the sale of slaves beyond the state's boundaries.

As practiced in Delaware, slavery was probably less repugnant than elsewhere in America. With the most liberal slave code, the state also claimed the lowest average of slaves per master. By 1860 only eight of Delaware's 587 slave masters owned more than fifteen blacks. Indeed, the twenty-eight bonded to Benjamin Burton of Indian River Hundred, Sussex County, made him the largest slave owner in the entire state. The low number of slaves per master insured that master-slave relationships in the First State were more personal and, therefore, more humane than found on the large plantations of the deep South.

But there were some examples of Delaware's slave owners physically abusing their servants. One extreme case involved Theophilus, a slave in the Lewes area, who ignored his master's injunction against attending church by going to a Sunday evening service in 1858. The next morning Theophilus was called into the master's home where he paid the price for disobedience: he was beaten so harshly by a whip, iron tongs, gun, and shovel that the last two instruments were broken in the process. Terrified and severely battered, Theophilus told his master that he was determined "to come out of that room." His master then drew a pocket knife and proceeded to lay open the unfortunate slave's stomach and stab him in the head. Somehow the desperate Theophilus broke free and headed for Georgetown, "carrying a part of my entrails in my hands for the whole journey, sixteen miles." Although not expected to live, Theophilus did recover thanks to the ministrations of an old black woman and some white physicians. Subsequently he made his way north via the underground railroad to Pennsylvania and freedom.

For Theophilus and the other slaves fleeing north through the Delmarva Peninsula, the last underground railroad station before the Pennsylvania line and freedom was the Wilmington home of Thomas Garrett, a Quaker iron merchant. In 1820 Garrett decided to devote his life to abolitionism and over the next four de-

Thomas Garrett, a Quaker iron merchant, is credited with helping over 2,000 slaves escape to freedom on the underground railroad. Courtesy, Historical Society of Delaware

cades, he helped more than 2,000 blacks reach freedom. Garrett was repeatedly threatened with physical violence by irate slaveholders and their sympathizers in the process. Moreover, because his actions were illegal, a U.S. circuit court fined him so heavily that he lost all of his property. Undeterred by this decision, Garrett turned defiantly to Presiding Judge Roger B. Taney, who was also Chief Justice of the U.S. Supreme Court. The Quaker abolitionist promised that although "thou has left me without a dollar, . . . I say to thee and to all in this court room, that if anyone knows a fugitive who wants shelter . . . send him to Thomas Garrett and he will befriend him." Thanks to business loans, the abolitionist made an economic recovery while simultaneously keeping his promise of continued aid to runaway slaves. After the Civil War Wilmington's blacks honored Garrett with a parade which included a banner proclaiming him "Our Moses."

As slavery declined, the number of free blacks dramatically rose from 3,899 in 1790 to nearly 20,000 in 1860. By the latter date, free blacks represented nearly one out of five Delawareans. Uneasiness among whites over the presence of so many free blacks reached new heights after Nat Turner's rebellion resulted in sixty white deaths in Virginia in 1831. Petitions demanding increasingly oppressive measures to curtail the liberty of free blacks were received by the Delaware legislature, and some became law. By 1837 a visiting representative of the American Anti-Slavery Society found that the state's free blacks enjoyed "a mere mock freedom."

Despite the 1847 abolition bill which came very close to passage in the Delaware legislature, white racial fears continued to be well pronounced, particularly in rural areas. With the collapse of the dominant Whig Party in the early 1850s, the Democrats seized the opportunity to capture the allegiance of white Kent and Sussex countians by opposing both equal rights for free blacks and the emancipation of Delaware's remaining slaves. Although the anti-Catholic American Party, made up of former Whigs, won the state election of 1854, the Democratic Party's willingness to pander to white racism brought victory at the polls in 1856.

Across the nation the increasing acrimony over race and slavery dramatically intensified regional differences, eventually leading to war between the North and the South. Just as with the American Revolution, Delaware's small size and geographic location limited its options during the Civil War. The First State's traditional loyalty to the Union and the decision of its much larger neighbors, Pennsylvania and Maryland, to oppose secession caused Delaware to cast its lot with the North and to reject overtures made by several representatives of the Confederacy.

Loyalty to the Union, however, didn't necessarily translate into statewide support for President Lincoln and his policies. This attitude was reflected in the election of 1860 when Lincoln captured only 24 percent of Delaware's vote and in 1864 when he won merely 48 percent of the ballots cast. During the latter contest, Delaware earned the distinction of being one of three northern states to support Lincoln's Democratic opponent, George McClellan. Indeed, suspicion of the Republican president and his policies probably led to the rejection of Lincoln's November 1861 proposal calling for the liberation of Delaware slaves. If the state legislature had approved this measure, all slaves would have been freed and their owners compensated from federal funds at approximately $500 per slave. As Lincoln told Sussex County slaveholder Benjamin Burton, he envisioned the Delaware initiative as a trial balloon. "If I can get Delaware to undertake this plan, I'm sure the other border states will accept it. This is the cheapest and most humane way of ending this war and saving lives." But Lincoln's hopes were dashed when the Delaware legislature failed to bring his emancipation plan to a vote.

In its reaction to this measure and to the president's prosecution of the war, the First State split along predictable geographic lines. Kent and, more particularly, Sussex were very vocal in their opposition to Lincoln's actions. U.S. Senator Willard Saulsbury, a Democrat from Georgetown, even rose on the floor of the U.S. Senate to call the president "a despot." A number of southern Delawareans—perhaps a few hundred—went so far as to join the Confederate army. Conversely, New Castle County supported Lincoln and gave him 53 percent of its vote in the 1864 election.

Despite the political tensions that divided the First State, Delaware provided thousands of recruits for the Union army, at first through voluntary enlistment and later by way of a lottery draft. Irish immigrants, attracted by enlistment bounties, were particularly numerous among the Delaware regiments. Although no battles took place on the state's soil, casualties to its servicemen—over one-third of the seven hundred members of the First Delaware Regiment were killed or wounded at Antietam—and rumor of Confederate invasion brought home at least some of the realities of the Civil War. Moreover, the festering prisoner of war camp at Fort Delaware, on Pea Patch Island, was yet another reminder of the terrible struggle between the Union and the Confederacy.

Although the Republican Party was founded in 1854, it didn't take root in Delaware and provide opposition to the dominant Democrats until the war years. The party of Lincoln particularly attracted New Castle County manufacturers because it stood for the same high tariffs and internal transportation improvements supported by the old Whigs. But it was the Republican Party's willingness to support the rights of blacks and the Democratic Party's sympathy for the South during the Civil War that set the tone and content for postwar political invective. Unabashedly proclaiming themselves "The White Man's Party," Delaware Democrats called Republicans "nigger lovers." Delaware Republicans countered that during the Civil War, their political opponents had clearly shown themselves to be "The Party of Treason."

Of particular concern to the state's Democrats was the projected impact of the Republican supported Fifteenth Amendment, ratified in March 1870, which guaranteed the right of black males to vote. Hitherto denied suffrage, approximately forty-five hundred Delaware blacks were now eligible to cast their ballots; and that would ensure a Republican victory because most blacks would definitely vote for the party of the Great Emancipator, Abraham Lincoln.

Fort Delaware was called the "Andersonville of the North" because of a high disease death rate. Courtesy, Historical Society of Delaware

But Delaware's Democrats weren't willing to surrender their political power without a fight. Back in the Civil War years, Lincoln's government had sent troops into Delaware to police elections, preventing Democrats from intimidating voters. The Democrats claimed, however, that the actual bullying came from the soldiers who kept some voters away from the polls and caused others to flee for their lives to the swamps of Sussex. Effectively using this example of federal interference to build up resentment against the Republican Party, the Democrats gained popularity during and right after the Civil War. But in 1870 they needed new tactics to win election contests. They consequently turned to voter intimidation and to an old state law which restricted suffrage to those males who paid either property or a capitation tax. Since the state's tax collectors were all Democrats, they prevented some blacks from paying taxes and refused to give receipts to others who were taxpayers. In addition, election day shenanigans by Democrats kept black voter participation to a minimum. At the request of irate Republicans, federal marshalls were positioned at polling places to assure black voting rights, but they proved ineffective and were even driven from the polls in Smyrna and Odessa. Needless to say, the Democrats won the election.

Because of the rough treatment of some of his federal marshalls in 1870, President Ulysses S. Grant sent troops into Delaware to police the election of 1872. Their presence at polling places, combined with a general dissatisfaction among Democrats with their own party's ticket, made some Republican candidates victorious. But the Democrats remained in control of the state legislature, and subsequently passed two measures that further restricted black voter participation and guaranteed Democratic domination of Delaware politics until the election of 1888.

The long-term success of the Democratic Party rested on its ability to attract the vote of the conservative,

The Bayard family dominated Democratic politics in Delaware for over a century. The son of Senator James A. Bayard, Thomas F. Bayard later occupied his father's seat, then became secretary of state and ambassador to Great Britain. His son, Thomas, followed the family political tradition, also rising to the U.S. Senate. Courtesy, Historical Society of Delaware

race-conscious, downstate farmers and, to a lesser degree the growing number of Wilmington's Irish immigrants who competed with blacks for unskilled jobs. Continually capturing both voting blocs through its image as "The White Man's Party," the Democrats pointed to success at halting Delaware's ratification of the Thirteenth (abolition of slavery), Fourteenth (equal rights for blacks), and Fifteenth Amendments (suffrage for black males). Indeed, thanks to Democratic intransigence, slavery persisted longer in the First State than anywhere else but Kentucky. It was only when the Thirteenth Amendment was approved by the requisite

number of states and took effect across the nation in December 1865, that both Delaware and Kentucky abandoned slavery.

Exercising power over the Democratic Party like medieval barons were the Bayards of Wilmington and the downstate Saulsbury family. Thomas Francis Bayard, scion of three generations of U.S. senators, was the most successful of these political power brokers. He served in the Senate (1869-85), then as U.S. Secretary of State, and Ambassador to Great Britain. In 1876, 1880, and 1884 Bayard was runner-up for his party's presidential nomination, a distinction that no other Delawarean has come close to sharing.

Three brothers who closed ranks when fighting with the Bayards for control of the Democratic Party, Eli, Gove, and Willard Saulsbury, also competed against each other for political office. Willard held a U.S. Senate seat from 1859 until 1871 when his serious drinking problem sparked senatorial ambitions in his two brothers. Just having completed a gubernatorial term, Gove narrowly lost the contest in the state legislature for Willard's seat to Eli, who went on to serve in the U.S. Senate for eighteen years. (U.S. senators were elected by Delaware's state legislature until the election of 1916).

The dynastic nature of the Democratic Party's leadership in the mid- and late-nineteenth century partly explains the Democrats' desire to maintain the old order and their reluctance to break new ground. But there were remarkable economic changes afoot that extended far beyond the booming industrial city of Wilmington, and these changes would one day set the stage for the defeat of the Democratic Party.

Initially, however, economic change came slowly to Delaware. Despite the rapid industrialization taking place along the Christina and Brandywine valleys, on the eve of the Civil War Delaware was still an overwhelmingly rural state with approximately seven times as many farmers and farmhands as factory workers. Although New Castle County farmers shared in the economic good times of nearby Wilmington, the rural economy farther south was in bad shape. Downstate agricultural lands had became unproductive after years of use and misuse. In Kent County alone, the wheat yield per acre was only one-third of what it had been in earlier years, and in Sussex many farmers simply ignored their played-out fields and turned to cutting timber. In 1850 New Castle County, containing less than one-third the combined land area of Kent and Sussex, produced twice as much wheat. No wonder so many young people from downstate Delaware recognized that better economic opportunities lay elsewhere and de-

WOODLAND BEACH.

HOTEL, PAVILION AND PARK
BOMBAY HOOK, DELAWARE BAY.

THE TERMINUS OF THE DAILY MORNING
EXCURSION BY THE STEAMER "THOMAS CLYDE."

Above
Like other resorts on the Delaware Bay, Woodland Beach boomed during the era of steamboat travel. Swift ships such as the Thomas Clyde encouraged day trips from Wilmington and Philadelphia. Courtesy, Delaware State Archives

Left
Blacksmiths like Glenn Truitt provided a variety of goods and services in the rural economy. They shod horses and repaired or built farm equipment, household tools, hinges, and hardware. Courtesy, Delaware State Archives

Above
"Alberta McNadd on Chester Truitt's farm. Alberta is 5 years old and has been picking berries since she was 3. Her mother volunteered the information that she picks from sun-up to sun-down." Reformer and documentary journalist Lewis Hine wrote these descriptions and took this picture in Cannon, Sussex County, on May 28, 1910. Courtesy, National Archives

Right
"James Loqulla, a newsboy, 12 years old. Selling papers for 3 years. Average earnings 50 cents a week. Sellings not needed at home. Don't smoke, visits saloons, works 7 hours a day." Wilmington, May 1910. Courtesy, National Archives

Above
"Group of girl workers at the gate of the American Tobacco Co. Young girls obviously under 14 years of age, who work about 10 hours every day except Saturday." Wilmington, May 1910. Courtesy, National Archives

Above
Reformer and documentary photographer Lewis Hine described his subject: "Richard Pierce, Western Union Telegraph Co. Messenger No. 2. 14 years of age, 9 months in service, works from 7 A.M. to 6 P.M. Smokes, and visits houses of prostitution." Wilmington, May 1910. Courtesy, National Archives

Left
"Daisy Langford, 8 years old, works on Ross's Canneries, Seaford, Del. She helps at the capping machine, but is not yet able to keep up. She places caps on cans at the rate of about 40 per minute working full time. This is her first season in the cannery." June 1, 1910. Courtesy, National Archives

Left
Documentary photographer
Lewis Hine wrote, "Michael
Mero, bootblack, 12 years of age,
working one year of own voli-
tion. Don't smoke. Out after 11
P.M. on May 21. Ordinarily
works 6 hours per day." Wil-
mington, May 1910. Courtesy,
National Archives

Top, facing page
"Mother and children hulling
strawberries at Johnson's Hulling
Station. Cyral (in baby cart) is
two years old this May and
works steadily hulling berries.
And Cyral would rest his little
head on his arm and fall asleep
for a few minutes and wake up
again commencing all over to
hull berries. This is an extreme
case by no means typical and
while it was found in this inves-
tigation that children of 3, 4, 5
years are accustomed to start out
before sun-up to pick berries,
we have not found cases like
this." Seaford, May 26, 1910.
Courtesy, National Archives

Right
"3 year old and 2 boys hulling
berries at Johnson's Canning
Camp." Seaford, May 26, 1910.
Courtesy, National Archives

Far right
Shoppers in 1928 could buy
fresh meat, eggs, and produce
from farmers at Wilmington's
King Street Market. Courtesy,
Historical Society of Delaware

Right
The introduction of railroads
and steamboats in the 1830s
made the widespread marketing
of an old Delaware crop,
peaches, lucrative. The peach
boom was short-lived, however.
Blight destroyed much of the
marketable crop by the 1890s,
and farmers switched to other
produce. Courtesy, Historical So-
ciety of Delaware

parted in very substantial numbers for the West or such urban centers as Baltimore, Wilmington, and Philadelphia. This large out-migration caused the combined population of Kent and Sussex to remain approximately the same from 1810 to 1850. For those who stayed, the only hope rested in the use of fertilizers to replenish the mineral-depleted soil and in the development of a transportation system that would provide quick and cheap delivery of perishable farm produce to the rapidly growing urban centers stretching from Baltimore to New York City.

The spreading of horse, cow, and sheep manure; guano (excrement of sea birds); and lime on the fields of northern Delaware was commonplace by the 1830s. The resulting increase in fertility of the area's farmland caused the *Baltimore Sun* in 1846 to call New Castle County "the paradise, the garden spot of Delaware," comparing it with the nation's most productive agricul-

much more remains to be done, particularly in the lower two counties."

Prior to the early nineteenth century, most of Delaware's bulk goods were moved slowly and erratically by sail on creeks and rivers. Transporting bulky cargoes over sometimes impassible roads via wagon was much costlier and neither faster nor markedly more dependable.

To improve land transportation, a number of turnpike companies were chartered in Delaware beginning in 1808. All of the toll roads subsequently built however, radiated out from Wilmington to service only northern New Castle County. In any event, water continued to be cheaper than turnpikes for moving most bulk cargoes. Water transport became more dependable when steamboats with fixed schedules connected many downstate Delaware towns with Philadelphia after the War of 1812. In addition to the usual corn and wheat, downstate farmers near steamboat landings could now think seriously about raising a perishable cash crop for shipment to northern urban centers.

Peaches had been grown in colonial times, but it wasn't until 1832 that Delaware's first commercial orchard was planted near Delaware City. By 1840 half of the surrounding land was covered with peach orchards. Philip Reybold quickly established himself as Delaware's peach king by growing 117,720 trees in the Delaware City area and sending 125,000 baskets via steamer to Philadelphia and New York markets in 1848. Two years later, one observer said: "There probably is not another place in the United States that supplies so

tural areas. From New Castle County, the new methods for restoring the soil spread southward, and in 1846 one observer found them being employed in Kent, "but not yet extended into Sussex." By 1851 a native of the Seaford area noticed that more Sussex farmers were using fertilizers. However, he also admitted that poor farming practices continued. Governor William Burton of Milford praised Delaware's recent agricultural advances in his 1859 inaugural address, but added "that

many peaches for market as Delaware City."

Peach orchards were slow to spread to Kent and Sussex because most downstate farmers were some distance from steamboat landings, and the connecting wagon ride over poor roads bruised the fruit before it could be loaded aboard a steamer. An extension southward of the already existing railroad in New Castle County was the obvious solution to the problem.

In 1859 the Delaware Railroad, which had been pushing south from Wilmington for more than a decade, finally reached Delmar on the Maryland border. Once south of Dover the line had cut through southwestern Kent and western Sussex, opening up for agricultural development some of the most isolated and neglected sections of Delaware. Economic life quickened all along the train route. New towns such as Clayton, Wyoming, Felton, and Harrington appeared, and older communities such as Middletown, Dover,

and Seaford grew more rapidly than the old port towns along the Delaware River and Bay.

A blight decimated the peach trees around Delaware City in the decade before the Civil War, but within proximity of the railroad in Sussex, and particularly in Kent, peach orchards dominated the landscape. During

The crew of the oyster schooner Doris *posed for this portrait in 1924 near the Delaware or Chesapeake Bay. Oyster boats might be at sea for a week or more before returning to harbor, where the catch was shipped—fresh or canned—to distant markets. Courtesy, Delaware State Archives*

the post-Civil War years, the rail network pushed into almost every corner of the state and touched almost every community, causing peach orchards to spread all over the southern portions of Delaware. By 1875, five million baskets of the fruit were annually shipped north by the Delaware Railroad.

The peach era was shortlived. Having decimated the orchards in the Delaware City area in the 1850s, the blight reached downstate Delaware three decades later. Due to this epidemic, the total number of Delaware peach trees was almost cut in half from 1890 to 1900, and by 1911 the apple had replaced the peach as the state's primary orchard fruit. Other perishable cash crops such as tomatoes, peas, beans, melons, and particularly strawberries helped fill the void. According to the census of 1900, more strawberries were produced in Sussex than any other county in the nation. As for northern Delaware, easy access to Wilmington's growing population caused many New Castle County farmers to turn to the production of milk.

A widespread rail network and a growing demand from nearby urban centers for fruits, vegetables, and milk, had caused a marked change in the economy of rural Delaware by the early twentieth century. Although farming continued to be the occupation of the overwhelming majority of downstate citizens, the increasingly volatile urban marketplace reshaped its nature.

And yet the pace and rhythm of daily life in the countryside remained virtually uninterrupted. Field work continued to follow the predictable patterns of an earlier era, dictated by the changing seasons and the closely tied cycle of clearing, plowing, planting, cultivating, and harvesting. As in the past, the mules and horses which did the pulling and hauling demanded daily attention. Although cash income rose over earlier years, farm life continued to offer little material reward. In fact, one-half of Delaware's farms in 1890 were worked by tenants, causing the state to rank sixth nationally in this category.

Conservative attitudes maintained their hold over the countryside as they had since time out of mind. The only real challenge to the status quo had come from the radical principles espoused by early Methodism; but that challenge largely ended in the early 1800s when Methodism began to modify some of its most revolutionary ideas. So uncomfortable was the typical Delaware farmer with new ways and attitudes that he could best be described as reluctantly and uneasily sliding his front foot forward into the twentieth century while keeping his back foot firmly planted in the eighteenth century.

Spring in Delaware traditionally meant the return of shad to the Delaware River. Fishing fleets at Bowers brought back boatloads at a time. Although pollution caused a decline in the catch by the 1950s, the shad population is now making a comeback. Courtesy, Delaware State Archives

The junction of Fourth and Market streets was Wilmington's busiest intersection in 1928. Businessmen, factory workers, and shoppers hastily shuffled about the sidewalks, and trolley lines converged from all points. Courtesy, Historical Society of Delaware

CHAPTER VI

THE AGE OF DU PONT

On February 14, 1902, Pierre S. du Pont of Lorain, Ohio received a long distance phone call from Wilmington, Delaware. On the other end, cousin T. Coleman du Pont's booming voice related some interesting news: the family-owned powder-making firm was for sale and he and cousin Alfred I. du Pont intended to purchase it. Wouldn't Pierre join them? Pierre, who had some premonition of the offer, took only three minutes before saying yes. He then made ready to return to Delaware. That three-minute phone call marked a turning point in the history of the Du Pont Company, the city of Wilmington, and the state of Delaware.

Pierre du Pont had been born in 1870 at Nemours, his family's home on the Brandywine, a few miles from downtown Wilmington. When he was eleven his family moved to Philadelphia where Pierre attended private school. Three years later his father was killed at work by a nitroglycerin explosion leav-

*Pictured here is Alfred I. du
Pont, who with his cousins,
Coleman and Pierre S., kept the
Du Pont Company in family
hands and greatly diversified its
operations. Courtesy, Delaware
State Archives*

modernize its archaic business practices, he moved to
Ohio in 1899 where he became a successful financier.
When Coleman's important phone call reached him
three years later, Pierre was confident that his two
cousins shared his own feeling; the Du Pont Company
needed a drastic overhaul if it was to meet the challenges of the twentieth century.

Cousins Coleman and Alfred each played a significant role in the modernization of first the company
and then the state. But it was Pierre who cast the largest shadow and who ultimately proved to have the
greatest impact on the lives of his fellow Delawareans.
Indeed, more than any other person, Pierre S. du Pont
shaped the development of twentieth century Delaware.

In the thirty-five years that followed the Civil War,
the First State underwent a remarkable economic transformation. By 1900 more Delawareans were employed
in manufacturing than in farming. Even downstaters
felt the impact of the Industrial Revolution. Soon after
Kent and Sussex turned to the growing of perishable
farm produce, factories began to appear along train sid-
ings to process food and build baskets, crates, and
boxes in which local fruits and vegetables could be
shipped to distant markets. In Georgetown during the

ing Pierre, as the oldest son, with considerable responsibility for nine brothers and sisters.

Like his two older cousins, Coleman and Alfred,
Pierre attended Massachusetts Institute of Technology.
But unlike his two Delaware cousins, he stayed long
enough to graduate. A painfully shy child, Pierre was
never totally comfortable with public speaking. Although he always regarded this personal trait as a
handicap, it made him a particularly sensitive listener,
and that proved to be an invaluable asset in later life.

Pierre returned to Delaware after graduating from
M.I.T. and spent nine frustrating years working for the
family's powder-making firm. Thoroughly disgusted
with the unwillingness of the Du Pont Company to

late 1880s, for example, several hundred workers were employed by local canning and basket-making firms.

The owners and managers of these new, downstate industries, such as Henry Richardson of Dover and Charles H. Treat of Georgetown, found the pro-business stance of the Republican Party far more to their liking than the ultra-conservative position of the Democrats. Under the leadership of this new class of entrepreneurs, the Republican Party experienced remarkable growth in Kent and Sussex.

The Republican Party's new appeal to downstate whites combined with traditional Republican strength in New Castle County and among Delaware blacks to produce some election victories in the last twelve years of the nineteenth century. Indeed, so rapidly did this strength increase that during the first three decades of the twentieth century, Republican candidates won most statewide elections from their Democratic opponents. But before Republican dominance could be firmly established, a serious split in party ranks had to be mended.

Shortly after 1:00 a.m. on January 1, 1889, John Edward Charles O'Sullivan Addicks, sartorially elegant in sealskin coat and tall silk hat, startled a group of celebrating Republican legislators at Dover's Hotel Richardson by suddenly announcing that he would be available if the U.S. senatorial contest became deadlocked. The legislators asked each other: "Who is this

Above
John Edward O'Sullivan Addicks is best known for his unsuccessful and shady attempts to become a U.S. senator. Having earned his fortune by investing in gas company stocks, the maverick spent about three million dollars trying to buy votes in the Delaware Republican party. He went bankrupt by 1906 and died a pauper in New York thirteen years later. Courtesy, Historical Society of Delaware

Left
Milton was noted for tomato growing and canning. At one time the town boasted four tomato canneries, though most of these factories only operated during a six-week canning season and closed down the rest of the year. Courtesy, Delaware State Archives

mystery man?"

The son of a Philadelphia Republican politician, Addicks had become an extremely wealthy manipulator of gas company stocks. In 1887, at the age of thirty-six, he established his official residence in Claymont, Delaware. Initially unfamiliar with the state and its boundaries, Addicks was convinced that Claymont was in Delaware County, Pennsylvania. In 1888, a division in the leadership of Delaware's Democratic Party helped the Republicans win a surprise victory and control of the state legislature. On reading about the political upset in a New York City newspaper, Addicks suddenly remembered that he was a Delaware resident and subsequently made his surprise New Year's offer to the victorious Republicans.

Although the Republican-controlled legislature elected Anthony Higgins to the U.S. Senate, Addicks was not discouraged. Over the next fifteen years he spent perhaps three million dollars in a futile attempt to buy a U.S. Senate seat. In the process, Addicks created considerable turmoil and division within the Republican Party, paralyzing election procedures in the state legislature to such a great extent that Delaware had no U.S. senators from 1901-1903 and only one for the years 1895-1897, 1899-1901, and 1905-1906. A respected magazine of the day called the Addicks fiasco "a national scandal," and the general denunciation of events in Delaware eventually helped spark passage of

Built in 1881 to accommodate visitors to Delaware's capital city, the Hotel Richardson proclaimed itself to be the finest hotel in the state. It offered guests reading areas, parlors, and dining rooms and featured steam heat, gas lighting, and a bathroom on every floor—indeed, the most modern facilities of the day.

the Seventeenth Amendment in 1913, which provided for the direct election of U.S. senators.

Despite his offer to the Republicans in 1889, Addicks' initial concern was to get the Delaware legislature to charter the Bay State Gas Company, a Massachusetts venture that would become the lynch pin of his financial empire. (Delaware's very liberal General Incorporation Law, which has led to the chartering of many American corporations in Delaware and resulted in considerable tax income for the state, wasn't enacted until 1899. But even prior to 1899, Delaware had liberal chartering procedures which caused a number of out-of-state companies to apply to Delaware for incorporation.) Convinced that the Democrats would bounce back to win in 1890, Addicks donated $25,000 to their campaign coffers and, after the predicted victory, the state legislature chartered his Bay State Gas Company.

Since he no longer needed the Democratic Party, in 1892 Addicks officially registered as a Republican. By 1894 the Republicans were desperate for money to meet delinquent poll taxes so that many of their impoverished downstate supporters might vote. J. Frank Allee, a Dover Republican, brought this urgent issue before the party's leaders, who just happened to live in New Castle County. These upstate power brokers proved unsympathetic and an angry Allee turned to Addicks, an already established party contributor. Addicks met Allee in Philadelphia and promptly wrote out a check large enough to pay most of the delinquent Republican poll taxes in Kent and Sussex. In return, Allee may have promised to compensate Addicks with a U.S. Senate seat. Whatever the case, Addicks' financial support contributed to the 1894 Republican victory. Addicks then began his unscrupulous drive for a U.S. Senate seat, only to fall short because of courageous opposition by principled Republican leaders—or so the story goes. Actually, the Addicks' phenomenon was a bit more complicated than that.

As the nineteenth century drew to a close, the increasing demands of Kent and Sussex Republicans for a stronger voice in party affairs were largely ignored by the New Castle County leadership. Frustration led many downstaters to join the Addicks faction, which was called the Union Republican Party. Those remaining loyal to the New Castle County leadership referred to themselves as Regular Republicans, and portrayed Addicks' followers as venal opportunists who played right into the hands of the Democrats. In truth, both Republican factions as well as the Democrats so freely engaged in the buying and selling of votes that the Addicks era was the most corrupt period in the state's political history.

By 1907 financial reversals and the subsequent desertion by J. Frank Allee and other supporters drove Addicks from Delaware's political stage and finally, in 1919, to a pauper's death in a cheap Brooklyn flat. But even after Addicks' political demise, the same corrupt practices continued, causing the *New York Evening Post* to characterize Delaware in 1910 as a "degraded and debased little rotten borough with a polluted and debauched electorate."

With Addicks gone, Republican unity was restored—but not before downstate Republicans had made their point. Amidst tremendous intrigue and corruption, the willingness of Kent and Sussex Republicans to align themselves with Addicks and against the "old guard" sent a warning message that state party leaders could not ignore. Henceforth, Delaware's Republican Party became increasingly sensitive to the needs of Kent and Sussex.

While corruption permeated the political system, optimism loomed elsewhere. Wilmington during the first decade of the twentieth century seemed to be a vibrant, growing city with a marvelous future. Its population increased from 76,508 to 87,411, and activity filled its newly paved streets. But developments along the north bank of the Christina, Wilmington's industrial heartland, were cause for considerable concern and cast a dark shadow over the years ahead. Some of the factories between the railroad tracks and the river lay idle. In the first five years of the twentieth century, Wilmington lost fifteen manufacturing establishments and almost 1,000 industrial jobs.

The reason for their city's industrial decline puzzled Wilmingtonians, but efforts to reverse the trend seemed futile. Shipbuilding and railroad car manufacturing, the key Wilmington industries, no longer represented economic growth areas and were particularly hard hit. In retrospect, Wilmington was heading down the dismal road to urban decay. At this juncture, however, the Du Pont Company entered the picture, redirecting and revitalizing the economic life of the city.

Having left behind the dangerous uncertainties of revolutionary France in early October 1799, Pierre Samuel du Pont and his two sons, Éleuthère Irénée (referred to as simply Irénée) and Victor, arrived with their families in Newport, Rhode Island on New Year's Day, 1800. The du Ponts fruitlessly looked up and down the eastern seaboard for a profit-making business venture in which to invest their money. In the fall of 1800 Irénée visited a friend who had also emigrated from France and was presently living just northwest of Wilmington along the road to Lancaster, Pennsylvania. The two men went hunting and stopped at a country

Above
The Wilmington Marine Terminal was constructed in 1923 at the junction of the Christina and Delaware rivers. International cargo—anything from automobiles to bananas—passed through these facilities, and some goods went into storage here. Courtesy, National Archives

Right
Horsedrawn wagons hauled the Du Pont Company's gunpowder, though this proved to be a dangerous method of transportation. In 1854 three such wagons exploded while rolling through the heart of Wilmington. Courtesy, Historical Society of Delaware

store for ammunition. Having been involved in the manufacture of gunpowder in France, Irénée was surprised at the high cost and inferior quality of the American-made gunpowder that he purchased. His friend assured him that all American-made gunpowder proved inferior to its European counterpart.

After touring an inefficient Pennsylvania gunpowder plant, Irénée convinced his father to back him in the establishment of a powder works along the west bank of the Brandywine several miles upstream from Wilmington. The site was chosen for its utilization of water power and access to the navigable waters of the Christina and the Delaware. But the considerable distance from Wilmington was also an important factor in site location: after the Du Pont powder works began operation in 1802, accidental gunpowder explosions often rocked the tranquility of the Brandywine Valley. One 1818 blast caused ground tremors as far away as Lancaster, Pennsylvania, and cost forty lives. By midcentury, the Du Pont Company averaged one accidental explosion and three deaths every fourteen months.

In order to make dangerous powder mill jobs more attractive, Du Pont paid good wages and took a paternal interest in its employees. Many men kept their jobs for forty or fifty years, and many of their children came to work for the company. Courtesy, Historical Society of Delaware

Generally Wilmington was far enough away to escape destruction. In 1854, however, three Du Pont wagons, loaded with powder, suddenly blew up while rolling through the heart of Wilmington. Three teamsters, two bystanders, and eighteen mules were killed; buildings were destroyed and a huge hole was left in the street.

To attract and keep workers under such hazardous conditions, the Du Pont Company paid good wages and took a paternal interest in their employees and their families. By the 1820s, approximately 140 men

were employed in the powder works along the Brandy-wine, and by 1900 the figure had climbed to approximately 400. As early as the late 1830s, all but a handful of these workers were Irish. They lived with their families in company-owned stone houses along the Brandy-wine in such tiny hamlets as Henry Clay Village, Hagely, and Squirrel Run.

Under the leadership of the shy and often despondent Irénée, the Du Pont powder works became the leader in an industry that was very vital to a young nation intent on blasting away tree trunks and rocks to clear farm fields, roads, canal and railroad beds, and mine tunnels. But it was the demand for ammunition—created by war—that yielded the highest Du Pont profits and eventually led critics to label both the company and the family "merchants of death."

Although Irénée died in 1834, the company that he founded continued to grow under the ownership and direction of other family members. By the late nineteenth century well over one hundred direct descendents of Irénée and his brother Victor lived in the vicinity of the Brandywine, and thanks to shares in the Du Pont Company, many had become quite wealthy.

And yet, more than wealth separated the du Ponts from other Delawareans. One characteristic was an intense sense of family loyalty which largely restricted social life to a circle of other du Ponts. Under those conditions it was not surprising that a number of du Ponts married first cousins, and that many seemed to lack social skills in meeting other Delawareans. This semi-isolation and clannishness caused at least one late

nineteenth-century Wilmington observer to speak of the du Ponts as "a race apart."

To assure stable profits in the chaotic and generally depressed explosives market following the Civil War, the Du Pont Company took the lead and exercised direction over a powder trust that controlled more than 90 percent of the nation's production by 1889. Further steps to insure increased profits and company stability included membership in an international cartel in 1897 and the 1899 incorporation as E.I. du Pont de Nemours. (Delawareans, however, continue to call it the Du Pont Company.)

Despite considerable growth and demonstrated leadership in the gunpowder and explosives industry, Du Pont was not one of the industrial giants of the international or national scene at the beginning of the twentieth century. Indeed, it was not even Delaware's leading industrial employer.

In 1902 company president Eugene du Pont died, leaving no suitable successor within the family. Du Pont elders were about to sell the business to a competitor when the three young cousins—Alfred I. and T. Coleman (both thirty-eight) and Pierre (then thirty-two)—stepped in and acquired controlling shares. Not only did these three keep the Du Pont Company in the family, but they also directed the firm through a period of unprecedented growth.

The cousins quickly discarded the antiquated business practices of their ancestors, thoroughly revamped company procedures, and simultaneously bought out competitors all over the United States. By 1906, only John D. Rockefeller's Standard Oil Trust was as well organized. Six years later, however, an anti-trust suit caused the breakup of part of the family-owned corporation into the Hercules Powder Company and the Atlas Powder Company, now a part of Imperial Chemical Industries Americas. But Du Pont's earning capacity remained largely unimpaired.

World War I produced an insatiable demand for explosives which meant enormous profits for the Du Pont Company. Realizing, nevertheless, that the end of hostilities in Europe would cause the bottom to drop out of the munitions market, the Du Pont Company used most of its World War I profits to make itself the world's largest chemical company. In 1917, as part of its planned diversification, the firm also purchased more than one-fourth of the stock of the General Motors Corporation. To protect the Du Pont Company's investment, Pierre served as president of General Motors from 1920-23, and as chairman of the board for thirteen years. (In 1957 the federal government ruled that the Du Pont Company had to sell its General Motors stock.)

Even before assuming direction of General Motors, Pierre S. du Pont was familiar with the trappings and prerogatives of executive power. He had already taken control of his family's firm by working with T. Coleman to reduce Alfred's influence in 1911 and four years later, by buying some of Coleman's stock. Maneuvers to diminish Alfred's role in the company produced such lasting mutual bitterness that Pierre's presence, brief though it was, at his cousin's funeral in 1935 surprised many Delawareans. (Coleman had died five years earlier).

The growth of the Du Pont Company dictated that headquarters be moved from the vicinity of the Brandywine powder yards to an urban center which could provide some of the amenities needed by a modern corporate giant. By the early twentieth century, the company's holdings spread across the nation, making New York or some other large metropolitan area a logical choice. The three cousins, however, decided on Wilmington. By the outbreak of World War I, a massive headquarters building, which included the splendid 100-bed Hotel Du Pont, dominated the city's skyline. Wilmington was becoming a corporate and banking center and, in the process, lost its image as a blue-collar, factory city. Indeed, by 1936 the *Sunday Star* agreed that Wilmington was "well on its way to becoming a white collar town."

In hindsight, the decision to locate the Du Pont Company's offices in Wilmington proved of enormous

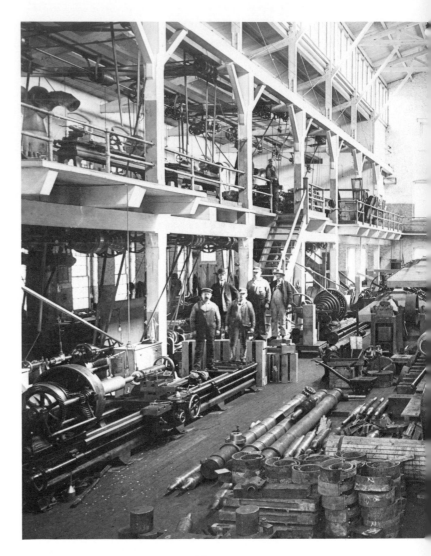

Above
A new Hagley yard machine shop, shown here in 1905, was used to build and repair equipment in the powder mills. Sixteen years later, Du Pont abandoned its century-old factories on the Brandywine in favor of more efficient western manufacturing sites. Courtesy, Historical Society of Delaware

Left
Employees at Green and Wilson's Shop, a keg mill that supplied containers for Du Pont black powder, posed outside their plant in the 1880s. Courtesy, Historical Society of Delaware

economic consequence to both city and state. Another accidental explosion ripped through the Brandywine powder works in 1920. Sensitive of the danger to increasing numbers of people who were building homes in the region as Wilmington expanded westward, the company decided to shut down the Brandywine powder works in 1921. Except for pigments plants at Edge Moor and Newport, and the Seaford nylon center built in 1939, almost all Du Pont production sites henceforth would be located outside Delaware. But the continued presence of the Du Pont headquarters in Wilmington acted as a magnet, attracting most of the company's research, experimental, and marketing facilities to northern Delaware. As it has in the recent past, Du Pont continues to be the single most dominant economic force in the First State. In 1984 it employed approximately 26,000 people or about 10 percent of Delaware's full-time work force.

In addition to being the major force behind the remarkable growth and diversification of his family's firm, Pierre S. Du Pont was also the founder of Delaware's modern school system. His efforts to revolutionize public education in the First State met with strong support from John G. Townsend, a Selbyville entrepreneur who had amassed a considerable economic empire of downstate food processing plants, banks, and farms. In contrast to Pierre's shyness, upper middle-class heritage, and lukewarm Episcopalianism, Townsend was an extrovert, a farm boy, and a deeply devout Methodist. Where du Pont possessed a degree from M.I.T., Town-

The Du Pont Company expanded and diversified into the production of chemicals and dyes during the early years of the twentieth century. Their plant at Newport yielded pigments for paints. Courtesy, Historical Society of Delaware

107

send claimed only six or seven years of formal education in a one-room school house. Moreover, Townsend, like many downstate Republicans, had been a supporter of John Addicks while Pierre and his family despised the maverick. And yet John G. Townsend and Pierre S. du Pont saw eye to eye on the need for a number of dramatic changes in Delaware, including a revamping of the state's public school system.

At the end of World War I, Delaware counted 425 local school districts and they weren't doing the job. Rather than the strong commitment to public education that typified New England, school districts in Delaware seemed apathetic and indifferent to their mission. One 1918 study ranked Delaware's educational system thirty-eighth among the states, and Pierre S. du Pont wrote a friend that "the schools of Delaware are a state and national scandal."

During World War I, Pierre organized and headed the Service Citizens of Delaware, a reform group urging significant changes in such areas as the state governmental structure and public health practices. But it was in public education that du Pont and his citizens' committee demanded the most drastic reforms and achieved the most stunning success.

In 1917 Republican John G. Townsend began his re-

Above
Selbyville entrepreneur John G. Townsend lacked Pierre S. du Pont's college training and distinguished lineage, but the two shared a strong commitment to advancing Delaware's public school system. Courtesy, Delaware State Archives

Right
Pierre S. du Pont, the soft-spoken president of the Du Pont Company, shaped the modernization of both his family's firm and his home state. Among Delaware's most generous philanthropists, he funded the rebuilding of the state's schools, and took an interest in libraries, public health, and the education of immigrants. Courtesy, Historical Society of Delaware

Facing page
These students at Delaware College (University of Delaware), among them several young World War I veterans, lounge in their dorm rooms. Except for the upper classes, post-secondary educational opportunities were limited until after the Second World War. Courtesy, Historical Society of Delaware

Above
Erected as a tribute to Delaware's patron of education, the Pierre S. du Pont High School in Wilmington boasted the most modern facilities, including a chemistry laboratory to train students for the state's leading industry. Courtesy, Historical Society of Delaware

Right
Black students at the Georgetown Colored School stand beside their one-room building in the 1920s. They received woefully inadequate education until Pierre S. du Pont enacted an ambitious program of reform in 1918. After the philanthropist paid for the construction of eighty-seven new schools for blacks, the state raised funds to build white schools. Courtesy, Delaware State Archives

markably active, four-year gubernatorial term. Thanks to the Delaware Constitution of 1897 (the state's present constitution), the powers of the governor had been considerably increased. Townsend used that new leverage to push through the state legislature a series of reform bills which included, at the urging of the Service Citizens, the reorganization of the public school system. By 1921 a more centralized state school system had been established. It featured the reduction of one-room school districts through merger, compulsory attendance rules, higher salaries and certification requirements for teachers, and the construction of new schools.

The major responsibility for financing the public schools was taken on by the state, and Pierre S. du Pont was appointed State School Tax Commissioner in 1925. By 1927-28 Delaware's government provided 85.5 percent of school tax revenue, a higher percentage than in any other state. Pierre S. du Pont also contributed approximately six million dollars from his own pocket to help build new facilities representing an estimated 30 percent of the total expenditures on school buildings in Delaware from 1920 to 1935.

In the process of reforming public education, Delawareans lost some control over their local schools to a group of professional educators in Dover, who dictated both curriculum and policy. But in return, per pupil average attendance climbed from 90 days in 1918 to 148 days in 1924; and the same study that ranked Delaware's school system thirty-eighth in 1918, ranked it tenth in 1930.

Some years before Pierre led the school reform movement, his cousin Coleman offered to give Delaware a modern highway that would connect Selbyville to Wilmington. The state's transportation routes certainly warranted such action. Downstate roads were unpaved and generally impassible much of the year. Moreover, the railroad took advantage of its downstate monopoly by routinely overcharging Kent and Sussex county farmers and manufacturers. And yet, downstate Delawareans greeted Coleman's offer with suspicion. After all, there were only a few automobiles south of the canal to make use of a modern highway, and downstate Delawareans distrusted Coleman's motives. Hadn't President William Howard Taft described him as "slippery as an eel and crooked as a ram's horn"?

But Coleman found a firm ally in Selbyville's John G. Townsend who resented the railroad's high freight rates and sensed that a modern highway would allow trucks to break this monopoly. Drawing on his considerable prestige in business and political circles, Townsend helped persuade downstate Delaware to be more receptive to Coleman's gift. When the road was finally completed in 1924, it cost Coleman four million dollars and, like the educational reforms, did much to alter the provincialism of downstate Delaware.

Despite the educational reforms and highway innovations which brought New Castle County and downstate Delaware closer together, traditional economic, ethnic, cultural, and religious differences still divided the First State along geographic lines. During the first half of the twentieth century, Kent and Sussex primarily continued to be inhabited by the descendents of Anglo-Saxon farmers and their slaves who had moved into Delaware from Maryland's Eastern Shore one or two hundred years earlier. By contrast, New Castle County's growing population resembled a potpourri of old, established families and newcomers, including European immigrants, Southern blacks, and whites from Kent, Sussex, and out of state. The latter group of whites was increasingly drawn to research and managerial positions offered by Du Pont and the Wilmington area's other large firms.

While most downstate whites continued to share the same Anglo-Saxon blood lines, commitments to traditional rural values, and a strong attachment to Methodism, New Castle County's white population represented a variegated patchwork of different ethnic groups, value systems, and religious faiths.

Irish immigrants (not to be confused with the Presbyterian Scotch-Irish) began arriving in Delaware during the eighteenth century, but were particularly attracted to the First State in the early nineteenth century, when they obtained positions as Du Pont mill hands, Chesapeake and Delaware Canal laborers, and workers on the New Castle to Frenchtown (Cecil County, Maryland) Railroad.

In the 1840s the Irish potato famine greatly accelerated immigration to America. Although earlier Irish newcomers had often lived in work camps and hamlets some distance from Wilmington, those who arrived after 1840 tended to locate in the city, finding employment as unskilled or semi-skilled factory laborers, construction workers, or domestic servants in the homes of Wilmington's upper middle class. Throughout the 1800s the Irish were Delaware's most numerous immigrant group. They and their children also became a very significant force in Wilmington's Democratic party and probably represented a majority of the state's rapidly growing Roman Catholic population by the turn of the century.

Italians began arriving in the Wilmington area in substantial numbers after 1880. Like the Irish, they were Roman Catholic and worked at low paying jobs. Some Italians were familiar with stone masonry, a skill

Right
T. Coleman du Pont (top, far right) stands with his family celebrating the state's 1924 completion of the Du Pont Highway from Wilmington to Selbyville. Du Pont financed this transportation improvement himself at a cost of four million dollars. Courtesy, Delaware State Archives

Below
Automobiles quickly gained popularity, replacing carriages and trolleys for local transportation. The construction of the Du Pont Highway created new links between upstate and downstate Delaware. Courtesy, Historical Society of Delaware

which drew them to the construction industry. Unlike the Irish, however, Wilmington's Italians didn't speak English and consequently had a greater tendency to congregate. They formed a large ghetto on the west side which was quickly dubbed "Little Italy," as well as some smaller pockets of settlement in other sections of the city.

When the Italians first came to Wilmington, they found that its Roman Catholic churches and parochial schools mainly responded to the needs of Irish and German Catholics. Unable to worship in their own language, these Southern European newcomers drifted away from Catholicism until 1924, when the dynamic J. Francis Tucker, a Wilmington-born priest of Irish ancestry, was assigned to serve the city's Italian population. Because Father Tucker had studied in Rome, he was fluent in Italian and familiar with Italian customs. He quickly marshalled the energies, skills, and resources of most of Wilmington's 4,500 Italians. Together, they completed St. Anthony's Church by Palm Sunday, 1926, and then made it the heart of "Little Italy's" social, cultural, and religious life.

Poles also began arriving in Wilmington during the late nineteenth century and generally worked at low paying jobs. They were particularly attracted to Wil-

Above
Many Italian immigrants who labored as stonemasons and in the construction trades volunteered their time and skills to build St. Anthony's, Wilmington's first church for Italians. Father John Francis Tucker, the energetic leader of the parish, is shown here with a worker and some neighborhood children. Courtesy, Historical Society of Delaware

Right
St. Anthony's Roman Catholic Church was dedicated on June 13, 1926, and became a source of pride and hope for Wilmington's Italian community. Courtesy, Historical Society of Delaware

mington's important leather industry, and like the Irish and Italians, were predominantly Roman Catholic. Most Poles settled in "Little Poland," located in southwestern Wilmington in what was known as Browntown. A much smaller group chose Wilmington's east side as their place of residence.

At first the Poles lacked their own church. Those who understood German attended Sacred Heart Roman Catholic Church, built in Wilmington's west side. In 1890 a Polish priest, Father John S. Gulcz, settled in Wilmington to begin fifty years of pastoral service to his countrymen. Under Gulcz's leadership, St. Hedwig's was completed in Browntown during the early 1890s, ministering to Wilmington's Poles in much the same manner that St. Anthony's served "Little Italy." Today, to the west of I-95, the gothic spires of St. Hedwig's and the Italian-style architecture of St. Anthony's offer mute testimony to the Roman Catholic Church's role in guiding so many immigrants through the initially difficult adjustment to a new life in the state of Delaware.

Although the Italians and Poles would soon outnumber them, at the turn of the century the Germans were second only to the Irish as the leading nationality among Delaware's immigrant population. Having entered the First State in considerable numbers since the mid-1800s, they organized German clubs and churches. Unlike the Irish, Italians, and Poles, however, some

Germans settled in downstate Delaware and attended Protestant as well as Catholic churches. Indeed, Germans founded Zion Lutheran Church on Wilmington's east side in 1848, the first Lutheran congregation in Delaware since Old Swedes became Episcopalian in the late eighteenth century. Many Germans were relatively unskilled and could find only low paying jobs, but others were well educated or highly skilled and quickly filled responsible positions in Wilmington's factories and businesses.

By 1900 Delaware counted approximately twelve hundred Jewish residents, most of whom lived in Wilmington. Split between the traditional eastern European refugees from the pogroms of czarist Russia and the more liberal, German-born Jews, these newcomers generally rejected factory work and turned, instead, to starting up small wholesale and retail businesses. Because Jews tended to live near their businesses, they maintained no large ghetto in the sense of a "Little Italy" or a "Little Poland."

In 1920 Delaware's foreign-born population reached an all time high of approximately 9 percent. Perhaps no one better exemplified their struggles and triumphs than Mary Feret. She left her native Poland in 1910 and, at the age of seventeen, sailed alone to America. Heading for Wilmington where a cousin lived, she departed from New York City by train wearing a tag with her destination plainly printed; Mary Feret knew

Skilled German craftsmen came to Delaware with the experience necessary to work in the woodworking and leather tanning trades. Others, like Jacob Swinger, started grocery stores, saloons, breweries, and similar businesses. Courtesy, Historical Society of Delaware

no English. She arrived safely in Wilmington, found her cousin, and then, like many other Poles, went to work in a leather tannery. Subsequently she married Stanley Babiarz, who had immigrated from Mary's section of Poland, and together they raised six children. Because Mary and Stanley lived in east Wilmington, which was somewhat distant from "Little Poland" and St. Hedwig's, they joined with Polish neighbors in building St. Stanislaus Roman Catholic Church (1913) to serve as the heart of their east side ethnic community. In 1961 a proud Mary Feret Babiarz looked on while her son John was sworn in as mayor of Wilmington.

Four years after Mary Feret left her native Poland, World War I engulfed Europe. In 1917 the United States entered the conflict and by 1918 a large contingent of Americans was fighting on the Western Front. Of the approximately 10,000 Delawareans who served in the armed forces, 270 lost their lives. While some Delawareans fought in Europe to "make the world safe for democracy," others at home engaged in the struggle to extend the right to vote to women.

After the Civil War a few men, such as the former abolitionist Thomas Garrett of Wilmington, joined Delaware's feminists in demanding equal rights for women. Perhaps the most colorful of the early feminists was Mary A. Stuart of Greenwood, Sussex County, who was described in 1881 by a Wilmington newspaper as dressed "in black, weighs 250 pounds, is good natured and can talk 10 hours a day at the rate of 200 words per minute." During the 1870s this formidable woman annually lobbied Delaware's state legislature for the extension of women's rights. Although she met with some success in expanding female property rights, she made no progress on the suffrage issue.

In general, the strongest support for female voting rights in Delaware came from the Women's Christian Temperance Union; Methodist church leaders; some of the women most actively involved in civic, philanthropic, and charity organizations; and many of the Republican Party power brokers, such as T. Coleman, Pierre S., and Alfred I. du Pont and Governor John G. Townsend. Downstate Democrats and, surprisingly, blue bloods like Mary Wilson Thompson, the leader of Wilmington society, offered the stiffest opposition.

Despite a number of appeals to the legislature and a petition presented to the 1897 state constitutional convention, Delaware's women were still without the right to vote at the end of World War I. In 1918 the U.S. Congress went on record as favoring women's suffrage by approving the Nineteenth Amendment which then needed ratification by thirty-six states for adoption. Two years later, Delaware's legislature began to consider the amendment, and suffragettes and their supporters had high hopes that Delaware would make history by becoming the decisive thirty-sixth state to cast an affirmative vote.

Both sides sponsored rallies all over the state. On March 25 a hearing on the Nineteenth Amendment was held before the General Assembly. Partisan Delawareans poured into Dover, and stores, hotel lobbies, and streets were filled with people heatedly arguing the merits of women's suffrage. Opponents sported a red rose, while supporters wore a yellow jonquil. Regardless of the fact that the rose only symbolized one viewpoint, the struggle in Delaware over women's suffrage has been subsequently labelled "The War of the Roses."

Despite optimism from suffragist quarters, opposition forces succeeded at blocking ratification. Disapproval by the powerful railroad lobby; the fear that so many more blacks would now be enfranchised; and the general linking, in the minds of many, of women's suffrage with other revolutionary changes—school reform, prohibition, and new highway construction—sweeping the First State, caused Delaware's very conservative Democratic Party to close ranks in opposition to the Nineteenth Amendment. Even a last minute telegram from President Woodrow Wilson asking three fellow Democrats in Delaware's lower house to support the amendment because "it would be the greatest service to the party" was of no avail. Joined by a few dissident Republicans, the Democrats prevented a vote on ratification in the lower house. Yet, despite the intransigence of the First State, the Nineteenth Amendment officially passed in August 1920 when Tennessee became the thirty-sixth state to ratify. Delaware was now forced to extend the franchise to women in the same manner that it previously had been forced to grant voting rights to black males.

The emerging "Roaring Twenties" found many Delawareans adopting the era's frenzied cultural fads. Young women—particularly in the Wilmington area—who rejected traditional dress and moral codes, were known as "flappers." They danced the Charleston with young men who wore long fur coats and owned automobiles with rumble seats. The flappers and their escorts used new expressions like "bee's knees" (superb), "hep" (wise), and "lounge-lizard" (ladies man).

But above all else, the 1920s was the era of Prohibition when bootleggers waited for moonless nights along Delaware's coast to smuggle in their contraband whiskey, and when even in the highest circles it became fashionable to flout the law. A waiter at the exclusive Wilmington Country Club recalled that at 12:45 p.m. daily, he was directed to provide a meeting room

with ice, glasses, ginger ale, and a mixing spoon. He had "strict orders not to reenter until all of the partici-pating members left the room." Later, when the waiter cleaned up, he always noticed the strong smell of whis-key. "This was my first actual observation of the disre-gard in which Prohibition was held by the upper crust of Society."

South of the Chesapeake and Delaware Canal, the zany behavior patterns and outlandish dress codes of the 1920s seemed far less evident. Also far less evident was the prosperity that had marked the decade in New Castle County. Depressed prices for agricultural com-modities caused downstate farmers to join with those from across America in experiencing a severe economic crisis. As one Kent County man pointed out, "though this period was the 'roaring' and supposedly ... afflu-ent twenties, for us times were hard and money almost nonexistent."

Understandably, when the Depression hit Delaware in the 1930s, many downstaters regarded it as just more of the same. By contrast, the economic collapse was a very traumatic experience for residents in urban and suburban northern Delaware. By 1934 approximately 11,000 Delaware families lacked working breadwinners. Of the families asking for relief, more than 90 percent lived in New Castle County.

Even before the onset of Depression-caused unem-ployment, Alfred I. du Pont came to the aid of one group of unfortunate citizens. In 1929 he urged the

General Assembly to make Delaware the second state in the Union to pass a pension bill for impoverished elderly people. When the legislators refused, Alfred I. personally financed his own statewide pension pro-gram. On November 1, 1929, 800 checks were sent out and by July 1931, the number of monthly recipients had climbed to 1,600. Because the ravages of the De-pression emphasized the critical economic needs of in-creasing numbers of senior citizens, Delaware finally instituted its own pension program in August 1931: it was based on a model conceived by an old age commis-sion. Not surprisingly, Alfred I. du Pont had chaired this group.

The Depression wreaked such economic havoc among northern Delawareans of all ages that emergen-cy church and private charity funds were soon ex-hausted. In 1932 Republican Governor C. Douglas Buck, a collateral descendent of John M. Clayton, pushed an important bill through the General Assem-bly to create the Temporary Emergency Relief Com-mission, with two million dollars to distribute. Three years later, New Castle County levied a special income tax for poverty relief.

These actions, plus a series of federally-funded pro-grams, helped the First State muddle through the Depression years—but with a certain lack of grace. Al-though it was rated fourth in per capita income, Del-aware's welfare payments to victims of the Depression ranked forty-second among the states. Part of the fault lay with the traditional antagonism between upstate and downstate. Kent and Sussex countians simply did not want to increase their taxes for unemployment relief, especially since most would-be recipients lived north of the Chesapeake and Delaware Canal. Indeed, a legislative committee reported that "it was almost the unanimous opinion of the people of Sussex County that each county should take care of its own."

Although upstaters and downstaters opposed each other on virtually every issue, by 1933 they did agree that Prohibition was a mistake. Thanks to the right of local option, the entire state (except Wilmington) had voted itself dry before the Eighteenth Amendment went into effect on January 16, 1920. But the corruption and disregard for the law which accompanied Prohibition soon changed the minds of most Delawareans. In 1933 Delaware became the seventh state to ratify the Twenty-first Amendment repealing national Prohibi-

tion. The next year every section of Delaware—Sussex, Kent, rural New Castle, and Wilmington—individually rejected the local option to ban alcoholic beverage sales.

The Depression years also marked the end of political domination by Delaware's Republicans. During the early 1930s, the First State's Democratic Party decided to reverse past practices in order to broaden its support base among voters. Subsequently, it abandoned its racist image as "the white man's party" and moved away from traditional opposition to women's rights. During the presidential election years of the 1930s, the shifting political allegiance of some blacks and many white females, combined with the presence of the widely popular Franklin Delano Roosevelt at the top of the ticket, produced Democratic victories in most state and local contests. Off-year elections, however, continued to give the previously dominant Republicans an edge.

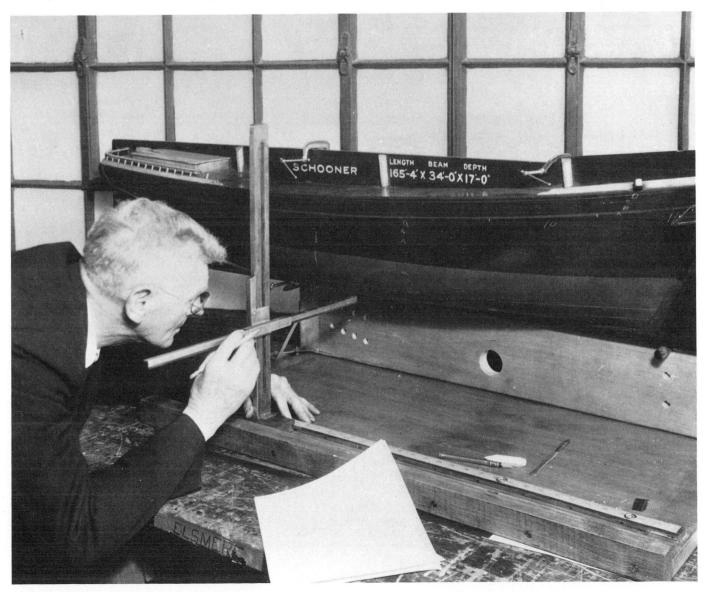

As white males engaged in World War II combat duties, civilian women and blacks gained access to the job market. It was several decades, however, before equal opportunity laws actually began to alter the nature and composition of the work force. Courtesy, Delaware State Archives

CHAPTER VII

TOWARDS A MORE DEMOCRATIC SOCIETY

On an early September morning in 1952 an anxious Shirley Bulah watched through a window in her home for a glimpse of the school bus which would take her to the opening day of third grade at Hockessin's elementary school No. 29. Later, when she entered her classroom, Shirley was very grateful to her teacher for "being kind and thoughtful and not singling me out as different." But Shirley was different—she was black.

About fifteen miles to the northeast, fifteen-year-old Ethel Belton, who was also black, attended her first day at all-white Claymont High School. The two girls were important, not only because they were among the first blacks to break the racial barriers that had existed in Delaware's public school system since its inception in 1829, but also because their presence in previously all-white schools marked the beginning of a number of historic changes which would sweep through the First State and make Dela-

ware a more democratic society.

❧

World War II brought an end to the economic stagnation and unemployment that marked the Depression years. More than 30,000 Delawareans served in the armed forces and 903 were listed as killed or missing in action.

On the home front, shipbuilding quickly became Delaware's largest industry. Defense contracts caused the Dravo Corporation of Wilmington to expand its work force along the Christina from 400 in 1940 to approximately 11,000 three years later. Other Wilmington shipyards, as well as those in Milford and Seaford, produced naval craft for war use. In order to further meet

Above
German prisoners of war incarcerated at Fort Miles near Lewes were put to work on Delaware farms and factories because of a critical shortage of wartime labor. Courtesy, Delaware State Archives

Left
The New Castle Army Air Base served as home to the Air Transport Command, a group that ferried important military shipments to U.S. stations here and abroad. Courtesy, Delaware State Archives

Facing page
The General Motors Boxwood plant, located outside of Wilmington, provided jobs to returning World War II veterans. Courtesy, Delaware State Archives

American defense needs, Du Pont, Hercules, and Atlas also hired additional employees, and many Delaware industries converted or altered their production procedures.

Although thousands of veterans returned at the end of World War II, Delaware's revived economy was able to provide most of them with jobs while simultaneously turning to peace-time production. The First State experienced an economic boom during the post-war era and, for a number of years, it ranked first nationally in per capita income. (The large number of resident millionaires helped skew the per capita income figures in Delaware's favor.)

While some traditional industries such as shipbuild-

ing and leather manufacturing faced hard times, the changing skyline of downtown Wilmington and the newly constructed laboratories and office buildings in the surrounding countryside testified to the dynamic expansion of Delaware's chemical industry. The postwar economic boom was also fueled by the decision of several industrial giants to locate plants in the state. A new General Motors facility on Boxwood Road near Elsmere turned out its first car in 1947 and employed more than 1,000 Delawareans. In 1950 Chrysler constructed a parts division in Newark which was subsequently converted into an assembly plant. General Motors and Chrysler together employed approximately 3 percent of Delaware's full-time work force by 1983.

Other companies to build in Delaware during the postwar years included International Latex and General Foods in Dover, and Getty Oil, which constructed a refinery outside Delaware City in 1957.

Delaware's farmers also experienced better times. Declining farm prices at the end of World War I and the resulting two decades of economic hardship were ended by World War II demands for agricultural goods. After the Second World War, the New Castle County farms which survived suburban homebuilding encroachments, continued to sell milk and the same field crops grown there since 1900. Downstate, however, a remarkable agricultural transformation had taken place.

By the end of World War I, Kent and Sussex farms raised increasing numbers of chickens and distributed their eggs to nearby urban markets. Young roosters, not required for breeding, were often culled out of the flock, then sold to satisfy an increasing culinary demand which first centered in Philadelphia and later, in the large, New York City Jewish community. In 1923

Cecile A. Steele of Ocean View (southeastern Sussex) decided to raise a flock of 500 chickens with the sole purpose of selling them as "broilers." When the birds weighed approximately two pounds, they were shipped off to market where they brought sixty-two cents per pound. Cecile and husband Wilmer doubled the size of their broiler flock the following year. So successful was this new enterprise that Wilmer left his job at the Bethany Beach coast guard station to devote full time to poultry raising. By 1927 the Steele farm reached a 25,000-bird capacity and was being duplicated throughout Sussex, in parts of Kent, and other locations throughout the United States. Delaware's annual poultry production skyrocketed from two million broilers (1928) to sixty million (1944) to 182 million (1983). By the latter year, Delaware ranked fifth among the states and Sussex, first among the nation's counties, in the number of chickens sold. In recent years over half of Delaware's agricultural income has come from broiler production.

Thanks to the rapidly increasing demand for chickens, relatively poor farmers could grow rich overnight. As historian Richard Carter points out, more millionaires were created during the 1930s and 1940s in Sussex when "the poultry business was at its prime than in all of the rest of the county's history." Some of these quick fortunes were amassed through illegal, black market sale of chickens during World War II.

Ironically, the enjoyment of this new-found prosperity ended the lives of Cecile and Wilmer Steele. In the fall of 1940, the two broiler industry pioneers were fishing a few miles off Ocean City, Maryland when an explosion ripped through their thirty-nine-foot cabin cruiser, killing both of them.

The industry which the Steeles helped to create had a ripple effect on Delaware agriculture. Increasing demands for chicken feed caused downstate farmers to expand corn acreage and begin growing soybeans. Today, a late summer drive through the flat, downstate farmland confirms the primacy of corn and drought-resistant soybeans as the First State's leading cash crops. The driver would also notice, on occasion, the vertical storage towers built by agribusinessmen to process corn and soybeans into mash for chickens.

With the move from truck crops to broilers, many of the canneries which once thrived in Sussex disappeared. Taking their place were chicken processing plants owned by Perdue, Townsends, Cargill, and others. Indeed, today's poultry growers are tied by contract to these large companies which provide them with newly hatched chicks and feed, then pick up the broilers after a few months and speed them through processing facilities and distribute the poultry to markets in Baltimore, Philadelphia, and, particularly, New York. Although the broiler is king in Sussex, truck farming survives, most notably in Kent County, where lima beans and green peas are important crops.

Clearly, agriculture and agribusiness generate enormous amounts of money in the First State. Yet, the percentage of working Delawareans actually dependent on full-time farming or farm labor for a living declined dramatically from a majority in the mid-nineteenth century to approximately 3 percent in 1984.

The development of the seashore from Lewes south to the Maryland line has also had a considerable economic impact on eastern Sussex County. At the center of this development lies Rehoboth Beach, originally rescued from the obscurity of a sandy, scrub pine wasteland by the decision of Methodists in 1872 to turn it into a camp-meeting site. Although camp meetings had ended by World War I, the completion of a railroad to Rehoboth Beach in 1878 assured a constant stream of summer vacationers from nearby urban centers. By the 1920s highways further opened up the Rehoboth area, but mosquitoes proved such a nuisance that local women often wrapped newspapers around their ankles for protection while doing yard and garden work. The Civilian Conservation Corps drained many of the marshes during the 1930s, largely controlling the insect problem. From then on it was almost

Mrs. Wilmer Steele, a Sussex County farm wife, first introduced the modern poultry industry to the Delmarva Peninsula. By the 1940s, broilers were raised on large farms, then processed and packaged on assembly lines. The Swift Company's plant, pictured here, handled thousands of broilers at a time. Courtesy, Delaware State Archives

Left
Students of Georgetown High School learned tree planting and soil conservation techniques on the Tunnell farm in 1948. Such progressive methods made the most of Sussex County land. Courtesy, National Archives

Below
Many New Castle County farms were sold to housing developers when property values in suburban Wilmington skyrocketed after World War II. Farmers north of the canal mainly raised dairy cattle, while those in Kent and Sussex counties utilized their larger acreage for corn, soybeans, and poultry. Courtesy, National Archives

uninterrupted boom, as vacationers vied with each other to bid up building lots and summer rental prices. After World War II, development spread southward to include Dewey Beach, Bethany Beach, and Fenwick Island.

It took the most destructive coastal storm in Delaware's history to force a brief pause in shore construction. On Monday night, March 5, 1962, the weather report out of Salisbury, Maryland assured Rehoboth television viewers that Tuesday would be cold and cloudy, but that the overcast sky would partially clear during the day. However, on Tuesday the confluence of two storms produced a northeast wind with gusts of up to 80 miles per hour. Combined with unusually high tides, huge waves destroyed or badly damaged Rehoboth's boardwalk, many of its oceanside hotels, and other buildings. For three disastrous days the storm pounded coastal Delaware, causing seven deaths and twenty-two million dollars in property damage.

Despite the fact that the storm of 1962 came close to wiping out their town, Rehoboth residents demonstrated resilience and confidence about the future. July 4 found the boardwalk completely rebuilt, and subsequent development of the coastal area has been spectacular. On a given summer weekend, sixty-five thousand sun worshippers—most from out-of-state— jam into the "nation's summer capital," and thousands

of others flock to the beaches that stretch from Lewes to Fenwick Island. Their free spending habits provide Delawareans with an increasing number of investment and employment opportunities.

There are, however, a few citizens who remember 1962 and consequently warn of the far more terrible destruction that a similar storm would cause along today's highly developed ocean front. Still others feel un-

Right
Sand dunes along the coastline support a wide variety of plant and animal life, including wild bayberry, dune grass, and migrating shorebirds. The phenomenal growth of beach resort communities threatens this fragile ecology. Courtesy, National Archives

Above
Bethany Beach was a small resort with boarding houses and seaside cottages in 1926. Founded by the Christian Church Disciples, the town forbade drinking, gambling, and amusement rides. Although some of those restrictions have long passed out of existence, the area retains much of its quiet nature. Courtesy, Delaware State Archives

Facing page
The Massey family of Wilmington enjoyed fishing and swimming excursions to Delaware's beaches. Still wet from the surf when this snapshot was taken at an unidentified beach, Bes and her sister Liz sport wool bathing suits. Courtesy, Historical Society of Delaware

easy about the extraordinary construction boom and the heavy seasonal population concentrations, viewing these factors as a threat to Delaware's entire coastal ecology.

In recent years other parts of the state also have experienced dramatic population increases. Until 1930, Delaware's growth rate had been significantly lower than in the rest of the country. From 1930 to 1970, however, it far exceeded the national average. But Wilmington didn't reflect this statewide pattern. After reaching 110,000 in 1920, the city's population held at approximately the same level until the 1950s, when it began a noticeable decline. By 1980 Delaware's largest urban center had only 70,000 residents.

Conversely, the population growth of the rest of New Castle County has been spectacular, increasing from approximately 54,000 in 1930 to almost 330,000 in 1980. Indeed, as early as 1960 the majority of Delawareans lived in the suburban sprawl that lay within a fifteen mile radius of Wilmington.

Delaware's suburbanization began in earnest in the years just prior to World War I. By 1912 trolley tracks had pushed out from Wilmington to the north, west,

and south, allowing workers to commute into the city from such communities as Elsmere, Richardson Park, and Montrose (Bellefonte). But it was increasingly common automobile ownership after World War I and, particularly, after World War II that made possible the remarkable demographic revolution which has turned the typical Delawarean into a suburbanite. New housing tracts almost immediately filled up with families who sought refuge from the noise, smoke, crime, and declining quality of public schools that seemed to characterize Wilmington. White flight to the suburbs was particularly spurred, after 1950, by Wilmington's rapidly growing black population. Only about 13 percent of the city's residents in 1940, blacks represented 44 percent by 1970.

White racial fears were particularly fueled by black unrest in Wilmington during the summer of 1967 and by more serious disturbances in April 1968, following the assassination of Martin Luther King, Jr. On April 9, 1968, black rioters set fire to a number of abandoned buildings on the city's near west side. Forty people sustained injuries and police arrested 154 others. That afternoon, terrified commuters, frantically trying to

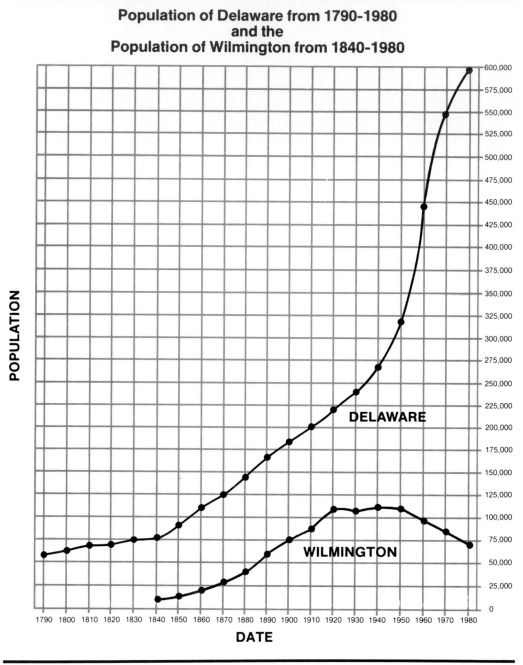

Population of Delaware from 1790-1980
and the
Population of Wilmington from 1840-1980

DELAWARE

WILMINGTON

POPULATION

1790 1800 1810 1820 1830 1840 1850 1860 1870 1880 1890 1900 1910 1920 1930 1940 1950 1960 1970 1980

DATE

Chart by Graphics, Etc., Newark, Delaware

Facing page
A deep sense of pride and digni-
ty appears on the faces of the
members of the Bethel A.M.E.
Church in Wilmington. Inde-
pendent churches were a vital
part of black life in Delaware
from the early years of the nine-
teenth century when Peter Spen-
cer founded the African Union
Church, the first independent
church for blacks in America.
Courtesy, Historical Society of
Delaware

escape to the security of their all-white suburban developments, caused massive traffic jams along some of the
city's major arteries. The clouds of smoke which hung
over Wilmington that day marked another chapter in
the troubled history of race relations in the First State.

Although 92 percent of Delaware's blacks were no
longer slaves on the eve of the Civil War, they were
treated as third class citizens by the dominant white
community. The racial mores of a deeply segregated society dictated virtually every aspect of black life from
education and job opportunities to church going. Indeed, it was not until the post-World War II years that

blacks could actually see dramatic progress in the low-
ering of racial barriers in the First State.

A series of early nineteenth-century incidents indi-
cate that Delaware's blacks didn't always meekly accept
discrimination. Although black Wilmingtonians had
been systematically excluded from most economic, educational, and social opportunities, they were invited to
join Asbury Methodist Episcopal Church, located at
Third and Walnut. But resentment over segregated
seating caused them to leave the congregation in 1805
and, under the leadership of Peter Spencer, to build
Ezion Methodist Episcopal Church at Ninth and

French. Now self-governing, Ezion's black worshippers thought they "could refuse any that were not thought proper persons to preach to us."

Eight years later, however, their assigned white pastor refused to recognize his black congregation's claim to self government. After the minister dismissed most of Ezion's lay leaders, Peter Spencer led thirty-one angry black families out of the congregation to build the African Union Church, or Old Union as it was called, almost directly opposite Ezion. Old Union's congregation completely severed ties with the white-dominated Methodist Episcopal Church, becoming the first independent black congregation to be established in the

United States. The Ezion and Old Union story illustrates that at an early date, Delaware's blacks found at least one way to maintain personal dignity in the face of white segregation policies: developing and centering their lives around a voluntary black organization.

Ironically, subsequently organized black churches and fraternal clubs further accentuated racial separatism. Throughout most of the First State's history there have been two Delawares: white Delaware which controlled all, or nearly all, the economic and political power; and black Delaware which worked hard to maintain some sense of self respect while carefully avoiding actions which would trigger the retaliatory

Right
Buttonwood School in New Castle was built by Pierre S. du Pont during the 1920s. Despite improvements in black education, Delaware's schools remained segregated for another three decades. Courtesy, Historical Society of Delaware

Below
The movement of middle class white families from the city to the suburbs, the decline in blue-collar jobs, and the influx of poor blacks from the south all contributed to the formation of slums. The northeast section of Wilmington, once a working-class neighborhood of neat row houses, became one of the city's most depressed areas. This block of Fourteenth Street between Claymont and Heald is shown in 1949. Courtesy, Delaware State Archives

wrath of the dominant white community.

Traditionally, schooling has offered Delawareans an alternative to a lifetime of poverty and menial labor. Prior to the Civil War, however, the overwhelming majority of blacks were denied formal educational opportunities. Indeed, the school law of 1829 specifically prohibited black children from entering Delaware's public education system. To partially remedy the situation, a group of white businessmen and clergy met in Wilmington in 1866 to form the Delaware Association for the Moral Improvement and Education of Colored People. Combining private donations with grants from the U.S. Freedmen's Bureau, this organization built thirty-two primary schools and imported black teachers who had been trained in the North.

Although the black community responded enthusiastically, some downstate whites used violence to halt the schooling of minority children. In Georgetown in 1867, for example, a black female teacher was chased out of town by a rock-throwing mob. Despite such interruptions, the efforts of the association continued. But at best they were regarded as only stop-gap measures until the state legislature could be persuaded to provide for the funding of black schools.

Initially, Delaware's lawmakers expressed little inter-

est in supporting black education. After becoming very concerned about interference from Washington, however, in 1875 the state legislature granted local government officials the power to tax black residents for the support of black schools. (Although the other former slave states had dual educational systems based on race, none had such a dual tax structure). Delaware's black schools, subsequently dependent on a very low tax base, proved very inferior to even the poorly regarded white schools.

Dramatic changes sweeping through Delaware during and after World War I ended the dual tax system. Although a racially unified tax would now support both black and white schools, the terrible physical condition of the former desperately urged an expensive, statewide school construction program. And because the costs of the new black schools would primarily fall on white taxpayers, Pierre S. du Pont decided to head off potential opposition by paying for the new black schools out of his own pocket.

Delaware's black schools continued to be the impoverished step-children of the state public education system despite a substantial improvement in funding and physical facilities. Equipment, textbooks, and other supplies were often, as a black from Lewes remembered, "hand-me-downs" from the white schools. Even more alarming was Delaware's reluctance to provide a high school education for most of its black teenagers. The black schools set up after the Civil War by the Delaware Association and subsequently taken over by the state, offered only a grade school education.

Towards the end of the nineteenth century, Wilmington's Howard High School and Dover's Delaware State College, which offered high school courses for much of its existence, provided a secondary curriculum for blacks. But those who desired a diploma and lived some distance away were compelled to find boarding in those two cities during the school year. For the black teenagers who chose to leave home, the stay in Dover or Wilmington often proved very traumatic. In 1932, for example, a young girl arrived at Dover from Lincoln in northern Sussex. After two years she gave up and returned. "I lost a lot of weight and cried, because I wanted to be at home. I was only fourteen and that was a very bad experience for me."

Even more difficult was the situation faced by the Nanticoke Indian community located in the Oak Orchard area of Sussex County. Categorized as "colored," their children could not attend white schools. Furthermore, most Nanticoke parents refused to send their offspring to nearby black schools because it was seen as a surrender of Indian identity and an acceptance of bur-

Left
*Big Quarterly, a traditional black
religious festival, occurs annually
in Wilmington on the first Sunday of August. The event dates
back to the 1820s, when Peter
Spencer's African Union
Church held quarterly meetings
in that city. Slaves and free
blacks from Delaware and the
surrounding states attended, and
the gathering became known for
worship, feasting, and celebration. Courtesy, Delaware State
Archives*

Facing page
*Howard High School was one of
only two Delaware high schools
for black students before the
Second World War. Many black
families placed their hopes for
the future on the education of
their children. Courtesy, Historical Society of Delaware*

densome racial stigmas. In response to pressure from
the Nanticokes, the state legislature as early as 1881 recognized the right of the Indians to erect and maintain
their own educational system. During the 1930s and
1940s, the Nanticokes maintained a one-room school
which served students through the eighth grade. The
lone teacher's salary was paid by the state beginning in
1935.

Few options existed for those Indian students who
wanted a high school diploma but did not wish to attend one of Delaware's two black high schools. If they
were lucky enough to have family in a state north of
Delaware, they might board there and attend an integrated high school. The other alternative was to head
for the Haskell Indian Institute in Lawrence, Kansas.
Only the most self-confident and venturesome of four-
teen-year-olds could follow either path. Although small
in number, the peculiar plight of Nanticoke teenagers
offers yet another perspective on life in racially segregated Delaware.

Wilmington's black community began to assert itself
at the turn of the century, despite numerous obstacles.
In 1901 Thomas Postles became the first in a continuous line of blacks to be elected to the Wilmington City
Council. The first Delaware chapter of the NAACP
also was organized in Wilmington just prior to World
War I, and in 1915 it convinced the City Council to

ban a public showing of the pro-Ku Klux Klan movie,
"Birth of a Nation." Moreover, the local NAACP led a
successful effort to defeat U.S. Representative Caleb
Layton's 1922 reelection bid, after the legislator refused
to support an anti-lynching bill in Congress. Nevertheless, Wilmington's NAACP chapter and the rest of the
black community were unable to prevent the Ku Klux
Klan from marching through city streets in the 1920s.

Outside Wilmington, Delaware's black population
exercised very little political power. As late as 1947, no
black held a significant position in the state government. It wasn't until 1948 that the first black state legislator, Republican William J. Winchester, was sent to the
House of Representatives and he hailed from Wilmington.

It was on education rather than on politics that
Delaware's blacks focused most of their energies to
bring about racial equality. By the early 1950s a small
black high school in lower New Castle County joined
with Howard in serving northern Delaware. Partly
fearing federal intervention if black educational opportunities were not improved, the downstate white community also finally supported the construction of two
black high schools, one in Kent and the other in
Sussex. Despite some physical improvements, however,
Delaware's black schools continued to lag behind their
white counterparts.

Louis L. Redding of Wilmington, a Harvard Law School graduate and the first black admitted to the Delaware Bar (1929), led the legal assault against the state's segregated school system. He was convinced that only through integration could racially-based educational disparities come to an end.

In 1952 two black girls, Shirley Bulah and Ethel Belton, desired to attend white schools in their neighborhoods. Chancellor Collins J. Seitz of Delaware's court of chancery, who had already ordered the University of Delaware to integrate, ruled that "the cold hand of fact is that the state in this situation discriminates against negro children." He then ordered Shirley's admission to Hockessin's elementary school No. 29 and Ethel's to Claymont High School. In spite of this legal breakthrough and the U.S. Supreme Court's famous *Brown vs. Board of Education* decision in 1954, massive integration of public schools didn't occur in Delaware until a decade later, when mandated by the Federal Civil Rights Act of 1964. In 1967 the state's last all black school was finally closed. The federal government then informed Delaware that it was the first former slave state to eradicate a dual public school system based on race.

In the years after Shirley Bulah and Ethel Belton began attending white schools, opposition to integration led to a few ugly incidents such as the 1954 demonstrations which briefly shut down Milford High School. But on the whole, most Delawareans followed the example of such public figures as Republican U.S. Senator John J. Williams (1947-71) of Millsboro, who opposed integration but even more vehemently rejected disobedience of the law as laid down by the federal courts. In nearby Virginia, where U.S. Senator Harry F. Byrd called for "massive resistance," public opposition to school integration was far more demonstrative.

The other shoe dropped for northern Delaware in 1978. Integration provided a racial mix in individual Kent and Sussex schools, roughly reflecting each county's demographic composition. In New Castle County, however, the disappearance of the dual public school system quickly led to white flight from Wilmington's increasingly black public schools. By the mid 1970s, almost 90 percent of Wilmington's public school students were non-white. Conversely, public schools in the rest of the county claimed a minority population of only 10 percent. De facto had replaced de jure segregation in New Castle County.

Although originally opposed to integration, U.S. Senator John J. Williams (1947-1971) encouraged Delawareans to accept and execute the Supreme Court's plan as outlined in Brown vs. Board of Education *and enforced by the Civil Rights Act of 1964. Courtesy, Delaware State Archives*

For reasons not entirely based on the educational needs of black children, both the city of Wilmington and some of its residents sought a judicial injunction to reverse the racial imbalance in the city's public schools. A federal court ruled that an approximate racial equilibrium should exist in each of New Castle County's public school systems. To achieve this goal, court-ordered, large-scale busing began in 1978. Only the Appoquinimink District, covering southern New Castle County, was exempt.

No contemporary issue has so roiled the waters in northern Delaware, nor caused so much perverse pleasure in southern Delaware. Because of the reluctance of Kent and Sussex to integrate their schools during the 1950s and 1960s, downstaters had long been the targets of self-righteous attacks from north of the canal. Now,

downstaters pointed out, the shoe was on the other foot.

White suburban parents vigorously protested the transportation of their children to inner city schools, while many inner city blacks were not so sure that an integrated education was worth the cost. Despite assuring words from administrators and the publication of test scores purporting to show that an integrated education justified its cost, many parents complained of school violence and of lower educational standards. Some frustrated suburban families moved out of northern Delaware; others turned to private and parochial schools for their children's education. This reaction to federally ordered busing combined with a steady decline since 1971 in the number of white school-age children in New Castle County to cause a dramatic drop in white public school enrollment north of the Appoquinimink District over the last fifteen years. By contrast, the number of nonwhite students has grown slightly, causing the nonwhite portion of the public school population in northern New Castle County to increase from approximately one out of five in 1971 to almost one out of three in 1984.

About the same time that Delaware's public schools were integrated, other racial barriers began to fall. Although libraries, trains, and buses had not practiced racial separation, colleges, restaurants, and theatres remained segregated. In 1948 the University of Delaware admitted its first black student. Two years later the facilities of the Hotel Dupont were opened to blacks, and most of Wilmington's movie theatres ended their discriminatory practices in the following year. Thanks to new federal guidelines and the infusion of federal funds during the 1960s, Delaware's blacks were being considered for jobs previously closed to nonwhites. Urban renewal, which began in a black slum area of Wilmington's east side in 1963, proved to be another positive step.

Despite progress on many fronts, deep frustrations lingered throughout Delaware's black community, but particularly in Wilmington. New agricultural technology and machinery had increasingly rendered traditional farm labor obsolete during the twentieth century. Needing jobs, large numbers of rural blacks from downstate Delaware and the South migrated to Wilmington and other northern cities. Except for the war years, however, Wilmington's new residents found that their adopted city offered few jobs because it was phasing out heavy industry and becoming more of a white-collar town. Although some white-collar positions were now open to blacks, most blacks possessed neither the educational background nor the requisite skills to take advantage of these opportunities. In 1960, for example, 80 percent of Wilmington's black adults had not finished high school.

With few blue-collar jobs available, unemployment among Wilmington's black males reached 13 percent by 1960; it was considerably higher among the city's black male teenagers. Adding to this frustration was the repeated refusal of the Delaware legislature to enact open housing legislation. Such a bill was approved by the House of Representatives in 1967, but the Delaware Senate blocked passage, while a tearful Herman Holloway, Sr., a black state senator from Wilmington, looked on.

Compared to the destruction and violence experienced by Washington, D.C. and many other northern cities, Wilmington's 1967 disturbances and the more serious 1968 riots did relatively little damage. But Democratic Governor Charles L. Terry, Jr., refused to take any chances. When in April 1968 Mayor John Babiarz asked for 1,000 national guardsmen to stop the chaos, Terry sent in 2,800 and then insisted that they remain long after Babiarz requested their withdrawal. The occupation of Wilmington didn't end until newly elected Republican Governor Russell Peterson, who had just defeated Terry, finally recalled the troops in January 1969. The guard's long stay drew the attention of the national media—no other American city spent so long a period under military occupation during the urban riot year of 1968—and further polarized Wilmington's black and white communities.

Yet, in spite of racial tension, a "back to Wilmington" movement began in the late 1960s during the Babiarz administration and was particularly encouraged by the succeeding mayors, Harry Haskell and Thomas Maloney. A city wage tax was levied in 1969, relieving some of the burden from overtaxed city real estate. To attract shoppers and concertgoers, part of Market Street was converted into a pedestrian mall and the Grand Opera House was restored.

With the election of Democrat Jimmy Carter to the White House in 1976, increased federal aid to the nation's troubled cities became available. Much of this new funding arrived in the form of Urban Development Action Grants, low interest loans to businesses willing to locate in inner cities. The federal program proved particularly timely for Wilmington because new construction in its struggling downtown area had become prohibitively expensive.

By 1984 businesses locating in downtown Wilmington had obtained almost forty million dollars in Urban Development Action Grants, with the building of the Raddison Hotel as the first example of the local impact of this federal loan program. Indeed, during Democratic Mayor William T. McLaughlin's administration (1977-85), Wilmington received a higher per capita percentage of Urban Development Action Grants than any municipality in the United States.

A second stimulant to Wilmington's recent economic renaissance has been the General Assembly's passage, at the request of Republican Governor Pierre S. du Pont IV (1977-85), of the Financial Center Development Act in 1981. Aimed at attracting out-of-state banks to Delaware by offering tax incentives and unlimited interest rates, the act had enticed branch offices and operations of thirteen lending houses (six in Wilmington) by the end of 1984. To make room for such financial giants as Chase Manhattan, more high-rise office buildings are being designed and constructed in the downtown Wilmington area. Indeed, one senses that Delaware's largest

Above
National guardsmen were called to Wilmington to quiet rioting and arson following the assassination of Martin Luther King, Jr. on April 4, 1968. The Guard remained in the city until January 1969, despite the black community's growing resentment and the request of Mayor Babiarz that they leave.

Right
Martin Luther King, Jr.'s assassination sparked violence in many American cities, including Wilmington. On April 9, 1968, thirty fires were set in abandoned buildings on the city's near west side.

Above
Modern homes, open spaces, new schools, and low-interest federal mortgage programs attracted urban dwellers to suburban housing developments north and west of Wilmington during the late 1930s and 1940s. Located north of the city near the Delaware River, Belleview witnessed a residential housing boom during this time. Courtesy, Historical Society of Delaware

Left
Republican Governor Pierre S. du Pont IV (1977-1985) sponsored a number of economic development measures and helped the state avert a likely financial crisis. Courtesy, Delaware State Archives

city is in the process of establishing itself as an important regional banking center while continuing to proclaim itself "the chemical capital of the world."

Particularly important to Wilmington's new vitality is the change in city school taxes that accompanied court ordered busing in 1978. Prior to that date, a larger property tax base per pupil enabled the suburbs to support first rate schools through real estate assessments which were only a fraction of the rates paid in Wilmington. But along with busing, the federal court established a unified school tax rate for Wilmington and the surrounding New Castle County areas. The suburbs subsequently lost the dual advantage of better public schools and lower tax rates. As historian Carol Hoffecker points out, the court-ordered desegregation plan of 1978 "has been the single most important step toward restoring the city's ability to compete successfully with its own suburbs."

Another struggle with the suburbs, however, did not bode so well for Wilmington. As of 1965, all of northern Delaware's general hospitals were located in the city. Seeking to avoid expensive duplication of services and to keep abreast of the newest advances in medical care and technology, Delaware's three largest hospitals—Memorial, Delaware, and Wilmington General—then merged to become the Wilmington Medical Center. Implicit in the merger was the recognition that a new medical facility, or facilities, needed to be built. Moreover, the site of the new facility, or facilities, should be chosen with New Castle County's rapidly growing suburban population in mind.

One option considered by the medical center in 1968—and endorsed by the city of Wilmington—was the construction of a large addition to the Delaware Division on the grounds of adjacent Brandywine Cemetery Association. But despite the pleas of such civic and political leaders as Mayor Harry Haskell, whose own parents were buried on the proposed construction site, the cemetery association refused to sell.

In 1969 Henry Belin du Pont's welfare foundation donated to the medical facility a 200-acre tract of former farmland near Stanton, southwest of Wilmington. The Medical Center then announced that "a major health complex" would be built on the suburban site. But it wasn't until 1975 that the center's board adopted Plan Omega which called for the construction of a major general hospital on the Stanton site, the closing of two Wilmington facilities, and the conversion of the Delaware division at Fourteenth and Washington streets to an emergency and routine care unit.

Plan Omega was strongly opposed by Wilmington's political leaders because its implementation meant the loss of medical services and jobs that were important to the city. The subsequent struggle between the suburbs and the city over the medical center's future site ended only after four years of litigation and the promise of a free shuttle service between Wilmington and Stanton. In addition, a pledge was made that the Delaware Division, the facility's only city hospital scheduled to remain open, would not become a racially identifiable unit. Despite concessions pleasing to Wilmington, the suburbs clearly had won the battle over Plan Omega. In January 1985 the new 780-bed Christiana Hospital, costing approximately 140 million dollars, opened for business on the Stanton site. Meanwhile, in Wilmington, the General and Wilmington divisions closed, while the Delaware Division was reduced to only 250 beds and renamed Wilmington Hospital. To add to the city's chagrin, the Wilmington Medical Center changed its name to the Medical Center of Delaware.

Before winning its fight over the location of the new medical facility, suburban New Castle claimed an even more significant victory. But this time the loser was rural Delaware.

By 1960 more than one half of the state's population lived in the New Castle County suburbs and, on the whole, were Delaware's best educated and wealthiest citizens. And yet, because of the antiquated election district lines drawn by the Delaware Constitution of 1897, the suburbs were scandalously underrepresented in the General Assembly. A case in point was the Brandywine Hundred Representative District north of Wilmington, which had thirty-nine times the population of the rural Blackbird District in southern New Castle County. Because of the extraordinary population growth in suburban northern Delaware, old election district boundaries increasingly ignored the concept of equal representation and gave disproportionate political power to rural and downstate residents.

In 1962 seven suburban Republicans went to court to challenge Delaware's antiquated election district lines. By doing so, they also contested downstate Delaware's traditional control of the General Assembly. After litigation reached all the way to the United States Supreme Court, the General Assembly was directed to reapportion election districts according to population. A statewide reapportionment, which went through several steps, was finally completed by the election of 1972, giving suburban New Castle control of a majority of seats in both houses of the General Assembly. As historian John Munroe points out, Delaware's politics—like housing, shopping, and even industry—had become "suburbanized."

In the late 1960s suburban New Castle began flexing

Right
In 1828 Jonathon Fell, a Philadelphia spice merchant, purchased this old mill on Mill Creek in the village of Faulkland, Delaware. The Fell family gained a worldwide reputation for their spices and they stayed in business until 1874. Courtesy, Hagley Museum and Library

During the eighteenth and nineteenth centuries, the Brandywine River in northern Delaware supported a variety of water-powered industries. Gilpin's Paper Mill operated until destroyed by a flood in 1822. Courtesy, Hagley Museum and Library

Above
The Republic, *a paddlewheel steamboat built by Harlan and Hollingsworth of Wilmington in 1878, could carry up to 4,000 passengers at a time on the Delaware-to-Philadelphia route. Courtesy, Historical Society of Delaware*

Left
Each spring, fishermen spread wide nets across the Delaware River in an effort to trap shad swimming upstream to spawn. Commercial plants salted and cured the meat, then packed it in barrels for winter use. Fresh shad and their roe, however, remained a seasonal delicacy. Courtesy, Historical Society of Delaware

James A. Bayard, U.S. senator from Delaware, greets Albert Gallatin, secretary of the treasury, and his son, James, as they arrive in New Castle. The three men boarded the ship Neptune on May 9, 1813, as part of a U.S. delegation which sought to end the War of 1812. Robert E. Goodier's painting looks east on Delaware Street, showing the stables and terminus of the New Castle and Frenchtown Stage Coach Lines. Courtesy, Bank of Delaware

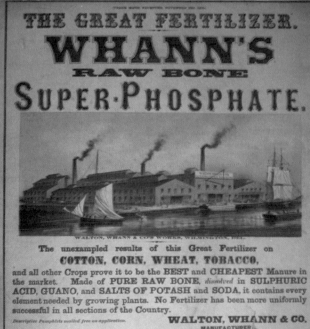

Above
A tin advertising sign used by the Du Pont Company during the nineteenth century associated gunpowder with the opening of the West. Courtesy, Hagley Museum and Library

Right
Fertilizers and improved farming techniques helped to revitalize Delaware acreage exhausted by centuries of cultivation. Whann's Raw Bone Super-Phosphate works in Wilmington, like downstate companies, produced fertilizers from agricultural by-products. Courtesy, Delaware State Archives

Facing page
Nineteenth-century advertisers used commercially-produced trade cards as prizes to attract shoppers to particular stores or products. Courtesy, Historical Society of Delaware

144

The Great Wilmington Fair,

Come, doggie, come, and go with me,
To see the grand new fair,
Prick up your ears, your nose keep clean,
For others will be there.

Tuesday, Wednesday, Thursday Friday and Saturday,
OCTOBER, 9, 10, 11, 12, & 13 1888.

PRESENTED BY **HENRY PIKE,**
304 Market Street, WILMINGTON, DEL.

EDWIN C. BURT, FINE SHOES.

Oh John I am so glad you brought that Cooked Corned Beef. We have had Company come and I did not know what I should give them to eat

Always keep on hand

LIBBY McNEILL & LIBBY'S COOKED CORNED BEEF

*Facing page, top, and left
These colorful cards were used
as advertisements by Delaware
retailers from the 1860s to the
1890s. Courtesy, Historical Society of Delaware*

FRESH TOMATOES

PUT UP BY
SAMUEL TOWNSEND,
TOWNS END, DEL.

Above
The most important Delaware crops during the nineteenth century were peaches and tomatoes. After blight destroyed many peach orchards in the 1890s, farmers switched to the succulent red vegetable. Samuel Townsend's cannery, a small factory similar to many others throughout the state, placed decorative labels on its products. Courtesy, Delaware State Archives

Right
Peter Sigfredus Alrichs, a Dutch settler, built a small frame house on the south bank of the Christina River near Old Swedes Church in the 1600s. The Alrichs family owned the house for over two hundred years. Over time, two brick sections were added to the house, leaving the original frame building as the rear wing. Painting by Robert Shaw. Courtesy, Historical Society of Delaware

148

Above
Robert Shaw (1859-1912) was one of Delaware's most talented artists. A resident of Penny Hill, he won fame for his many etchings, as well as book and magazine illustrations. This exacting work led to temporary blindness. Upon regaining sight, Shaw took up watercolors, capturing some fine landscape scenery. Courtesy, Historical Society of Delaware

Above
The rolling hills of northern Delaware gradually give way to flat, open fields and marshlands in the southern and coastal regions. "A View Near Newark," painted by Kevin McLaughlin, depicts a tranquil New Castle County vista. Courtesy, Kevin McLaughlin

Facing page
Return Day in Georgetown is more than simply the announcement of election results. It is also an opportunity for voters to meet the candidates, and for the candidates to "mend fences" and to gather support. Courtesy, John Purnell

Left
Delaware's soil has supported agriculture from the time that the Swedes first cultivated crops to the present era of large-scale farming. "Cut Fields, Hockessin," by Kevin McLaughlin, evokes a feeling of the state's agricultural heritage. Courtesy, Kevin McLaughlin

Following page
Encouraged by the movement for historic preservation, urban professionals have renovated Victorian row houses once owned by factory workers. These homes on Sixteenth Street in Wilmington are a short walk from the Hercules Corporation headquarters. Courtesy, Carolyn Stallings

151

its newfound political muscle by supporting the Republican Party. Since the Depression, neither Democrats nor Republicans had been able to dominate Delaware's elections for any extended period of time. In 1968, however, suburban New Castle helped elect one of its own, Du Pont Company scientist and executive Russell Peterson, as Republican governor. Suburbanites were also partially responsible for Republican majorities in both houses of the General Assembly.

Governor Peterson reflected the priorities of many of his constituents when, for the sake of efficiency, he decided to reorganize the executive branch of Delaware's state government. He also pushed legislation to protect the state's coastal ecology. In 1970 Peterson replaced approximately 140 commissions and agencies with a ten-agency cabinet. The next year, he signed the Coastal Zone Act, prohibiting oil refineries and certain other types of industrial development from locating along Delaware's shoreline. Responding to Shell Oil's plans for a refinery in southeastern New Castle County, the governor's "To hell with Shell" remark made him a hero to ecologists across the nation.

But Republican domination was brief, in part because the party couldn't consistently depend on overwhelming support from suburban New Castle. Many blue-collar workers and unionized clerks now lived outside of Wilmington and, more often than not, supported the Democrats. By the 1950s most black Wilmingtonians had turned against the party of Lincoln in local elections. With few exceptions they could also be counted on to pull the Democratic lever during statewide contests. Adding to Republican woes, downstate Delawareans became increasingly resentful of the new political power exercised by suburban New Castle and personified in the active governorship of Russell Peterson. After turning back a primary challenge that

The introduction of electric trolley cars in the 1880s originally expanded the bounds of Wilmington. Distinct "streetcar suburbs" were developed along these transportation lines. Courtesy, Historical Society of Delaware

*First elected to the U.S. Senate
in 1972 at age thirty, Delaware
Democrat Joseph R. Biden, Jr., is
seen as one of his party's up and
coming leaders.*

split the Republican Party, Peterson was defeated in his 1972 reelection bid by Democrat Sherman Tribitt of Odessa. Two years later the Democrats won control of both houses of the General Assembly.

But Democratic control in Dover was just as short lived as Republican political domination. With the state government facing a financial crisis, Delaware's voters turned to Republican gubernatorial candidate Pierre S. du Pont IV, grandnephew of education reformer Pierre S. du Pont, to lead the state government to solvency in 1976. Belt tightening and a recovering economy worked so well that within eight years, near the end of du Pont's second term, his administration announced a very sizeable surplus for the fiscal year ending June 30, 1985. By the time du Pont turned the governor's office over to Republican Michael Castle in January 1985, he was assured the same respect that Delawareans accord two other former governors, Democrat

Elbert N. Carvel (1949-53, 1961-65) and Republican J. Caleb Boggs (1953-60).

Since 1940 the First State has sent a number of capable men to Washington, D.C., but with the exception of U.S. Senator John J. Williams (1947-1971), no Delawareans in recent memory have exercised more national influence than the tandem of Democrat Joseph Biden (1973-) and Republican William Roth (1971-). At the 1984 Return Day celebration in Georgetown, Delaware's Democratic Congressman Thomas Carper (1981-) paid tribute to the growing national reputations of Senator Biden and Governor du Pont by predicting that in 1987, the two would be slogging their way through the snows of New Hampshire, wearing Delaware "Small Wonder" buttons and campaigning for votes in the first of a long series of presidential primaries.

Since World War II the state of Delaware has considerably increased its commitment to public education. Of particular importance was the General Assembly's 1968 decision to institute kindergartens throughout the state. That same year, legislators passed the Educational Advancement Act, which forced many of Delaware's smaller school districts to consolidate and established an equalization formula which provided increased funding for the state's poorer districts.

Consolidation didn't sit well with many downstate Delawareans. To some communities, it meant the loss of the local high school and necessitated busing local children to other towns. A poll taken in Georgetown in 1968, for example, showed that a clear majority of the local school district's residents opposed any form of consolidation. Educational authorities in Dover countered this opposition by arguing that the enlarged districts would offer a greater variety of courses, provide specialized services to meet the peculiar needs of a heterogeneous student body, and do it all in a cost efficient manner. Moreover, they pointed out, consolidation merged many poorer districts with wealthier ones, thus reducing the disparity in educational opportunities throughout the state.

During the last two decades, falling test scores and reports alleging lack of discipline and serious purpose have evoked considerable criticism of public education in Delaware and across the nation. Amidst the recriminations, however, there was a growing realization that positive action, legislative and otherwise, was immediately necessary. Recommendations by a state education task force, for example, led to a 1984 hike in teachers' salaries, which improved Delaware's 1983 national ranking of twenty-second among states.

Despite widespread criticism of their schools, in recent years Delaware's students generally have scored well on standardized examinations. Their 1984 performance ranked Delaware fifth out of the twenty-one states emphasizing the Scholastic Aptitude Test. Dr. William B. Keene, superintendent of Delaware's Department of Public Instruction, reflected a new optimism about the future of the state's elementary and secondary schools here when, in late 1984, he confidently predicted that Delaware "will emerge as one of the significant education leaders in the country."

Extraordinary growth by the University of Delaware and the founding of Delaware Technical and Community College have highlighted recent developments in post-secondary education. Undergraduates at the University of Delaware's Newark campus increased dramatically from less than 1,000 prior to World War II to approximately 13,000 in 1984. By the latter year, the school employed 800 full-time faculty and a total of 2,400 full-time employees—almost one percent of the First State's work force. Graduate programs also began to proliferate in the 60s, and the university offered forty-one different doctoral degrees by 1984. Over the same period the school demonstrated an increased willingness to cater to the needs of the market place, adding new colleges in nursing, business and economics, urban affairs, and marine studies. Much of this recent growth was made possible by the University of Delaware's large endowment which, according to a recent study, ranked among the top thirty of all higher educational institutions across the nation.

Even more sensitive to the needs of the market place than the University of Delaware has been Delaware Technical and Community College. The school opened its first campus at Georgetown in 1967 under the aegis of Democratic Governor Charles L. Terry, Jr. Offering two-year vocational degrees, Delaware Technical and Community College's 1984 enrollment numbered 2,940 full-time and 3,699 part-time students on four campuses.

Many museums and restored historic buildings have also expanded educational opportunities to Delawareans. Founded in 1951 by Henry Francis du Pont and located on his estate northwest of Wilmington, the Winterthur Museum opened to the public a world famous collection of early American furniture and decorative art. The Hagley Museum and the Museum of Natural History are two other educational institutions recently spawned by du Pont money and located just northwest of Wilmington. In Wilmington, the Delaware Art Museum (1938) exhibits Delaware illustrator Howard Pyle's works, plus a marvelous Pre-Raphaelite collection once the property of Wilmington textile

manufacturer Samuel Bancroft, Jr. Other museums, restored homes, and public buildings open to the public can be found throughout the state, but especially in New Castle, Odessa, Dover, and Lewes.

Women have been particular beneficiaries of the expansion of educational opportunities in the First State. It wasn't until the twentieth century that the barriers restricting women to domestic duties and to a lesser extent, factory jobs, secretarial work, nursing, and public school teaching, began to disappear. A crucial first step in breaking the shackles of tradition was for Delaware women to acquire a post-secondary education.

Contrary to the mores of his day, President William Purnell of Delaware College (University of Delaware) initiated coeducation on the Newark campus in 1872, only to have the experiment abandoned fourteen years later, after his resignation. When opening its doors in 1892, all-black, Dover-based Delaware State College introduced the first permanent coeducational program in the state. For white women seeking a college education, however, it was necessary to go outside of Delaware. Those few who did leave generally attended two-year normal schools which prepared them to become public school teachers. Prior to World War I, the Delaware General Assembly annually appropriated $4,500 in scholarship aid to help defray the costs of tuition at out-of-state normal schools.

Led by Emalea Pusey Warner, the Delaware State Federation of Women's Clubs and other women's organizations convinced legislators in 1911 to direct the State Board of Education "to evolve a feasible plan for the higher education of women in Delaware." Three years later, under the leadership of Dean Winifred Robinson, formerly an assistant professor of botany at Vassar, the Women's College of Delaware admitted its first students. This fledgling female college was built on grounds adjacent to all-male Delaware College in Newark and shared the older institution's administrative staff. Although the men's and women's colleges merged to become the University of Delaware in 1921, it wasn't until after World War II that the classroom integration of male and female students established itself as a permanent policy on the Newark campus.

In recent years there has been a remarkable increase in the number of women pursuing college degrees in Delaware and across the nation. Consequently, the percentage of female undergraduates at the University of Delaware has climbed from 33 percent in 1950 to 57 percent in 1984. As older, stereotyped images of a woman's proper place in society gave way to new perceptions, larger numbers entered Delaware's graduate and professional schools. At the University of Dela-

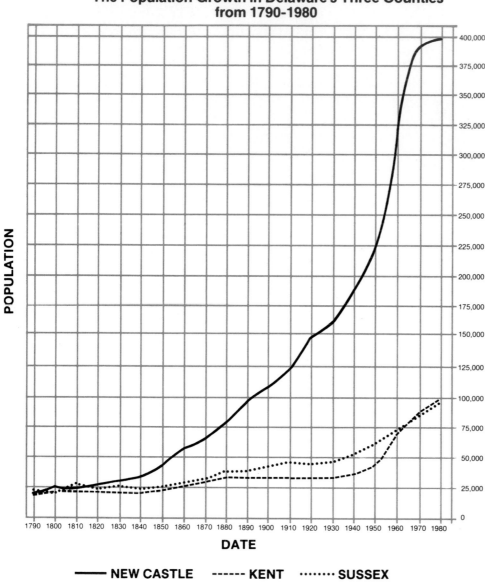

The Population Growth in Delaware's Three Counties from 1790-1980

POPULATION

DATE

—— **NEW CASTLE** ------ **KENT** ········ **SUSSEX**

ware, female graduate students increased from 26 percent of the total in 1960 to 46 percent in 1984. Delaware Law School also experienced an impressive rise in its full and part-time female students from 6 percent in 1974 to 33 percent in 1984.

Well educated, capable, and aided by federal affirmative action guidelines, Delaware women have moved quickly into responsible positions that were all but closed to them only a few decades ago. From 1960-64, for example, women accounted for less than one percent of newly admitted attorneys to the Delaware Bar and 13 percent of newly licensed Delaware physicians. By contrast, in the years 1980-84 almost 30 percent of newly admitted attorneys and 19 percent of newly licensed physicians were females. Women have also been making remarkable employment advances in the First

State's large corporations. For example, only a few women were found among the Du Pont Company's managerial and professional staff two decades ago. In 1984, however, Du Pont reported that women occupied 23 percent of its Delaware-based managerial and professional positions. Recent gains in the professional and business spheres have been most evident among white females.

Since 1920 Delaware women also have exercised their right to vote, but few have run for elective office. In 1924 Republican Florence M. Hanby became the first female elected to the state's House of Representatives. But another twenty-two years elapsed before Republican Vera G. Davis pioneered her way to the Delaware Senate. After serving as Senate president pro tem and later as majority leader of the House of Representatives,

Davis claimed another distinction: the first Delaware woman to win a statewide position when she was elected Treasurer of Delaware in 1956. In recent years the number of Delaware women elected to public office has increased. Sixteen percent of the 1985 General Assembly was female, yet no Delaware woman has ever been elected to the U.S. Senate, U.S. House of Representatives, or served as governor.

❧

Today, most Delawareans are as confident of their state's future as they are proud of its past. The Chesapeake and Delaware Canal continues to geographically divide downstaters and upstaters, but the actual differences between the two groups are considerably less than they were fifty years ago and surely less than politicians and writers, intent on telling a good story, care to admit. One suspects that Delawareans, like the proud inhabitants of small states and nations throughout the world, have a tendency to exaggerate sectional differences because this somehow makes their state seem a bit larger than it really is.

Delaware's dimensions—only Rhode Island is smaller and only Vermont, Wyoming, and Alaska have fewer people—define both its charm and its potential. As a number of Delawareans have pointed out, the First State's small size lends itself to innovative ideas which would be difficult to implement in larger states.

But history indicates that Delaware hasn't always been receptive to innovative ideas. Although the first state to ratify the U.S. Constitution, Delaware was among the last to abandon slavery and grant women's suffrage. Indeed, for much of its history, Delaware has been reluctant to address significant social, educational, racial, and economic problems. Because the First State so often refused to take the initiative, the federal government or certain members of the du Pont family felt compelled to act. By 1985, however, most of the du Ponts lived outside of Delaware and the Reagan Administration had curtailed federal intervention in the affairs of individual states. Now more than ever before, the future of the First State rests with ordinary Delawareans and their elected representatives.

Among the issues that must be addressed to ensure Delaware a better tomorrow is what, if anything, can be done to more directly involve the black community in the First State's economic, political, and cultural life. Because legal racial barriers have disappeared, many blacks have matched white women in dramatic personal advancement. A large segment of Delaware's minority community, however, seems mired in apathy and contributes less than it might to the state's economic and social well being. If some way can be found to stimulate the energies and ambitions of this black underclass, all Delawareans will benefit.

A second issue concerns the development of downstate Delaware. Although Wilmington is in the midst of an economic resurgence and the majority of Delawareans continue to live in suburban New Castle, much of the state's economic future will depend on the dramatic expansion of lower Delaware's business, industrial, and tourist base. Already in Kent and Sussex, population is increasing at a more rapid rate than in New Castle County. But without proper control over future development, the bucolic fields and forests of downstate Delaware will eventually give way to the ugly jungle of signs, stores, and parking lots that scar New Castle County's Kirkwood Highway. At stake is a certain quality of life which Kent and Sussex residents have traditionally taken for granted, but which may be hard to preserve.

If the past serves as a guide, Delaware's future governments will be reluctant to confront these and many other significant issues. Even when previous General Assemblies addressed important problems, they often opted for a cosmetic cure while ignoring the fundamental question at hand. Delaware's continued use of the whipping post long after it had been abolished in every other state is a case in point. In 1935 a Philadelphia newspaper published a photo of a public whipping in Delaware which stirred strong protests in and outside of the First State. The General Assembly's perverse response to the humanitarian outcry was to outlaw, not the whipping post, but the photographing of public whippings. The last public whipping occurred in 1952 and Delaware law finally abolished the whipping post twenty years later.

Three and one-half centuries ago, David de Vries first set eyes on southern Delaware. He marveled at Delaware Bay "with whales so numerous," and at the land "so fine for cultivation." Shortly thereafter, Peter Lindestrom waxed euphoric about the Christina River "so rich in fish," and the surrounding countryside so fertile "that the pen is too weak to describe, praise and extol it." History demands of Delaware's past generations an accounting for what they have done with the state's bountiful natural and human resources since the days of De Vries and Lindestrom. A century from now, history will demand a similar accounting. The long life of Delaware's whipping post, however, makes clear that when Delawareans and their public officials choose perversity and shortsightedness over empathy and vision, the accounting can be painful.

*"Southern Approaches," a paint-
ing by Kevin McLaughlin, depicts a scene familiar to most
residents of Northern Delaware.
Commuters make their daily
trek from their suburban homes
to work in Wilmington along
well-traveled routes such as Interstate 95. Courtesy, Kevin
McLaughlin*

CHAPTER VIII

PARTNERS IN PROGRESS

Delaware's fortunes have always been strongly tied to its hundreds of miles of shoreline along the Delaware River Bay and Atlantic Ocean. The fertile coastal plain, combined with waters teeming with marine life, attracted European settlers as early as 1631.

The first settlers, a small band of Dutch fishermen, lived briefly near Lewes before being massacred by Indians. They were followed in 1638 by Swedish and Finnish settlers, who sailed farther into the bay to establish New Sweden at the mouth of a deep-flowing river they named the Christina.

Later the Scotch, Irish, Welsh, and English arrived, as well as other settlers from Western Europe. By the early 1700s another community, Willingtown, was established nearby. When chartered in 1739 the two settlements were renamed Wilmington.

During and after the American Revolution, the city prospered. Lumber, grains, paper, and textiles were milled along the plentiful streams that were the sources of power for the mills as well as conduits to outlying areas.

In 1801 a French immigrant named Éleuthère Irénée du Pont began operating gunpowder mills on Brandywine Creek. His choice of location was to have a profound effect on the state. The powder mills were the forerunner of the modern-day enterprise that bears his name, the E.I. du Pont de Nemours Company, Inc., the state's largest employer.

In the lower counties, forests of cypress, cedar, and white oak provided a thriving lumber trade. Fishing, crabbing, and oystering provided food as well as goods for trade.

By the beginning of the nineteenth century shipbuilding had become important to the state's commerce. Shipyards in many coastal and river towns produced wooden sloops, schooners, and fishing boats.

The railroad brought profound changes to lower Delaware. In 1856 the first train from Wilmington reached Seaford on a new line built by the Philadelphia, Wilmington & Baltimore (PW&B) Railroad. The downstate line opened all of Delaware to trade.

Farmers in Sussex and Kent counties planted large fruit orchards and strawberry fields and sent the crops to city markets. Lower Delaware was a major producer of peaches, pears, and strawberries well into the twentieth century. The development of a year-round broiler industry in the late 1920s was also furthered by the new overland access.

Today Delaware is known worldwide as headquarters for three major chemical firms. Nearly half of the nation's *Fortune* 500 companies claim Delaware as their corporate home. During the early 1980s an increasing number of banks and insurance companies have built large offices and computer operations here. Tourism is also a growing industry, and the Port of Wilmington draws ships from around the world.

In Kent and Sussex counties the broiler industry is still king, and the fertile land continues to yield vegetables and grains. The coastline provides towns like Rehoboth, Lewes, and Bethany with a thriving tourism business.

Today First Staters enjoy the same riches that attracted the earliest settlers. The rich land provides plentiful grains and food, and the Delaware Bay still yields a rich marine harvest for table and trade.

The organizations whose stories are detailed on the following pages have chosen to support this important literary and civic project. They illustrate the variety of ways in which individuals and their businesses have contributed to the state's growth and development. The civic involvement of Delaware's businesses, institutions of learning, and local government, in cooperation with its citizens, has made the First State an excellent place to live and work.

DELAWARE STATE CHAMBER OF COMMERCE

The origins of the Delaware State Chamber of Commerce go back to 1837, when the Wilmington Board of Trade was formed by local businessmen. The city was a bustling manufacturing center, producing railroad cars, wheels, and sailing ships, as well as gunpowder and dynamite at the fledgling DuPont Company Powder Works.

The early business coalition was responsible for several improvements, including expansion of rail service, widening of city streets, and construction of the city's first elegant hotel, the Clayton House, at Fifth and Market streets.

By 1913, when the Board of Trade was renamed the Wilmington Chamber of Commerce, the city's importance as a business center had increased due to the move of the county seat from New Castle to Wilmington. In 1953 the organization changed its focus and assumed a new statewide role as the Delaware State Chamber of Commerce.

While influential, the Chamber remained small. Until 1979 membership remained at less than 500. Today it is a strong and effective

organization with nearly 3,000 members. The Chamber's president, William C. Wyer, attributes its success and strength to a successful legislative program and drastically increased membership services.

The Chamber's hub is its new Wilmington headquarters at One Commerce Center—the state's first center-city high-rise condominium office complex. When it opened on November 3, 1983, with much fanfare, the site of the new offices had a mixed history. It was purchased in 1964 by the DuPont Company from the Grand United Order of Odd Fellows, a black fraternal organization that had used the building since 1927. At one point it was the location of the cavalry unit of the Delaware National Guard. During the Revolutionary War it was the home of the Bellachs, a Quaker family. By 1981, when the DuPont Company donated the site to the Chamber for its new headquarters, it was being used as a parking lot.

Members now enjoy well-organized conference and seminar facilities, complete catering services, a state-of-the-art computer, and teleconfer-

William C. Wyer, president of the Delaware State Chamber of Commerce.

encing capabilities.

The Chamber is the state's oldest and largest business advocacy agency, providing an organized voice to the community and legislature for industry and business leaders while offering an ever-growing selection of seminars and educational programs. Services include an annual Economic Summit and regularly scheduled small business education forums. There are monthly luncheons on employee relations topics, monthly dinners devoted to discussion of business and economic development, and export seminars to acquaint members with the ins and outs of foreign markets and trade financing.

The Chamber represents its members at all levels of government through its Government Relations staff, which has been successful in a wide spectrum of issues, ranging from reduction of personal income taxes and unemployment compensation reform to mandatory deposit legislation and the Financial Center Development Act.

The Delaware State Chamber of Commerce is nearly 150 years old. Today, with a 40-member board of directors comprised of talented men and women from the state's three counties, the Chamber faces the future with confidence and great pride in its past accomplishments.

One Commerce Center, the Chamber's home since 1983.

UNIVERSITY OF DELAWARE

Memorial Hall, University of Delaware.

The stately, handsomely landscaped campus of the University of Delaware lies within the boundaries of the city of Newark in northern New Castle County. This modern-day center of learning can trace its roots to a school operated by renowned clergyman/scholar Dr. Francis Alison in 1743, but its charter as a college wasn't granted by the Delaware legislature until 1833.

In 1834 Newark College opened in the building now known as Old College Hall. During its first ten years the institution was supported by a state lottery.

The Middle States Association of Colleges and Secondary Schools has accredited the University of Delaware continuously since 1921. Professional accreditation is held in business administration, chemistry, clinical psychology, dietetics, education, engineering, medical technology, music, physical therapy, and nursing.

In 1921 the name University of Delaware was adopted for the combined institutions of Delaware College and Women's College. Until 1938 males and females attended separate classes. That year coeducation was permitted in junior and senior classes only. In 1944 coeducation was adopted as a permanent policy of the university.

Today approximately 13,000 students gather in Newark every September for the opening of the fall session. The university also has 2,000 graduate students and 2,300 part-time students in its Division of Continuing Education.

The eight undergraduate and two graduate colleges comprise 130 major and 39 minor areas of study. The Newark campus embraces 1,100 acres. There is an additional 360 acres in Lewes, where the College of Marine Studies has facilities and a 310-acre Agricultural Substation in Georgetown.

The eight undergraduate colleges are Agricultural Sciences, Arts and Science, Business and Economics, Education, Engineering, Human Resources, Nursing, and Physical Education, Athletics, and Recreation. The College of Marine Studies and the College of Urban Affairs and Public Policy are concerned primarily with graduate education and research.

The university's $251-million physical plant consists of approximately 2,700 acres, with 354 facilities, including 132 major academic buildings. Students participate in a semester system of study with an optional five-week winter session. Summers are divided into two five-week sessions with an overlapping seven-and-one-half-week session.

In 1983-1984 the university held a celebration of its 150th anniversary. A highlight of the celebration was the groundbreaking for a $15-million expansion of the Morris Library. When completed in 1986 the renovation will double the study seating, triple faculty study areas, and double storage space for collections.

Major academic events during the anniversary celebration were symposia held by each of the ten colleges on the present and future of their respective disciplines. The fifteen months of the 150th anniversary celebration were used by administration and personnel for critical self-examination and evaluation.

Today men and women attend the University of Delaware to prepare themselves for careers, self-sufficiency, and the business of life. The institution's philosophy emphasizes the development of the total person, with students encouraged to participate in all programs of the university community.

GILPIN, VAN TRUMP & MONTGOMERY, INC.

Ferdinand L. Gilpin

The year is 1865.

The U.S. Civil War has finally come to a close. The last few miles of the Atlantic Cable are completed. The first few miles of the first oil pipeline are opened.

And Edwin A. Van Trump opens the doors of his new insurance business in Wilmington, Delaware, offering accident, death, and fire insurance to city residents.

That same year another man who was to be instrumental in the growth of the state's insurance industry, Ferdinand L. Gilpin, opened his insurance business in Wilmington.

Within a few years John A. Montgomery entered the insurance business. Times were good.

1904. The three entrepreneurs merge their interests to better serve the community and to offer expanded lines of insurance.

1909. A new corporation is registered: Gilpin, Van Trump & Montgomery, Inc. The corporation provides new channels for the entrepreneurial spirit of the founders and their rapidly growing number of associates. It provides new avenues for growth throughout the century.

1941. Gilpin, Van Trump & Montgomery, Inc., begins to specialize in real estate sales, development, and mortgage banking.

1946. Gilpin becomes an FHA-approved mortgagee.

1950. Gilpin is a loan correspon-

dent for Metropolitan Life Insurance Company and services the loans in-house.

Since 1865 the Gilpin family tree has grown in many directions. Today its branches spread wider than ever. Five central divisions are continuing a tradition of growth as Delaware's only full-service real estate organization.

For years the Gilpin corporate color has been green, a color that symbolizes vibrant, healthy growth. What better color for a corporation with a history of putting down roots in areas that other companies have yet to discover!

When America moved to the suburbs, Gilpin was already there. As a developer. As a mortgage banker. As residential brokers. Communities such as Brookmeade, Willow Run, Capitol Trail Farms, Limestone Gardens, Pinecrest, Church Hill, Fairthorne, Barleymill, West Riding, Lambeth Riding, Limestone Hills, and others all have their roots beginning with Gilpin.

When America rediscovered its inner cities, Gilpin was already there. As investors. As risk-takers. The sweeping transformation of Wilmington has not come overnight. Nor has it been the result of one company or one city administration.

Yet one real estate company has contributed more than any other to change the face of the city, to build the new city of Wilmington: Gilpin.

In the mid-1950s the Wilmington

Edwin A. Van Trump

John A. Montgomery

Planning Commission reported that a tract of eight square blocks in the heart of the downtown business district must be improved: from Fourth to Eighth streets, between King and Walnut.

After twenty-one years of planning, negotiation, and clearing the land, the commission found a company that was willing to accept the challenge of redevelopment: Gilpin.

Working closely with the city, Customs House Square Associates, a Gilpin joint venture, was able to achieve the results that many other developers had dismissed as impossible.

Within one year of breaking ground, the Customs House Square office complex and underground parking garage was open for business.

Two years later the new Radisson Hotel welcomed its first guests.

The development has continued to move rapidly south, as new buildings are rising to create a new Wilmington skyline. The Alico Building. The Christina Gateway Building. A future new wing of the Radisson Hotel.

From land acquisition, through financing, construction, leasing, and management, once again Gilpin has proven its ability to do it all.

1985. No other real estate company in the state can match Gilpin, Van Trump & Montgomery, Inc., in depth, diversity, or the Gilpin track record of results.

In residential sales, more than 100 professional real estate sales person-

estate.

The Gilpin Relocation Center coordinates out-of-state referrals, helps companies relocate employees and their families, and, as a third-party buyer, offers home equity advances to the employees of corporate clients.

The firm has also established an enviable track record in joint ventures including office buildings, apartments, condominiums, shopping centers, resort property, and a major hotel. Its major accomplishments include the development of the Radisson Wilmington Hotel, the Kirk Building, One Customs House Square,

Reconstruction of Customs House Square.

nel help clients find both homes and buyers.

As Delaware's oldest and largest mortgage banker, Gilpin is a leader in finding new, innovative ways to accommodate requests for mortgage loans of almost any size.

Gilpin property-management professionals lease, promote, manage, and maintain all types of commercial, office, residential, and industrial real

the DuPont Street Shopping Center, the Millcreek Shopping Center, English Village in Dover, Kinnaird Point on Maryland's Eastern Shore, and Gilpin Place Apartments in Wilmington, besides the residential developments mentioned earlier.

You can trace the track record of Gilpin, Van Trump & Montgomery, Inc., all the way back to when it began, in 1865.

Small wonder that Gilpin knows how to take care of business. The firm has been doing it for a long, long time.

From land acquisition through financing, construction leasing, and management, Gilpin has been involved in creating a new Wilmington skyline.

BANK OF DELAWARE

Bank of Delaware is the great-grandfather of the state's financial institutions. It was born in 1795 in an era of dislike and suspicion. It wasn't easy for a bank to survive in those days, less than two decades after the American Revolution.

Living conditions were primitive, and travel was limited and hazardous because most roads were desolate and impassable in bad weather. Outside the towns and villages land was heavily wooded and often inhabited by highwaymen. There was widespread counterfeiting, and the use of unstable and often worthless currency contributed to the disdain in which banks were held.

In this forbidding atmosphere, several Wilmington businessmen gathered at Patrick O'Flynn's hotel to organize a bank. The first stockholders included several of Delaware's most illustrious citizens: James A. Bayard, Caesar A. Rodney, Joseph Tatnall, John Ferris, William Hemphill, and Eli Mendenhall. Tatnall was elected the first president of "The President, Directors & Company of the Bank of Delaware."

Within a year the institution purchased property at Market and High (now Fourth) streets, built a vault, and opened for business. That same year the Delaware General Assembly passed an incorporation act that gave the bank its status as the first state-chartered commercial institution.

In 1815, because larger quarters were needed, the bank built a facility at the corner of Hanover (now Sixth) and Market streets. (As was customary in those days, the cashier's residence was attached.)

In 1816 the bank formed an association with four other state institutions to study the problem of free circulation of various bank notes. It was not until 1863, when President Abraham Lincoln signed the National Currency Act, that the problem was solved.

This act made possible the dual system whereby banks could operate under either a state or a federal charter. Notes of the national banks be-

Joseph Tatnall, one of the organizers of the original Bank of Delaware and its first president. Courtesy, Historical Society of Delaware

came the national currency, uniform in design and engraved under government supervision, but circulated by individual institutions.

In 1865 the bank sought and received a national charter, becoming The National Bank of Delaware. By 1866 there were more than 1,600 nationally chartered institutions.

Through mergers and acquisitions, the bank has enjoyed considerable growth. In a 1930 corporate reorganization the Security Trust Company acquired the business, assets, and goodwill of The National Bank of Delaware.

That was also the year the brick Bank of Delaware Building at Market and Hanover streets was sold to Delmarva Power and Light Company. The structure was removed and rebuilt at Lovering Avenue and Union Street. It remains today as the Delaware Academy of Medicine.

In 1952 Security Trust Company merged with Equitable Trust Company to become Equitable Security Trust Company. In 1958 it was renamed Bank of Delaware. The most recent merger, with The Milford Trust Company, was in 1982.

Other components of the twentieth-century Bank of Delaware include Wilmington Morris Plan Bank, acquired in 1944; The Central National Bank of Wilmington, 1951; The First National Bank of Dover, 1954; The New Castle County Bank of Odessa, 1956; and The National Bank of Smyrna, 1957.

Between 1956 and 1983 the institution expanded through mergers with The First National Bank of Seaford in 1959, Millsboro Trust in 1970, and Commercial Trust Company in 1974. Today the institution is a principal subsidiary of Bank of Delaware Corporation, a bank holding company.

In the late nineteenth and early twentieth centuries Bank of Delaware survived bank panics, depressions, recessions, and financial crunches that caused many other financial institu-

A facsimile of a 1795 Bank of Delaware note. Courtesy, Historical Society of Delaware

The National Bank of Delaware, located at Hanover (now Sixth) and Market streets in Wilmington, after its rechartering. The cashier's adjoining residence is at the rear of the building; the directors' meeting room is shown in inset at top. Courtesy, Historical Society of Delaware

tions to collapse. Even the stock market crash of 1929 left the bank largely unaffected. It is a healthy survivor of numerous mergers and name changes. Bank of Delaware now has thirty-two branch offices and more than 1,000 employees working to serve customers throughout the state.

In 1983, for the first time in the institution's history, total assets reached the billion-dollar mark, making Bank of Delaware one of only 240 commercial banks in the United States to achieve this position. In a world of billion-dollar banking, Bank of Delaware's leaders continue to be acutely aware of the institution's status as a local bank. Throughout its 190-year history the institution's officers have possessed a strong sense of corporate responsibility toward the communities it serves.

Today the bank's officers are active in community service organizations. A 1984 survey found that 187 officers were represented in 318 organizations, volunteering over 30,000 hours to these groups. Bank of Delaware also contributes many thousands of dollars to diverse community services organizations.

Many changes have occurred and continue to occur in the financial services industry as a result of modification in regulations. In a letter to stockholders in 1983, Jeremiah P. Shea, chairman of the board and chief executive officer, and David McMillan, president and chief operating officer, explained, "Good people, working in a less inhibited environment, took advantage of new regulatory and organizational freedoms to produce one of our best years in modern history."

Deregulation gave Bank of Delaware the opportunity to offer interest-bearing checking accounts as well as other consumer services such as financial management accounts. Other new products and services initiated include a new Small Business Unit in the Commercial Loans Department; computerization of the cash management information system; new certificates of deposit, IRA, and Keogh options; and the reintroduction of "no-frills" checking. During this same period, Del-Vest Inc., a subsidiary of Bank of Delaware Corporation, was formed to offer the bank's customers investment, advisory, and management service.

Bank of Delaware Corporation is proud of the part it has played in shaping banking and state history, and its officers look forward with confidence to playing a major role in the future of its communities.

Current executive officers are Jeremiah P. Shea, chairman of the board and chief executive officer (left), and David McMillan, president and chief operating officer.

DIAMOND STATE TELEPHONE

On January 1, 1985, Diamond State Telephone celebrated its first year of operation as a Bell Atlantic Company. After more than a century of service as a part of the Bell System, Diamond State and other local companies were spun off from AT&T in 1984 and regrouped into seven small, regional organizations.

Diamond State Telephone's mission, now more than ever, is to be the preferred source of low-cost, high-quality telecommunication services. This goal has been encouraged in many ways, with a spirit fostered by changes in the corporate structure and customer/employee relations.

All employees are encouraged to think, act, and conduct themselves as proprietors of the new business. Several new programs have been introduced in an effort to maximize employee participation, new ideas, and entrepreneurial spirit. One of the most successful, the Employee Participation Plan, encourages and rewards employees who have submitted suggestions that have been adopted. Another innovation, the Achievement of Excellence Award, provides recognition by corporate officers for exceptional, individual effort and performance by employees made to further corporate goals of providing better customer service, reducing costs, and increasing revenues.

"Equal Access," a term from the court-ordered divestiture, became important to Diamond State customers

Diamond State Telephone's largest central office, built on the Tilton Hospital site, today serves over 100,000 customer circuits.

in 1984. The local company is required to provide equivalent connections for all long-distance companies. Some 72,000 lines in sixteen Wilmington central office codes were equipped to give callers easy dialing access to the network of their preferred long-distance company. By late 1986 all Delawareans will be able, on an easy dialing basis, to use the service of any of the long-distance firms

The 380-bed Tilton Hospital, at the corner of Ninth and Tatnall streets, cared for wounded soldiers during the Civil War.

that will be vying for their business.

Other technological advances are ensuring that by mid-1986 all Delawareans will be served by the computer-controlled switching system that is already utilized by nearly 90 percent of the state's population.

Marketing its services to individual

and corporate customers has become an important aspect of Diamond State's long-range planning. Recognizing that different customers require different services, the firm has carefully tailored programs for different accounts. The largest customers have marketing account executives assigned to them on a full-time basis. Other corporate clients are assigned operations managers.

Diamond State Telephone's goals include providing individualized customer service, the integration of personal needs of employees with those of the company, reducing cost to become the low-cost supplier of superior telecommunication services, financial viability through sustained revenue growth and profitability, and encouraging two-way communication that stresses understanding and support with each person having a stake in Diamond State's operations. Today's goals will help Diamond State meet tomorrow's challenges.

Installers wait in front of the Delaware & Atlantic Telephone office at Sixth and Shipley streets. Photo circa 1899

GENERAL MOTORS

In May 1945 the nation was preoccupied with news of the ending of World War II and the anticipation of the return of thousands of veterans. That same month another announcement was made in Delaware that was to have a profound impact on the state's economy.

A local newspaper announced that the General Motors Corporation was planning to build an assembly plant in Wilmington. It forecast that GM's operation, on a site in the Homestead section five miles southwest of Wilmington, would mean much to the state's economy by offering employment to thousands of area residents, including many returning GIs.

Groundbreaking ceremonies for the $9.5-million facility at the 145-acre site were festive. Governor Walter Bacon turned the first shovel of earth, signifying the start of construction of the three main structures for manufacturing, administration, and a powerhouse that today enclose over 2.2 million square feet of floor space.

After completion of the plant in the spring of 1947, over 800 workers began production of 1947 Pontiacs in the fall. The first eight cars, all black, were shipped to Philadelphia area dealers in October of that year. Plans were for the plant to produce forty cars per hour—or 640 cars per sixteen-hour production day.

By 1952 there were 2,234 employees at the Boxwood plant and an annual payroll of $10.4 million, and by 1955 the plant was assembling sixty cars per hour. That year a second shift was added to step up production, and by mid-1955 employees numbered 4,400.

The one-millionth car rolled off the assembly line at Boxwood in 1957, just a decade after the plant had opened. Before the end of its second decade the plant would produce its two-millionth car. In 1968

General Motors' Wilmington plant.

Boxwood workers began producing the first of many Buicks. By 1970 one million Buicks had been assembled at the plant, representing 20 percent of the total national Buick production.

After producing more than 3.7 million standard-size cars, the plant started assembling the subcompact Chevrolet Chevette in 1975. Production of the Chevette continued until 1984 with slightly over two million being produced. In 1984 the plant resumed production of the standard-size Oldsmobile and Chevrolet models. By the end of 1984 the plant had produced a total of over 5.8 million cars with estimated sales of more than fifteen billion dollars.

In the summer of 1985, a $300-million modernization project was announced. When the project is completed in 1986, the Wilmington plant will be among the most highly automated facilities in the world with leading edge state-of-the-art technology. This investment will result in the production of the Chevrolet "L" car.

DELMARVA POWER AND LIGHT COMPANY

Delmarva Power provides electricity and service throughout most of the Delmarva Peninsula, which includes all of the state of Delaware, portions of nine Eastern Shore Maryland counties, and two Eastern Shore Virginia counties. In addition, the firm provides gas service to northern Delaware residents.

The Delmarva Peninsula stands out as one of the most distinctive geographical features on the East

utilities have merged with the firm, including New Castle County Electric Company, Seaboard Electric Company, Wilmington Automatic Telephone Company, Wilmington Light & Power Company, Wilmington City Electric Company, United

One of Delmarva Power and Light Company's major generating facilities is situated on the Indian River.

adopted for the parent corporation.

Delmarva Energy Company, a totally held subsidiary, was formed in 1975 to explore for natural gas. Currently it is producing gas in Texas and Pennsylvania under two separate joint ventures.

Effective at the close of the business day on December 31, 1979, the Maryland and Virginia subsidiaries were merged into the parent company. Since 1981 Delmarva has acquired the Centreville, Maryland, electric light, heat, and power system and has signed a 25-year lease with the St. Michaels, Maryland, electric system.

Delmarva Industries, Inc., a totally held subsidiary, was formed in 1981 to evaluate appropriate business opportunities. Currently it is producing oil and gas in Pennsylvania and Ohio under joint ventures.

During the mid-1960s joint ventures in large projects offered the most economic and efficient means

A lineman in Virginia repairs power lines after a storm.

Coast, with a historical and cultural background to match. Centrally located between major East Coast markets, the peninsula has a blend of industrial, agricultural, commercial, and recreational services.

To provide service to this 5,700-square-mile peninsula, Delmarva's operations are divided into Northern and Southern divisions. Each has a general office headquarters: Southern Division is located in Salisbury, Maryland, and Northern, in Christiana, Delaware, near Wilmington.

Major generating facilities are located in Edge Moor, Delaware City, and Indian River in Delaware, and in Vienna, Maryland. In addition, the company receives generation from two coal-burning stations in Pennsylvania and from nuclear power stations located in Peach Bottom, Pennsylvania, and Salem, New Jersey.

Delmarva Power and Light Company was incorporated in Delaware on April 22, 1909, as the American Power Company. Since then, several

Gas Improvement Company, Stockton Light & Power, and Chestertown Electric & Light. In December 1928 the firm's name became Delaware Power and Light Company.

During 1947 and 1948 the company and its subsidiaries disposed of all ice and refrigeration properties. And in 1966 the present name, Delmarva Power and Light Company, was

of adding to electric capacity. During that time Delmarva purchased a small interest in two coal-burning power stations in Pennsylvania.

Together with three neighboring utilities, Delmarva Power and Light Company constructed four nuclear generating units. Two are located at Peach Bottom, Pennsylvania, and two near Salem, New Jersey.

NANTICOKE HOMES, INC.

The roots are deep in Delaware soil for the Mervine family of Greenwood, owners of Nanticoke Homes, Inc., the largest builder and distributor on the Eastern Shore of customized, high-quality sectional homes.

In the years before their energies created this unique manufacturing business, John and Peggy Mervine ran a successful chicken-brokerage company on the property where Mervine's father started the business in 1936.

In 1971 their lives were changed by a chance investment in a local contractor's building business. The Mervines also offered the builder the use of an abandoned chicken-feeding station behind their house so that the contractor could begin construction of a model unit. It was February, the ground was frozen, and time was short if the model was to be completed by spring. The work began indoors with the 28- by 40-foot home being constructed in sections on blocks. Even the plumbing, wallpaper, and wiring were completed before the Mervines and their partner moved the model on site in Seaford later that year.

That was the beginning of Nanticoke Homes. By the end of the first year the local contractor had pulled

Nanticoke Homes' Rancher.

out, and the Mervines were sole partners. In the first year they constructed seventeen sectional homes in the formerly abandoned building.

Today Nanticoke Homes, Inc., has sales offices in Delaware, Maryland, New Jersey, Pennsylvania, and Virginia, all of which are served from the Greenwood plant. More than 400 employees, plus about 100 full-time subcontractors, build offices, garages, porches, multifamily units, town houses, and single-family homes. The custom-created buildings are produced at the rate of three houses per day.

Today's modern facility is a far cry from the original chicken-feeding station. Prior to 1979 the Mervines expanded the original facility four times. In February 1979 the entire plant burned to the ground. The

tragedy also destroyed all company records. The Mervines wasted no time in rebuilding. Plant No. 1 was put up immediately, and in 1983, with help from a Sussex County bond issue, the Mervines rebuilt Plant No. 2. The new, 6,000-square-foot office was erected in four days and set on site in four hours.

The new structure includes a model house, complete drafting department, cabinet shop, prefinishing department, a molding shop, vehicle maintenance shop, interior door assembly operation, and the corporate offices, where records are initiated and filed with an IBM System 36 computer.

Nanticoke Homes' two-story Colonial.

RLC CORP.

RLC Corp. was founded in 1954 as Rollins Fleet Leasing Corp., Inc., to incorporate the automobile-leasing business established in 1946 and operated as a sole proprietorship in Lewes, Delaware, by John W. Rollins, who continues to serve as RLC's chairman of the board of directors and chief executive officer.

The automobile-leasing business was started by Rollins, a pioneer in the industry, to help corporate America build its sales forces after World War II. He recalls, "Until that time nearly all want ads for salesmen specified that job applicants had to own a car, but I convinced companies that owning a car should no more be a condition of employment for a salesman than owning a typewriter should be for a secretary."

In 1968 the company became publicly held and its common stock was listed on the American Stock Exchange. The firm's common stock is now listed on the New York Stock Exchange (since 1978) and the Pacific Stock Exchange (since 1977).

Also in 1968 RLC formed a subsidiary, Rollins Environmental Services, Inc., which is engaged in the industrial waste treatment and disposal business. In 1982 RLC spun off to its shareholders the common stock of Rollins Environmental Services, Inc. This company is also listed on the New York Stock Exchange.

RLC Corp. is headquartered in the fifteen-story Rollins Building (which opened in 1972) on the Concord Pike north of Wilmington. Its principal subsidiaries are Matlack, Inc., and Rollins Leasing Corp. and, in the three decades since its incorporation, RLC has become one of the nation's leading highway transportation companies. RLC currently employs nearly 4,000 men and women at almost 250 locations throughout the United States and has more than 15,000 vehicles in operation on the nation's highways.

Matlack, Inc., which began operations in 1888, was acquired by RLC in 1968. Matlack is the nation's leading motor carrier of commodities in bulk and is known by its slogan, "Pipeline on Wheels." Operating as both a common and contract carrier, Matlack provides services on shipments throughout the United States and through agreements with other carriers, to and from Canada, Mexico, Europe, and the Caribbean. Based at nearly 100 strategically located terminals, Matlack's fleet of 1,500 tractors and 4,000 trailers is tailored to meet the needs of shippers of liquid, powdered, and gas chemicals; food; petroleum and forest products; and building materials.

Rollins Leasing Corp. was created from a base of small truck leasing businesses acquired in the late 1960s and early 1970s. One of the leading nationwide truck-leasing and -rental companies, Rollins Leasing services nearly 10,000 vehicles at 140 company-operated facilities across the United States. Rollins Leasing's principal revenue producer is Full Service Truck Leasing, providing, on a long-term basis, all the truck transportation equipment and services necessary for private carriage operations. Rollins Leasing also rents vehicles on a short-term basis, provides fleet operators with administrative services (Truck Control Services), and designs and operates specialized distribution systems for its customers.

John W. Rollins, chairman of the board.

One of the leading nationwide truck leasing and rental companies, Rollins Leasing Corp. services nearly 10,000 vehicles at 140 company-operated facilities across the United States.

ROLLINS ENVIRONMENTAL SERVICES, INC.

Rollins Environmental Services, Inc., was the nation's first high-technology hazardous waste management company. Today it is the only firm listed on the New York Stock Exchange devoted exclusively to the proper and safe management of hazardous waste. Since its inception in 1966 it has provided a complete spectrum of hazardous waste treatment and disposal services through subsidiaries in Texas, Louisiana, and New Jersey. Its national headquarters is located in New Castle County, in a distinctive high-rise building just north of the intersection of routes 100 and 202, north of Wilmington.

Rollins has more experience, involving nearly 30,000 different hazardous waste streams and the application of a greater variety of hazardous waste management techniques, than any other U.S. firm. The company continues to spend millions of dollars to continually improve, upgrade, and expand its facilities.

RES' principal service is incineration, the only effective large-scale method for the destroying of materials contaminated by toxic chemicals, including PCBs. Rollins operates three high-temperature, high-residence time incinerators. The first such incinerator was built in 1969.

The firm also offers a wide variety of PCB management services, including full analytical capabilities and service teams specializing in cleanup, packaging, and transportation. The Rollins facility outside Houston, Texas, was awarded the first-ever permit by the Environmental Protection Agency to incinerate PCBs in 1980. Since that time the company has safely destroyed over 100 million pounds of PCB-contaminated material.

Rollins' experienced personnel specialize in finding creative, cost-effective solutions at the nation's Superfund sites and other abandoned hazardous waste sites and facilities. In 1984 RES created its fifth subsidiary, Field Services, to concentrate exclusively on environmental cleanup problems.

Whatever solutions are required, Rollins' expertise is available to carefully plan and execute major cleanup projects. The firm's experts can sample, identify, and isolate materials, then remove, treat, or dispose of problem wastes in the most sound manner.

At its sites in Baton Rouge, Louisiana, and Deer Park, Texas, Rollins operates controlled land disposal facilities. These secure landfills represent the best available design, engineering, and monitoring technology for the final disposal of industrial hazardous wastes.

To reduce toxicity or to form innocuous compounds, Rollins can treat wastes chemically or physically. Other materials can be treated in specially designed biological degradation systems to accomplish the same purpose. A wide variety of inorganic and organic liquid wastes, ranging from oily to acidic wastewaters, can be received, treated, and disposed of at Baton Rouge and Deer Park. The combined capability at the two sites is 700,000 gallons per day.

Some industrial wastes must be injected into deep wells such as those maintained by Rollins in Louisiana. That site is accessible by barge and/or truck for direct off-loading, storage, filtration, and injection of aqueous saline wastes and wastes that have been cross-contaminated with more than one chemical. The deep-well injection disposal system is inexpensive for large-volume waste streams.

While laboratory wastes are normally generated in small quantities, their potential hazard can be just as serious as the large quantities of materials generated by industries. Rollins anticipates rapid growth in this area beginning in mid-1986, when new federal requirements will affect more than 90,000 small and medium-size businesses that heretofore have not had to account for the proper handling of hazardous wastes. Laboratories and businesses of any size can avail themselves of Rollins'

The Rollins Environmental Vault, patented by the environmental services company in 1984, has virtually eliminated any chance of groundwater or surrounding land contamination because of its above-ground design.

expertise in handling collection, packaging, transportation, and treatment programs.

Since the beginning RES has always been in the forefront of advanced technology for the safe handling of hazardous waste. A prominent example of this is the Rollins Environmental Vault, which the company won a patent on in 1984.

Because of its above-ground design, the Rollins Vault virtually eliminates any chance of groundwater or

exterior structure. The essence of the vault, however, is its multiple protective layers, which insulate the hazardous waste from the environment and capture potentially damaging leachate should it escape from the containment structure.

As a company, RES has consistently been committed to operating its facilities and field service projects in full accordance with all health, safety, and environmental regulations and standards. Compliance with all permit and regulatory requirements of federal, state, and local authorities has been and will continue to be the top priority at Rollins Environmental Services, Inc.

The Rollins Environmental Services (TX) facility outside of Houston, Texas. © Houston Chronicle

surrounding land contamination by making the laws of nature work for it instead of against it.

In conventional landfills, gravity is the principal enemy because it can drive accumulated leachate from the waste through the liner and toward the groundwater. Any corrective actions must work against this gravitational pull by pumping leachate or contaminated groundwater to the surface. With the above-ground Rollins Vault, gravity works for environmental protection, directing any possible leachate into collecting and monitoring devices before groundwater or surrounding earth is contaminated.

The Rollins Vault is constructed on a reinforced concrete base. Concrete walls, of any geometry, form the

MITCHELL ASSOCIATES, INC.

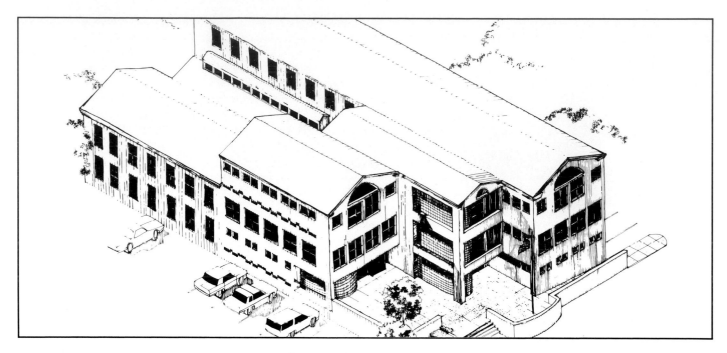

Just two decades ago three associates in a Philadelphia firm relinquished the security of working for someone else to become partners in a space planning and interior design business. Mitchell Associates was incorporated in Delaware, and the three partners completed their first projects from a rented farmhouse in Hockessin. Today Mitchell Associates, Inc., is a highly successful corporation, operating from two offices and with billings that place it as one of the top interior and graphic design firms in the United States.

In fact, most Delawareans have probably stepped into at least one Mitchell-designed environment. Interiors created by the firm include many of the DuPont Company's facilities, Wilmington Trust headquarters building on Rodney Square in Wilmington; Cokesbury Village, Hockessin; the Health Maintenance Organization (HMO), Stanton; Legislative Hall, Dover; and the Christiana Hospital of the Medical Center of Delaware, Stanton. The firm has completed numerous design projects in the state, representing only a portion of its diverse client list which includes projects in twenty-four states, the District of Columbia, Saudi Arabia, and Brazil.

Mitchell Associates was incorpo-

Mitchell Associates' new location at One Avenue of the Arts in Wilmington's Christina Gateway on the city's waterfront.

rated in 1965, and has moved its office several times as the staff and needs of its clients grew. The three founders were the sole employees the first year, but by the following year it was necessary to move to larger offices in Wilmington's Independence Mall.

As the firm moved again to even larger facilities in the mall, the corporate structure of Mitchell Associates changed drastically. One partner left the firm, and the partner for whom the business was named, Donald Mitchell, was tragically killed.

In 1979, after Mitchell's death, Louis B. Rosenberg, the remaining partner, became president. The company, now totaling seventeen employees, moved to new offices in Trolley Square. In 1984, less than twenty years after its founding, Mitchell Associates had forty-one employees working in the main office in Trolley Square and a branch office in Baltimore, Maryland.

In 1985 the firm moved again, this time to another area of Wilmington experiencing a building boom—the Christina Gateway on the city's

waterfront.

Situated on the railroad's northeast corridor and within easy commuting distance of other major cities, Mitchell Associates is able to successfully compete with design firms nationwide. In 1984 the high volume of annual business placed the company on a nationwide list of interior design giants cited by *Corporate Design* magazine. Rosenberg's goal is to see the firm's name in the top 100 list in 1985.

The interior and graphic design firm accepts only commercial projects and specializes in creating interiors for corporate health care, hospitality, banking, educational, and municipal facilities. By design and necessity, it is a people-oriented business. Each project is developed by a team of Mitchell staffers, selected on the basis of their expertise, be it graphics, interior design, architectural space planning, medical equipment specification, signage design, textile design, or donor recognition programs.

Each assignment is approached as a new challenge with the needs, desires, and financial commitment of the client providing the direction. Mitchell Associates applies the common principle that the creative design must fit the people, both those who work in the space and those who visit it.

THE NEWS-JOURNAL COMPANY

The ancestry of the newspapers of The News-Journal Company goes back to a weekly publication started in Wilmington 200 years ago, known as the *Delaware Gazette*. It eventually became a daily, and in the 1880s it was absorbed by the *Every Evening*. It was the first and longest-flourishing daily newspaper in Delaware until it merged with the *Evening Journal* on January 1, 1933.

The News-Journal Company's

The Every Evening, *first published in 1871, is one of the predecessors of today's News-Journal Company newspapers.*

The Sunday News Journal *began rolling off the presses in 1975 under the editorial guidance of Norman E. Isaacs, one of the country's most respected journalists.*

papers are the largest and most influential in Delaware and adjacent counties in Maryland, New Jersey, and Pennsylvania. Today they are part of a billion-dollar information corporation, the Gannett Company, which bought them for sixty million dollars from the DuPont Company on January 30, 1978. The papers include the *Morning News* and the afternoon *Evening Journal,* published five days a week; the *News Journal,* published on Saturday; and the *Sunday News Journal.*

Although the story of the *News Journal* is usually traced to the *Delaware Gazette,* it really began in 1871 when the *Every Evening* was established by William T. Croasdale to rival another afternoon daily known as the *Wilmington Daily Commercial.* Six years later the *Every Evening* absorbed the *Daily Commercial.* Other newspapers that were to become part of the firm were *The Morning News,* founded in 1880, and

the *Evening Journal,* founded in 1888.

In the late nineteenth century Delawareans had a wide choice of newspapers, including the three dailies published in Wilmington and a number of weeklies issued in various southern Delaware towns.

The Morning News, owned by the late Alfred I. du Pont in the early 1900s, became an active rival of the *Evening Journal,* which was owned by several of his cousins. The News-Journal Company was created in 1920 when Alfred du Pont sold *The Morning News* to his cousins, Henry A. and Coleman du Pont, who had owned the *Evening Journal* since 1912. The two publications merged in 1933. The combined afternoon news-

paper was called the *Journal-Every Evening* for many years, but it again became the *Evening Journal* in 1960.

During this period The News-Journal Company was owned by the Christiana Securities Company, a holding company chiefly for members of the du Pont family. In the 1960s staff members and editorial writers began to demand more autonomy and frequently clashed with the owners of the papers. Eventually Christiana Securities was phased out of existence, and ownership fell to the DuPont Company, which announced its plans to sell the papers.

It was during this period that the *Sunday News Journal* was created. Its founding editor was Norman E. Isaacs, one of the country's most prominent journalists.

The process of getting the papers ready for sale lasted more than five years but eventually five bidders submitted proposals, and the highest bid, from Gannett, was accepted. The first president and publisher under Gannett was Brian Donnelly, who served until 1979. He returned to Wilmington in 1982 to succeed John J. Curley, who became editor of *USA Today,* and is now president and chief operating officer of the Gannett Company.

J. Donald Brandt is the editor of The News-Journal papers, John H. Taylor, Jr., serves as editor of the editorial page, and Norman A. Lockman is the managing editor.

ASSOCIATION OF DELAWARE HOSPITALS, INC.

The Association of Delaware Hospitals, Inc., is the common thread that links nine of the state's diverse and geographically widespread hospitals. Each facility serves the specific needs of its community while the ADH provides a collective voice for issues that affect all of them. The association's office is in Dover, near Legislative Hall, where president Eugene H. Wolinsky can keep up with legislation that affects its members.

The member hospitals include Alfred I. du Pont Institute of the Nemours Foundation, Beebe Hospital, Kent General Hospital, Medical Center of Delaware, Milford Memorial Hospital, Nanticoke Memorial Hospital, Riverside Osteopathic Hospital, St. Francis Hospital, and Veterans Administration Medical and Regional Office Center.

The A.I. du Pont Institute, for the care and treatment of crippled children, opened in July 1940 under the auspices of A.I. du Pont's will. It has earned an international reputation for excellence in pediatric orthopedics. In late 1984 the institute opened a new, multimillion-dollar facility, and through the generosity of its governing body, the Nemours Foundation, it provides young patients with care using the latest technology

Featured here is Milford Memorial Hospital's new emergency outpatient treatment center, scheduled for completion in 1985.

and administered by a professional staff.

Beebe Hospital in Lewis opened its doors in 1916 with three beds and an operating room to serve the residents of this coastal Sussex County community. Named for its founders, Dr. James Beebe, Sr., and Dr. Richard C. Beebe, the hospital today is a five-story facility complete with 150 beds and modern equipment for its X-ray, pathology, pharmacy, and operating units. The oldest section was built in 1921, a year before its School of

Nursing opened. Today Beebe has the only nurse diploma program in southern Delaware.

Kent General Hospital in Dover opened in 1927 following an ambitious fund drive by the local Rotary Club. In its first year it admitted 583 patients to the forty-bed facility.

Over the years increasing demands for services required three more major fund drives. Kent General has recently embarked upon its fifth major building project that will result in a four-level addition to the present structure, as well as improvements to the older section of the hospital. Kent's modern facility features an inpatient psychiatric unit, state-of-the-art radiology and imaging department, six operating suites, and a birthing room.

From the time Wilmington Medical Center (presently known as the Medical Center of Delaware) was created by the merger of the Delaware, Memorial, and Wilmington General hospitals in 1965, its trustees and board of directors have planned a rebuilding program to replace and modernize facilities. By late 1985 the new, 780-bed Christiana Division in Stanton will be fully operable. It has been designated the region's only Level I Trauma Center, capable of handling any type of critical illness

Workers began construction on the 100-bed Milford Memorial Hospital in 1936. It remains on the same site today but has grown to 185 beds.

or injury.

The Medical Center of Delaware is the tertiary and specialty care center for all of Delaware and nearby areas of New Jersey, Pennsylvania, and Maryland. It offers specialized diagnostic and treatment services to cancer patients, patients with heart problems, burn patients, critically ill infants, stroke victims, and paraplegic and quadraplegic patients. There are special facilities for neurosurgical patients and for family-centered maternity care.

When the new Christiana Division opened in 1985, the Memorial and Wilmington General divisions were closed. The remaining Delaware Division, located at Fourteenth and Washington streets, is undergoing extensive renovations. The 250-bed inner-city hospital has operating rooms, coronary and intensive care units, lab and X-ray facilities, emergency room, and outpatient clinics.

Milford Memorial Hospital in Milford opened in 1918, and its forty-three beds served the community until 1938 when a modern, 100-bed facility was built. By 1946 the need for more space resulted in the addition of a rear wing which accommodated a new pediatrics unit and operating rooms. Several more additions were made in 1953, 1969, and 1973, and today the hospital has 185 beds. An extensive renovation program is scheduled for completion in 1985 and will feature new and expanded radiology, lab, emergency, and outpatient departments.

Milford Memorial Hospital was the first in southern Delaware to initiate several services particularly important to a small, rural town: hospital-based home health care services, C-T scanning, a two-tier pricing structure for outpatient lab tests, and a nonemergency transport service. Milford Memorial Hospital is a member of Voluntary Hospitals of America—

Riverside Osteopathic Hospital, which opened in 1946, was then housed in the Sellers estate near Governor Printz Boulevard in Wilmington.

Mid Atlantic, and has initiated many cost-containment programs that have resulted in the hospital's ability to maintain the lowest cost per patient stay of any Delaware hospital.

Nanticoke Memorial Hospital in Seaford has provided modern, comprehensive care to the 50,000 residents of the Delmarva Peninsula since 1952. Its medical staff of more than seventy admitting/consulting physicians and dentists provides skilled care for surgical, medical, pediatric, and obstetrical patients. The hospital's modern emergency care unit is staffed twenty-four hours per day by specialists.

Nanticoke Memorial also has one of the region's most modern coronary/intensive care units, serving up to ten patients with computerized monitoring and individualized personal care. Facilities include a highly automated clinical and pathological laboratory, respiratory, and physical therapy, and radiology departments.

Riverside Osteopathic Hospital in Wilmington was established in 1946 by the Osteopathic Hospital Association of Delaware. The first facility, in Clifton Park Manor, had a patient

capacity of forty-eight. In December 1970 a new, 100-bed hospital was opened at 700 Lea Boulevard.

Riverside was established to provide treatment facilities for the patients of local osteopathic physicians. In 1971 staff membership was opened to doctors of medicine in the community, and today more than 120 physicians admit patients. It provides services in outpatient surgery, obstetrics/gynecology, respiratory therapy,

Today Riverside Osteopathic Hospital is located at 700 Lea Boulevard.

stress testing, hearing, and outpatient myelography.

St. Francis Hospital has served the city from its hilltop location in western Wilmington since 1924, when the Sisters of St. Francis of Philadelphia opened the doors with a staff of nine doctors, ten sisters, and five volunteers.

Throughout its history St. Francis Hospital has attempted to respond to the community's health-care needs. A school of nursing was built in 1925 then closed in the mid-1970s. A thirty-bed obstetric unit was built in 1936 and closed in 1975 when the demand for maternity service waned. By the early 1980s the hospital reopened its maternity unit. In 1979 a Family Practice Residency Program was begun, providing solid clinical experience for residents as well as meeting the medical needs of the community.

St. Francis has a bed capacity of 400 in its seven-story hospital, as well as a connecting four-story medical office building. It is staffed by more

The Veterans Administration medical center provides modern and comprehensive medical, surgical, neurological, and other specialty care.

than 2,200 sisters, physicians, employees, and volunteers.

The Veterans Administration Medical and Regional Office Center has been serving the veterans of all wars since the early 1950s. Located in Wilmington, the VA medical center provides modern and comprehensive medical, surgical, neurological, and other specialty care to a regional catchment area of Southern New Jer-

The Veterans Administration Medical and Regional Office Center serves a wide area around Wilmington.

sey, the Eastern Shore of Maryland, contiguous counties of Pennsylvania, and all of Delaware. Referral and admission to the medical center occurs through an extensive catchment area referral network with community-based organizations identifying those veterans who might not otherwise be medically treated. Emergency admissions are accepted on a 24-hour basis with many self-referrals.

Educational affiliations have been established with the Jefferson Medical College of Thomas Jefferson University and the Temple Dental School of Temple University, along with many other allied health affiliations. A unique maxillofacial training program provides both training and a highly specialized treatment program that is authorized to accept veterans, nonveterans, and children. Additionally, the outpatient clinics present many specialties, including orthopedics, mental hygiene, general surgery, urology, oncology, ophthalmology, and others. Applicants for hospital treatment may be treated as outpatients to either obviate the need for inpatient care or to shorten the hospital stay.

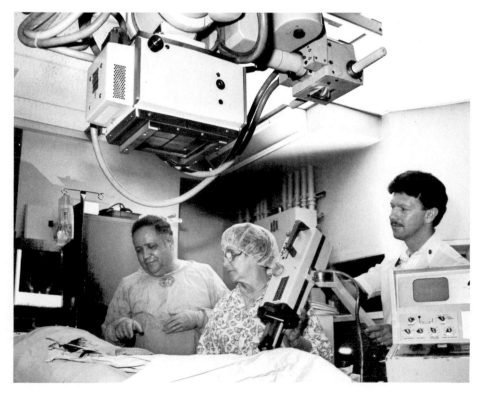

ALL AMERICAN ENGINEERING COMPANY

As interstate travelers whiz by on I-95, workers in the Newark plant operated by All American Engineering are busy building equipment used by the military in countries all over the world.

Its aircraft arresting systems are installed at airports in thirty-five countries to protect pilots and aircraft from overrun accidents during landing and take-off emergencies. Smaller airborne arresters are installed in fixed- and rotary-wing aircraft to recover satellites or drones in mid-air.

The firm started nearly fifty years ago when Richard C. du Pont developed energy-absorbing winching mechanisms that made possible in-flight delivery and retrieval of mail that was particularly useful in rural areas. He founded All American Aviation in 1937 and operated an in-flight airmail delivery service until World War II, when the armed services realized the possibilities of the winching system for aircraft to pick up and tow troop-carrying gliders.

Although du Pont was killed

USAF F-15 just after engaging (with tailhook) the arrester cable of All American's Mobile Arresting Gear (MAG). The arrester cable is connected between trailerized MAG units (foreground) that will bring the aircraft to a safe stop on a short or damaged runway.

during the war in a glider training accident, the company continued to operate through the 1940s as All American Airways.

By 1951 All American Airways was flying more passengers than any other airline in the world. However, in 1952 new federal regulations made it necessary for the airline to spin off its development operations as All American Engineering (AAE), and All American Airways became Allegheny Airlines. That same year AAE began to develop aircraft arresting gear, which has become its premier product. And the retrieval system developed by du Pont was further refined, leading to its use today for satellite pickups and the recovery of drones.

Edward J. Fahey, who has managed All American since 1969, also has

All American's HP-33 trailer-mounted launcher with a "Sky-Eye" remotely piloted vehicle (RPV). RPV's are small, unmanned aircraft that can be used on a variety of military or civilian missions.

high hopes for the company's new line of launch and recovery systems for remotely piloted vehicles (RPVs). Demand for RPVs and related equipment should increase as it is no longer tolerable to expose men in the dangerous role of military aerial reconnaissance.

Until 1970 AAE operated independently as a publicly held company. That year it became a subsidiary of International Controls Corporation. AAE also operates an assembly plant in Shannon, Ireland, and markets outside of the Americas from an office in London, England.

GOLDEY BEACOM COLLEGE

H.S. Goldey, co-founder.

Goldey Beacom College will be 100 years old in 1986. For a century it has provided students with a varied, high-quality business training and education, using advanced technology. Today it offers programs through the bachelor's degree in accounting, business administration, secretarial science and word processing, and computer information systems.

The college's remarkable 100-year history is attributable to two leaders of vision—men who combined business acumen and educational foresight to produce successful ventures. One was pioneer business educator H.S. Goldey, who opened Wilmington Commercial College to five students on September 1, 1886.

Fourteen years later the second pioneer, W.H. Beacom, founded the Wilmington Business School. Beacom, who had been one of Goldey's finest instructors, introduced the now-standard Gregg shorthand system to his Wilmington students at a time when the traditional Pitman method was prevalent.

For fifty years the two successful schools were strong competitors. On June 25, 1951, Goldey and Beacom consolidated forces in a merger that, with a new charter, gave rise to to-day's Goldey Beacom College.

By 1951 Wilmington was also growing as a major corporate center, and the college benefited its students through cooperative education programs sponsored by many Wilmington firms, including the DuPont Company, the former Atlas Powder Company, and Joseph Bancroft & Sons.

When the institutions joined forces in 1951, classes were held at Tenth and Jefferson streets. The school remained at that location until 1974, when Goldey Beacom

---

W.H. Beacom, co-founder.

College moved to its new multilevel facility in Pike Creek Valley on the western outskirts of Wilmington.

The entrepreneurial spirit of the institution continues to be embodied by an active and progressive leadership. Goldey Beacom College has achieved and maintained a prominent position in the First State and beyond as a result of its leadership, its progressive faculty and business curriculum, and the success of its graduates.

Beginning in 1978 the college began offering bachelor's degrees. By 1979 special academic programs were created to serve the economically and educationally disadvantaged. A new Business Skills Training Pavilion was opened in 1982 to house computing, word-processing, and learning resource laboratories.

The college returned to downtown Wilmington in 1983 by opening the Business Training Center, an extension campus, that offers flexible program options in entry-level and advanced business skills. Goldey Beacom College also has six advisory boards that provide links with business, industry, government, and various academic and administrative departments of the college.

Goldey College, forerunner of today's Goldey Beacom College. For nearly 100 years the institution has provided students a varied, high-quality business education.

WILM NEWSRADIO

WILM radio was licensed by the FCC in 1923, when two young entrepreneurs, Brandt Boylan, and his brother, Donald, went on the air as WTBQ. At that time commercial radio broadcasting was less than a decade old. Don Boylan, at age sixteen, and Brandt, twenty-two, were described in a 1929 newspaper article as "the youngest men in their line of work in the country."

Over the years the state's second-oldest continuously licensed broadcast station has moved from 1210 to 1420 to 1450 on the radio dial. Today it is powered twenty-four hours a day by 1,000 watts from offices at 1215 French Street in Wilmington.

The call letters were changed from WTBQ to WILM a few months after the Boylans began broadcasting through a transmitter on the top of the Equitable Trust Company building at Ninth and Market streets.

The station was acquired by the Delaware Broadcasting Company in 1929 and operated independently for ten years. In 1939 it became affiliated with Intercity network through a sister station, WDEL. A year later WILM changed its affiliation to the Mutual Broadcasting System. A short time later its frequency was changed to 1450, the spot on the dial it still occupies.

In 1949 a group headed by Ewing B. Hawkins acquired the Delaware Broadcasting Company. Hawkins became WILM's president and general manager. By 1959 Sally V. Hawkins had joined her husband's firm as treasurer. Today she also serves as president, a position she has held since 1972.

Mrs. Hawkins has continued her husband's tradition of applying vision and an adventurous spirit to plans for the radio station. During the years the Hawkins have taken extraordinary steps for a small local radio station. WILM had one of the first two-way talk shows in the country. Many Delawareans will remember the controversial Joe Pyne, who manned talk show lines in the 1950s; he was on the WILM staff for five

Sally V. Hawkins is president of WILM NEWSRADIO.

years.

It was in September 1976, the year WILM switched to an all-news format, that the station won a major victory for taped-delay broadcasts of political debates. WILM NEWSRADIO won an appeal to the Federal Communications Commission that gave all radio stations more flexibility in scheduling programs of importance to the public. The victory made it possible for stations to tape, then broadcast later for the convenience of its audience.

Today, with a newsroom staff of eighteen, WILM NEWSRADIO broadcasts news and information twenty-four hours a day, seven days a week. It has been a 24-hour broadcast station since 1952, when its format was contemporary music.

Mrs. Hawkins says that she considers it the mandate of WILM NEWSRADIO to continually seek ways to make its audience think and respond to the events that shape its world.

GEORGE & LYNCH, INC.

Road crews for George & Lynch, Inc., are shown laying a road in Kent County in the 1930s.

George & Lynch, Inc., is a hot-mix paving contracting firm that has been in business in Delaware since 1923. Started by Hyland P. George and John P. Lynch, who worked out of Dover as road contractors, the respected company is now headquartered at 113 West Sixth Street in New Castle.

George & Lynch, Inc., has been responsible for building or resurfacing a good portion of the roadways in Delaware and on the Eastern Shore, but well-paved roads are not its only concern. The firm has enlarged or built a large number of the water treatment and water line distribution systems in the Delmarva Peninsula. As general contractors, the company also builds bridges, marinas, utility plants, landfills, tennis courts, and running tracks.

The original partners sold the firm to Richard M. Appleby, Sr., and Joseph C. Pennington, Sr., in 1955. Pennington died in 1962 and Appleby in 1973. Today the business is owned by Appleby's sons, Richard M. Appleby, Jr., and Robert S. Appleby.

George & Lynch moved from Dover to Wilmington in the late 1930s, establishing offices in the Delaware Trust Building on Market Street. In 1968 a new headquarters was opened on the present site in New Castle.

Most of George & Lynch contracts are for jobs in Delaware, Mary-

This was a familiar scene along Kent County roads in the 1930s as crews from George & Lynch paved former dirt roads with concrete.

land, and Virginia, but it has done work from Pennsylvania to Georgia. The firm has also completed some rather unusual jobs such as the test bunkers built at Aberdeen Proving Ground in Maryland and the runways at Dover Air Force Base, which were built during World War II.

More than 300 men and women

work at George & Lynch and it's not uncommon to see several paychecks issued with a common surname. Longtime employees number in the dozens with sons and daughters, nephews and nieces working alongside their parents.

Through a subsidiary, Dover Equipment and Machine Company, the general contracting firm is also

the largest hot-mix, sand and gravel producer in the state with plants in Wilmington, Dover, and Seaford.

The modern and efficient headquarters in New Castle includes a completely computerized bookkeeping system. All bidding estimates and billings are also computerized.

George & Lynch, Inc., which began in 1923 employing three or four men to lay power lines and dig sewer systems, today employs more than 300 in a diversified general contracting business.

Modern-day road crews supervise the machinery that paves roads for George & Lynch, Inc.

COMMONWEALTH TRUST COMPANY/ COMMONWEALTH MANAGEMENT CORPORATION

Trusteeship, through development and management of the real properties of others, is the primary service offered by a unique Delaware family-owned firm, the Commonwealth Trust Company. Commonwealth Trust and its Commonwealth Management Corporation are managed by Benjamin Vinton, Jr., and his son, Brock J. Vinton. They continue a tradition that began with their father and grandfather, respectively, Benjamin Vinton, Sr.

Vinton Sr. was a World War I Army Air Corps flier. That experience demonstrated Vinton's willingness to take risks, a skill he combined with a down-to-earth business sense that served him well in later years.

Vinton arrived in the First State in 1918 to manage a branch of the Delaware Trust Company in Delaware City. Soon thereafter he formed his own bank, St. George's Trust Company, which was later sold to Wilmington Trust Company.

Vinton founded Commonwealth Trust in 1936 in order to administrate the investments of people who had financial interests in oil and gas

Benjamin Vinton, Jr., president, Commonwealth Trust.

properties in the American West. Commonwealth received the income from the oil and gas companies and then disbursed the monies to individual investors.

The services offered were unique in 1936 and are still unique today. The firm is not a bank; there are no vaults, deposit slips, or tellers. The policy of trusteeship continues with the addition of a satellite company, Commonwealth Management, which develops and manages real properties held in trust.

Until 1945, when Benjamin Vinton, Jr., joined his father's firm, the mainstay of the business was oil and gas trusteeships. The younger Vinton recognized the burgeoning development of New Castle County by purchasing real estate through newly organized trusteeships for property developers. Many of the Exxon gas stations, Holiday Inns, and Sheraton Hotels were brought to Delaware as the result of efforts led by Vinton Jr.

Benjamin Vinton, Jr., is now president of Commonwealth Trust. Except for a short stint in the U.S. Navy during the Korean War, he has worked for Commonwealth since returning from World War II in 1945. Under his leadership many of northern Delaware's shopping centers were developed, including Milltown Road, University Plaza, Stanton, and Ogletown Road.

In 1973, a year after Brock J. Vinton left the U.S. Navy to join the firm, Commonwealth Trust moved to its present site in University Plaza near Route 273. The move, after nearly forty years in various Wilmington locations, was accomplished after purchasing nearly 100 acres there. Today eleven buildings have been completed toward a planned business park consisting of eighteen buildings.

Through the efforts of Brock J. Vinton the family firm has moved in

new directions. He organized, and became president of, Commonwealth Management Corporation in recognition of the need to have real estate assets managed properly. In recent years the firm has begun to act as a property developer, acquiring land with other investors. Since 1983 one of its major projects has been the completion of Omega Professional Center in Christiana and the continued development of New Castle Corporate Commons.

In 1986 another major development will be completed. Rockland Mills, a 34-acre site on historic Brandywine Creek, will be opened, con-

Brock J. Vinton, president, Commonwealth Management Corporation.

sisting of luxury condominiums and town houses. Rockland Mills is the site of paper mills that date back to 1700. Commonwealth first renovated and restored several of the old buildings, then incorporated new housing south of the old mill. The final phase of development will be new housing to the north of the original mills.

W.L. GORE AND ASSOCIATES, INC.

Teamwork, characterized by a "lattice" working structure, is the management strategy that distinguishes W.L. Gore and Associates, Inc., from the majority of U.S. businesses. The Newark-based manufacturing company employs over 4,000 people in the United States and overseas to make chemical- and plastic-based products. The firm is a vital addition to Delaware's industry because its products reflect exciting solutions to high-technology problems in heavy industry, medicine, communications, computers, and other science-related fields.

The company was founded in 1958 by Wilbert L. and Vieve Gore. They launched the business partnership on January 1, 1958, their twenty-third wedding anniversary.

There are no ranks, no pyramid of managers, and no titles (except those mandated by law) at Gore. Workers, called associates, participate in a team or project group where each make specific commitments to the group's success. Associates relate one-on-one, interacting in a lattice-like manner.

Inc. magazine, in an August 1982 cover story, called Gore's management technique a theory of "un-

GORE-TEX® filter bag

management." In another cover story, in October 1983 *Industry Week* magazine recognized Wilbert L. Gore's "outstanding efforts in implementing and maintaining sound labor-management relations" by presenting an "Excellence in Management" award. By any standard the lattice technique is successful. It works because it encourages each associate to

MULTI-TET® insulated wire and cable

GORE-TEX® catheter

GORE-TEX® surgical gowns and drapes

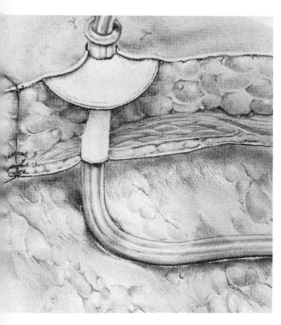

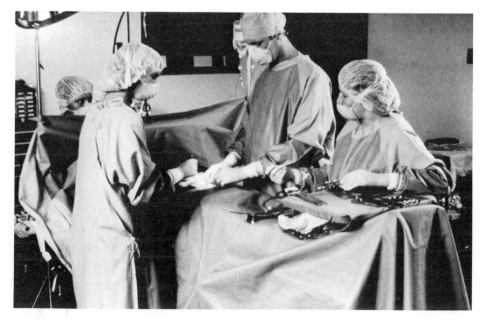

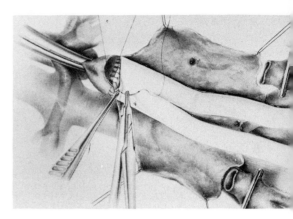

Above:
GORE-TEX® bifurcated vascular graft

Left:
GORE-TEX® fabric laminates

make and keep commitments.

The Gore lattice is based upon four principles: fairness, freedom, commitment, and "water line" discretion. These tenets, the founders believe, are basic to the creativity and productivity that has brought so many exciting successes to the associates. In just over a quarter-century Gore has grown from a family-basement operation to a multimillion-dollar venture with manufacturing plants in thirty locations in the United States and abroad.

Products range from rugged GORE-TEX® fabric outerwear, to

Left:
GORE-TEX® microwave coaxial assemblies

Below:
GORE-TEX® cardiovascular patch

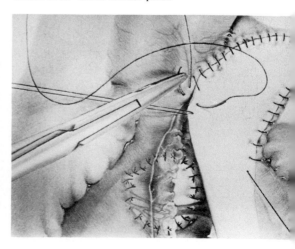

GORE-TEX® fiber used in NASA spacesuits

vascular grafts used in artery replacement surgery, to microwave equipment for defense systems.

Most of Gore's products are manufactured using patented inventions based upon the PTFE resin (Teflon®). Gore's first application was a ribbon of electrical conductors insulated with PTFE resin. The utilization of preformed strips of the resin in making the insulation was proposed by Gore's son, Bob, then in his junior year of chemical engineering studies. It was patented in 1963.

In 1969 Bob also discovered that PTFE-extruded articles could be stretched at high rates to produce a very strong but porous material. This discovery led to a multitude of GORE-TEX® expanded PTFE products: tents, shoe uppers, glove liners, sleeping bag covers, and garments designed for outdoor activities. Delaware residents can see and purchase many of these items at the company's retail outlet, The Lattice Works, in Newark.

Chemical vessel covered with Fluoroshield® coating.

Working in product-related groups of no more than 200 people at each manufacturing site, Gore associates have developed an impressive array of sophisticated uses for GORE-TEX®-expanded PTFE. The firm has produced a synthetic microfiltration membrane that removes bacteria and other microorganisms from air or liquids. It is used chiefly in medical devices, pharmaceutical manufacturing, and chemical processes.

One of Gore's most exciting prod-

GORE-TEX® transmission line cable assembly

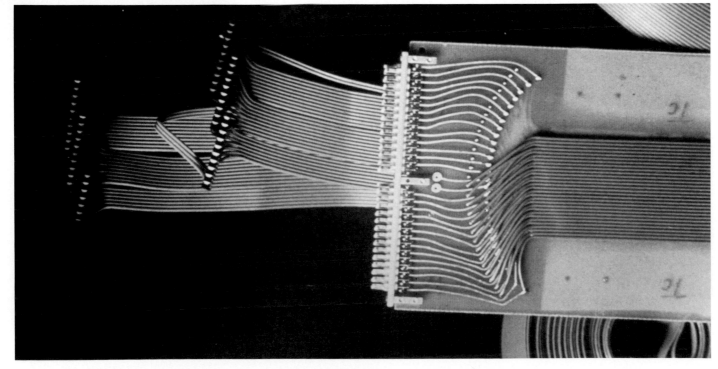

ucts is used by surgeons to replace human arteries plugged with deposits that interrupt the normal flow of blood. Diseased portions of the arteries are replaced with GORE-TEX® vascular grafts. The biocompatible GORE-TEX® PTFE is not rejected by human body tissue.

The firm's Electronic Products Division is a leader in the advancement of industry technology. Its products are used as a key computer component for signal distribution, in microwave equipment for defense systems, for switching equipment in support of telephone systems, for a seismographic instrument on the moon, and as flexible interconnections for high-speed printers and robotics.

GORE-TEX® fibers are impervious to sunlight and chemicals, can be used over a wide range of temperatures, possess high strength, and are highly resistant to abrasion. For these reasons, NASA selected a fabric woven with GORE-TEX® fiber for the outermost layer of the space suits worn by the Space Shuttle astronauts.

The fiber also has a multitude of uses in heavy industry. It is braided into packing for sealing high-speed pump shafts. It is also woven into fabric that is used in filter bags for industrial filtration.

In Gore's Coatings Division, layers of fluoropolymer coatings are applied to steel and other metallic articles used in corrosive chemicals.

Another GORE-TEX® fiber is used to manufacture two related sealants that reduce labor costs, material wastes, and downtime in a variety of process plant applications. The first, GORE-TEX® joint sealant, is used as a gasket by laying it on the surface to be sealed. Because it conforms to existing surface imperfections, it can be used on damaged or irregular sur-

GORE-TEX® industrial seals

faces.

GORE-TEX® valve stem packing is a less compressible cord of PTFE that is wound around the stem of a valve, then compacted. Liquids or gases will not leak through the packing, and the low surface friction of PTFE makes it possible to easily turn the valve.

Wilbert Gore is chairman of this family-held company. Vieve Gore is its secretary/treasurer, and Bob Gore is president. Howard Arnold is vice-

president. The titles are maintained to meet legal requirements for corporations, but the Gores believe that all are "associates" in their egalitarian enterprise. Their method of management is unusual in twentieth-century corporate life. Yet, for the Gores and their thousands of associates, it works.

Wilbert L. (left) and Vieve Gore (center) founded the family-held firm, W.L. Gore and Associates, Inc., in 1958. They are chairman of the board and secretary/treasurer, respectively. Son Bob Gore (right) is president.

DELLE DONNE & ASSOCIATES

The name Delle Donne has been associated with building in the Brandywine Valley for nearly forty years. Eugene Delle Donne's Fairfield Construction Company built many well-known New Castle County housing developments, including Fairfield, Holly Hill, Stone Haven, Carrcroft Crest, Forest Hill Park, and Alapocas. He retired several years ago but reentered the business in 1983.

It was his father's example of integrity and courage, as well as his forty years of expertise in the construction field, that led Ernest Delle Donne to a real estate career. His firm, Delle Donne & Associates, was founded in 1983 when Ernest was twenty-six years old. His father, Eugene, is chairman of the board.

Delle Donne & Associates is a real estate development company, specializing in structuring creative financial, leasing, and construction packages for commercial firms requiring office, warehouse, and industrial space tailored to their needs.

Ernest Delle Donne has assembled a creative and hard-working team that takes pride in the quality of its product. Key personnel in the company, in addition to father and son, include Elliott Golinkoff, former City of Wilmington commerce director who orchestrated the city's considerable economic development from 1974 to 1984. Golinkoff markets and sells the real estate development packages created by Delle Donne.

Thomas A. Conigliaro, former president of Chase (USA), has been a successful banker and businessman for more than twenty years. As chief financial officer for Delle Donne & Associates, he is responsible for new business development, project financing, and internal financial management.

John E. Greer, a former Hercules Company executive, administered the construction of the $80-million Hercules Plaza, the firm's world headquarters in Wilmington. At Delle Donne & Associates he is project executive, directing the construction projects.

Edward Lacy, project supervisor and vice-president at Delle Donne & Associates, is responsible for the daily supervision and implementation of the company's construction projects. At Hercules, he worked with John Greer in supervising that corporation's headquarters project.

Anthony D. Barba, property manager, is responsible for managing and coordinating completed projects and administering all tenant-related work.

James P. Collins, Jr., an attorney, is general counsel for the business and the in-house executive responsible for guiding the firm's projects from inception to fruition.

The company's president, Ernest F. Delle Donne, is a quietly aggressive entrepreneur who started his real estate career in New York City. While a student at Columbia University in the late 1970s, he bought and sold commercial and residential properties. In a 1984 newspaper interview, Delle Donne explained, "I'm just fascinated by numbers. I like to see what happens with slight changes of the variables. You can see what effect it will have on the deal—and you can be wiser in decision making." He believes, "There are twenty-five ways to create a financial package. I help potential customers pick their plan by walking them through all of the options."

Delle Donne & Associates is located at 800 Delaware Avenue in Wilmington, next door to the $38-million Chase Manhattan Bank (USA) headquarters that is being constructed by the Delle Donne organization. It was Delle Donne's financial acumen that was a deciding factor in convincing Chase Manhattan to locate its expanded operations at this site.

Delle Donne & Associates has recently completed renovations on a building at 801 West Street. That structure stands on a site of personal and historical significance to the elder Delle Donne. It is the site of the original Salesianum High School where he attended school. Most recently it was occupied by the Department of Labor. Delle Donne

renovated the building to be used as offices and it is currently occupied by Chase Manhattan Bank (USA) for back office operations.

Other proposed projects include One Corporate Plaza, adjacent to the Chase Manhattan project on Delaware Avenue. Delle Donne & Associates owns virtually all the land in the block surrounded by Adams Street, Delaware Avenue, and Eleventh Street. Ernest Delle Donne predicts that his firm will eventually have more than one million square feet of office space on that downtown block of land.

Additionally, Delle Donne & Associates is working on a 60,000-square-foot flexible warehouse/office space facility at Hares Corner near Route 13, that will include a major new warehouse facility for Chase USA's Delaware operations. Delle Donne & Associates has recently completed Concord Pike Village north of Wilmington. This $3.4-million project included the renovation of an existing store and the construction of a shopping center.

Delle Donne & Associates is also developing a major suburban corporate office park located at one of the most prestigious sites in Delaware. Across from DuPont's suburban office complex, the E.A. Delle Donne Corporate Center is a 180,000-square-foot office complex offering the highest level of amenity and convenience available in New Castle County. The location at the juncture of routes 48 and 141 is easily accessible and offers corporate clients a unique environment only minutes from downtown Wilmington. Delaware Charter Guaranty and Trust Co., Corporation Service Co., and J.A. Montgomery are all occupants of this prestigious facility.

Another successful Delle Donne project involves the corporate headquarters for Mitchell Associates, Inc., Wilmington's largest interior design and space-planning firm and Moeckel-Carbonell, the state's largest architectural concern. Both firms had been seeking a way to build new

headquarters on the Christina waterfront. Delle Donne created a financial package that has enabled Mitchell and Moeckel-Carbonell to relocate in the rapidly expanding waterfront area. In addition Delle Donne & Associates conceived of this project as part of a larger performing arts center and also included the new home of the Delaware Theater Company in this pioneering riverfront development.

Delle Donne attributes the success of his firm to two primary factors. The first is his father, who provided

Delle Donne & Associates' management team. Standing, left to right: James P. Collins, Jr., general counsel; Anthony D. Barba, property manager; Ernest F. Delle Donne, president; John E. Greer, partner in charge/construction; and Elliott Golinkoff, vice-president/marketing. Seated: Eugene A. Delle Donne, founder and chairman of the board. Not pictured (new partners) are Thomas A. Conigliaro, vice-president/finance, and Edward F. Lacy III, vice-president/marketing.

wisdom, a well-respected name, and financial backing. The second factor is the team he has put together to market and oversee the firm's devel-

opment projects.

Delle Donne & Associates is one of the city's biggest land owners, highly visible in the development of commercial properties. Ernest Delle Donne explains, "We have made a major investment in the city. We are not builders, but we know construction. We prepare real estate packages that are a combination of our building know-how and our financial expertise."

By the end of 1986 Delle Donne & Associates' financial holdings in real estate will reach $150 million.

CITIBANK (DELAWARE)

Citibank (Delaware) is a recent addition to the state's business roster. It came to the First State in 1982, under the venerable aegis of its parent, Citicorp, and in three years has established itself as a respected corporation heavily involved in the life of the community.

As a subsidiary of Citicorp, the New Castle office of Citibank (Delaware) is part of a dynamic worldwide organization employing more than 70,000 people. The Delaware facility's main business charter is the delivery of cash management services to corporate clients electronically, to assure clean, cost-effective services delivery.

Citibank (Delaware) uses state-of-the-art systems to tailor services for corporate treasurers and cash managers concerned with the disbursement, collection, and mobilization of funds and the delivery of timely information about these activities. Customers have direct access via their office terminals to their account information in New Castle.

Citibank's offices are seven miles from downtown Wilmington in the New Castle Corporate Commons, near the Greater Wilmington Air-

Located seven miles from downtown Wilmington in the New Castle Corporate Commons, Citibank (Delaware), a subsidiary of Citicorp, is part of a worldwide organization.

port. The office opened on October 6, 1982, with thirty-one employees installed in the 75,000-square-foot building. Dignitaries broke ground on an adjacent site for two additional buildings in September 1985. By the end of its first year Citibank's payroll stood at 100, and today there are more than 200 permanent employees.

The Cash Management Operations Center was founded to service the rapidly growing needs of corporations to manage the daily flow of funds for investment purposes and to manage the timely updating of accounts receivable/accounts payable. Using sophisticated electronic balance reporting systems, Citibank (Delaware) provides direct access to corporate treasurers to information regarding their corporations' net cash position each day. Decisions to invest excess funds overnight or to purchase funds when the corporation

experiences a shortfall in funds availability for the day are readily made at the earliest possible time of day in order to obtain the most advantageous interest rates. Later in the day, detailed information on a transaction level is available for accurate, labor-free updating of corporate accounts for receivables and payables. This, too, is delivered electronically by way of data transmission to the clients' systems.

Both management and employees are a composite of local Delawareans and people transferred from New York. All now view themselves as Delawareans and have plunged into community life. This sense of citizenship is displayed through employee involvement in many community organizations concerned with education, health, social welfare, and charity.

Citibank (Delaware) president Barry Keane says, "Our people are very happy here. The quality of life, the hospitality, the "can-do" attitude found in Delaware have caused our employees to readily adopt Delaware as home. We're excited about our future in Delaware."

ARTESIAN WATER COMPANY, INC.

The Artesian Water Company's beginnings go back to 1905 when home owners in the Richardson Park area west of Wilmington needed a reliable source of water.

From the beginning it has been a family operation. Aaron K. Taylor, grandfather of Artesian's current chairman of the board, Ellis D. Taylor, was a prominent merchant and the owner of a slaughterhouse in Richardson Park. When a new railway line opened in 1901 adjacent to his property, he divided a large portion of the sixty-acre site into building lots to attract Wilmingtonians who wanted to move out of the city.

The rocky subsoil made locating water on each site nearly impossible, so Taylor agreed to furnish a water supply plant. In order to concentrate on the real estate aspect of his business, he handed the operation of the water plant over to his 23-year-old son, W. Howard Taylor, who presided over the company from its inception until 1958, when Ellis D. Taylor took over the reins of leadership.

In 1912 W. Howard Taylor formed the Richardson Park Water Company, which was superseded by Artesian Water Company in 1927. Three years later the firm was serving nearly 1,000 homes. Today it serves al-

W. Howard Taylor, founder of Artesian Water Company, presided over the firm until 1958, when his son, Ellis D. Taylor, took over the presidency.

most 40,000 customers in an area covering more than 100 square miles of New Castle County.

It was during the 1930s that the supply of water for fire protection became as important as the supply for residential use. Artesian's huge water storage tanks began to pepper the skyline, assuring New Castle County home owners an adequate supply of water for emergency as well as residential use.

Until the late 1940s business was conducted from a building on Ashton Street, directly behind the Taylor home on Maryland Avenue. In 1947 the company began building a modern office and warehouse that opened for business on Newport Gap Pike the following year.

As New Castle County has grown, so has its need for water supply. During the 1960s the easy access to good roads had a profound effect on Artesian. The burgeoning of housing developments along Kirkwood Highway, into Pike Creek Valley, and along Interstate 95 added approximately 8,000 new customers to Arte-

sian's system. In order to provide them with water, the company added 100 miles of water mains.

In 1972 the firm moved into its present office/operational complex on Churchmans Road. By that time its customer base had grown to 30,000.

The past twenty-five years have seen tremendous changes in regulations governing water utilities and the quality of water service. Artesian's laboratory facilities enable personnel to monitor water quality throughout the system and assure compliance with federal and state standards.

In 1984, following a trend in the water utility industry, Artesian formed a holding company, Artesian Resources Corporation, to separate the utility from the nonutility aspects of its operations in order to diversify. The goal of Artesian Water Company, Inc., now a subsidiary of the parent organization, remains to provide quality water service to its customers at the lowest possible cost.

Artesian Water Company operates from a modern complex of buildings, housing both office and operational facilities centrally located adjacent to the Stanton exit of Interstate 95.

E.I. DU PONT DE NEMOURS AND COMPANY

The gunpowder mills that were the forerunners of the modern DuPont Company were built along the Brandywine River near Wilmington in 1802 by Eleuthère Irénée du Pont de Nemours, a 31-year-old French immigrant. The young Frenchman was a chemist who had learned to make gunpowder in the laboratories of the great French chemist, Antoine Lavoisier.

A hunting expedition with a friend brought him to the Delaware Valley soon after arriving in America. Recognizing the poor quality and high prices of local gunpowder, du Pont decided to use his own gunpowder-making experience to start a new business.

With the backing of his father, Pierre Samuel, and other French investors, du Pont bought a parcel of land on the Brandywine and built the first powder mills. The first du Pont powder was produced in 1804.

Manufacturing gunpowder was a dangerous business, and explosions were a constant threat. This danger engendered one of the DuPont Company's strongest traditions—concern for employee safety. The rigorous safety practices instituted and enforced at the Eleutherian Mills were the beginning of safety programs

The DuPont Company buildings dominated the skyline of downtown Wilmington in this photograph taken in the 1970s.

By 1880 the du Pont mills on the Brandywine were strung below and across the stream from the original mill. This sketch was originally published in the 1881 issue of the Railroad Atlas and Pictorial Album of American Industry.

that are still a major concern of the company.

By the time du Pont died in 1834 the mills were producing more than one million pounds of powder annually. Soon after his death the original investors were bought out, and the du Pont family became sole owners.

In 1902, when there seemed to be no family member ready to take over the running of the firm, the family decided to sell. Three du Pont cousins, determined to keep the business from competitors, joined forces and bought the firm. They were T. Coleman du Pont (who became president), Pierre S. du Pont, and Alfred du Pont.

The firm was reorganized in 1903, and the first public stocks were issued that same year. The new leadership was to usher in an era of growth as DuPont began to diversify,

partly through research and development and partly through acquisitions.

In 1910 DuPont began marketing materials based on nitrocellulose chemistry, a logical extension of its explosives chemistry. Acquisitions and innovations led to plastics, rayon, cellophane, lacquers, and photographic film products.

During the next twenty years the firm also moved into the area of basic industrial chemicals. Then came production of the first fluorocarbons (Freon® refrigerants) and tetraethyl lead antiknock compounds. DuPont purchased a business that manufactured electrochemical and ceramic enamels, and another that produced synthetic organic chemicals.

DuPont was one of the first domestic manufacturers of fixed nitrogen, basic to the production of fertilizers. By 1931 the company was producing synthetic urea for fertilizers. Additional expertise in agrichemicals led to its emergence by mid-century as a major manufacturer of insecticides, fungicides, and herbicides.

The polymer chemistry era began in the 1930s. The first polymers were developed in 1931, the same year that neoprene, the first commercial syn-

The latest building to open at the Experimental Station was the Life Sciences Building, in late 1984.

thetic rubber, was discovered. In 1939 commercial production of nylon heralded the polymer revolution. From DuPont's research and development came fibers, plastics, and films, which spawned new industries.

DuPont became a leader in industrial research and development. New products in the following decades include such household names as Lucite® acrylic resin, Teflon® fluorocarbon resin, Orlon® acrylic fiber, Lycra® spandex fiber, and Dacron® polyester fiber.

Through 1940 the firm was headed by family members. Pierre S. served from 1915 to 1919, Irénée from 1919 to 1926, and Lammot from 1926 to 1940. Walter S. Carpenter, Jr., who led the company during World War II, was the first chief executive who was not a family member. In 1948 Crawford H. Greenewalt became president.

Significant overseas growth began in the 1950s. Today chemicals and allied products are marketed around the world through exports from domestic facilities and through manufacture in twenty-four countries outside the United States.

Greenewalt's tenure ended in 1962, and Lammot du Pont Copeland became the new chief executive. He was a great-great-grandson of the founder and the ninth family member to head DuPont. He was succeeded in 1967 by Charles B. McCoy.

The major thrust into electronics came in the late 1960s and 1970s with such developments as Crolyn® chromium dioxide high-resolution recording tapes, precious metal thick film compositions, and Riston® photoresist for high-quality printed circuits. Berg Electronics, a manufacturer of miniaturized connectors, was acquired by DuPont in 1972.

In 1973 Irving S. Shapiro became head of the company. A lawyer, he was DuPont's first chief executive without a technical or scientific background.

DuPont entered the pharmaceuticals business in 1964, with a new ethical drug, Symmetrel® amantadine hydrochloride, for the prevention and treatment of A strain influenza. The 1969 acquisition of Endo Laboratories (now DuPont Pharmaceuticals), the 1973 acquisition of Sorval Instruments, and the introduction of the aca® discrete clinical analyzer signaled the firm's commitment to becoming a major factor in the health care field.

DuPont had been in the medical X-ray film business since 1932. The acquisition of New England Nuclear Corporation in 1981 moved the corporation into radiopharmaceuticals and radiochemicals, used in health research and diagnosis.

Shapiro retired in 1981. Edward G. Jefferson, Ph.D., a physical chemist whose entire career had been with DuPont, became chief executive officer.

That same year the merger with Conoco virtually doubled the size of the firm. Conoco's petroleum and coal give DuPont a strong diversification into natural resources and assure competitively priced energy and feedstocks vital for some 70 percent of its chemicals and allied products.

Today DuPont is a worldwide enterprise and the seventh-largest manufacturing company in the United States. Some ninety major businesses and 1,700 products generated sales of more than thirty-five billion dollars in 1984.

DuPont's primary research and development facility is the Experimental Station, built on a site overlooking the Brandywine where the company's gunpowder mills were located long ago.

HOTEL DU PONT

The Hotel du Pont opened a century too late for George Washington to sleep there, but the flawlessly elegant and prestigious inn on Rodney Square has had its share of well-known guests from around the world.

In addition to the thousands of businesspersons who consider a stay in Wilmington synonymous with the Hotel du Pont, the company-owned hostelry has turned down its bed linens for General Douglas MacArthur, Jesse Owens, entertainers Bob Hope and Elizabeth Taylor, artist Norman Rockwell, and First Ladies Eleanor Roosevelt and Rosalynn Carter. Eight of the thirteen Presidents elected since the hotel's opening in 1913 have also been guests.

The overwhelming majority of overnight guests are not famous, but the hotel staff of more than 400 are thoroughly trained to render courteous and discreet service to everyone who passes through its doors.

In 1911 Pierre S. du Pont, the president of E.I. du Pont de Nemours and Company, was approached by developers who wanted financial support to construct a hotel in downtown Wilmington. Two years later, on January 15, 1913, the idea became a reality, when 295 men and women dined for the first time in the new hotel's dining room. In its first week 25,000 visitors toured the Hotel du Pont.

In 1919, 118 additional guest rooms were added to the original 150. That

The original lobby.

The elegant Hotel du Pont, housed in the DuPont Company headquarters building, opened in Wilmington in 1913.

same year a new lobby was constructed, adding the intricately designed ceiling, patterned after a Venetian ducal palace, that is still admired by visitors today.

Each of the hotel's public rooms has been designed to present an aura of elegance and timelessness to its visitors.

The high-ceilinged Green Room, reopened in 1984 after extensive restoration, continues to be a model of elegance and refinement. It is noted for its elaborately carved, beamed ceiling and the beautifully restored mosaic floor in the entrance.

The walnut-paneled Brandywine Room opened in 1941 in space that had served over the years as brokerage office, writing room, and telephone exchange.

The Christina Room was originally the hotel's Club Room. Visitors used it for reading, relaxing, and occasional afternoon teas. It reopened in 1964 as the Christina Room and today boasts a priceless collection of Wyeth

family art.

The Gold Ballroom was opened in 1919. It took thirty artisans imported from Italy to complete the walls of Sgrafitto (hand-cut or scratched designs made through multiple layers of colored plasters).

The Hotel du Pont also houses the Playhouse, which opened in 1913 in what had been known as Pinkett's Court. The 1,200-seat theater was built completely within the walls of the hotel, and still presents quality theater to Wilmington residents.

The Lobby Lounge, completed in 1983, was designed according to the unique concept of a "café with a living room atmosphere." Here visitors can enjoy simple breakfasts, light lunches, and high teas. It is also a popular after-hours place for cocktails and music by accomplished pianists.

Another new addition, built to meet Wilmington's needs as an emerging corporate center, is the Conference Center. It offers state-of-the-art facilities including simultaneous translation capability.

At the hotel's initial planning meetings held in 1911, DuPont Company executives stressed the importance of "high quality {service} with no compromises" as their primary objective. It is a goal the Hotel du Pont continues to meet.

GRAND OPERA HOUSE

Mime Marcel Marceau is a frequent performer at the Grand Opera House.

The story of the Grand Opera House began in the optimistic post-Civil War years, when the Wilmington Board of Trade was formed with the idea that "men, not natural advantages, make great and prosperous cities" and that Wilmington could become an important East Coast port and rail center. In 1869, recognizing that Wilmington needed a

first-class theater if it was to become a major city, the Delaware Lodge of Ancient Free and Accepted Masons decided to build a Grand Opera House on the ground floor of its new temple.

The theater was completed in December 1871, and Delawareans flocked to the "splendid new ornament on Market Street." Joseph Jefferson, Fanny Davenport, James O'Neill—all the great stars of the day appeared here. The best comedy, drama, comic opera, and minstrel troupes stopped here on their national tours.

Until 1910 the Grand Opera House was Wilmington's performance and meeting center. Then moving pictures, the newest entertainment rage, were substituted for the rich variety of live performances, and the Grand declined into a second-rate movie theater, reaching its nadir as a home for horror films in the late 1960s.

But the theater was not destined for oblivion. A centennial gala, held on December 22, 1971, proved there was widespread community interest in the facility. Performing arts enthusiasts realized the Grand could enhance the arts scene in Delaware by

presenting outstanding artists as well as by serving as a first-class performance center for local groups. Urban developers recognized the Grand could be a focal point for the revitalization of the city, just as it had been a key to its 1870 development. Preservationists saw the value of restoring an important Victorian building.

By January 1973 the nonprofit Grand Opera House, Inc., had been established to enrich the cultural life of Delaware and to restore the Grand Opera House to its original artistic splendor. Between 1973 and 1983 world-class symphony and chamber orchestras, renowned soloists, country western, jazz, and pop musicians, dancers, singers, actors, films, and children's shows thrilled capacity audiences. Eugene Ormandy announced "the Grand Opera House is an acoustical gem." Marcel Marceau called it "one of my favorite theaters in all the world."

An enthusiastic public, foundations, business, and governments contributed more than six million dollars to the project to fund restoration of the theater and its ornate facade, one of the nation's finest extant examples of cast-iron architecture.

In spite of all this success, overwhelming financial problems threatened the Grand's survival until 1984, when stability was achieved with the completion of a $5-million endowment fund, which will help support building operations.

The future of the Grand Opera House is now assured. Each season more than 100,000 people attend performances at the theater. Thousands of others tour the historic landmark or attend seminars, parties, and meetings in the two second-floor parlors. The Grand Opera House is proud of the vital role it has played in Delaware's cultural life and looks forward to more "grand" centuries.

—Toni Young

During the 1890s, when this photograph was taken, the Grand Opera House had one of the most elegant facades on Market Street.

195

MELLON BANK DELAWARE

"We have a law passed establishing a Farmers Bank which excites much expectation," a Delawarean wrote in a letter to a friend on February 4, 1807.

That same day the general assembly of the state of Delaware passed "An act to establish a Bank and incorporate a Company, under the name of the Farmers Bank of the State of Delaware." It was only twenty-six years after the first commercial bank in America was founded, and only twenty years after Delaware became the first state to ratify the new U.S. Constitution.

Today that pioneering institution has evolved into Mellon Bank Delaware, a subsidiary of Mellon Bank Corporation, the nation's eleventh largest, with $30.6 billion in assets.

Farmers Bank pioneered by organizing a principal office and two branch banks, probably the first bank branches in the nation. These offices functioned with virtual autonomy. Branch autonomy was necessary when the trip from Dover to Wilmington took a full, long day over dusty roads in hard-seated, springless coaches. Delaware's first bankers had to take care of themselves in every

Henry Moore Ridgely, first president of Farmers Bank of the State of Delaware.

Lower Market Street at Third Street in Wilmington in the latter half of the nineteenth century. The second Wilmington banking house of Farmers Bank is shown at the corner with columns on the second-floor facade.

way. One of the organization's first acts was to buy twenty muskets and cartridge boxes and issue them to the bank's directors, creating a blunt but effective security system.

The principal bank was at Dover, with branch banks at Georgetown and New Castle. A Wilmington branch was added in 1813. Today Mellon Bank is still serving the consumers in these communities.

The institution's first president was lawyer Henry M. Ridgely. Through the first 133 years of the bank's existence, there was always at least one Ridgely on the board, and three generations of Henry Ridgelys served as president at different intervals, for a total of 118 years. The last Henry Ridgely, though blind, was president of Farmers from 1918 to 1940, while simultaneously practicing law.

The first Henry Ridgely and his two branch presidents, Kensey Johns and Thomas Cooper, followed the examples set in nearby Philadelphia by the Bank of North America, the nation's first bank, and by the Bank of the United States, established as a federal institution by Alexander Hamilton. Its charter echoed many provisions of the government bank's rules. But, unlike many banks of that era, which were structured to deal primarily with the wealthy, Farmers specifically declared a policy of granting six month loans of up to $2,000 to "any farmer, mechanic, or manufacturer" in Delaware.

Kensey Johns, Sr., first president of the branch bank at New Castle.

The nineteenth-century headquarters of the Farmers Bank at Georgetown was located on South Bedford Street.

Founded by Delawareans who felt that their state should have a local institution to serve its own citizens, Farmers Bank was feisty toward the large Philadelphia banks in the early years. The big-city institutions attempted to discount bank notes issued by Farmers, honoring them at less than face value, but most of the Farmers branches refused to allow it. The Delaware bankers maintained their independence and developed their own style.

When currency issued by state banks was no longer viable in 1865 because the federal government had clamped a 10 percent tax on it, Farmers Bank began withdrawing its bills from circulation and burning them. The last quantity burning of the old currency took place in 1891. Today the few Farmers Bank notes in existence are collectors' items.

The state of Delaware started to change at the beginning of the twentieth century, as New Castle County industrialized and became the dominant chemical industry center of the United States. In the 1950s Farmers merged with or acquired seven other institutions and began a modern branching system. One office was opened at the Wanamaker store in Wilmington, believed to be the first bank branch ever established inside a department store.

The Girard Company (a Philadelphia financial institution) acquired Farmers Bank in December 1981 by virtue of an act of the Delaware Legislature. The institution was renamed Girard Bank Delaware. Girard merged with Mellon Bank Corporation in April 1983, and on June 25, 1984, the Girard name was changed to Mellon.

Today, under the leadership of president H. Harrison Kephart, Jr., the bank operates at twenty-nine locations throughout the state, offering complete financial services to checking, savings, trust, investment, and business customers, both large and small. A heritage of nearly 180 years has not been diluted. Delawareans, particularly downstate, remain fiercely loyal to Mellon Bank, the institution that has served many families for generations.

An 1813 bank note issued by Farmers Bank. This is the earliest form of note used by the institution, and it is signed by Henry M. Ridgely.

An 1815 bank note issued by Farmers Bank.

197

AMERICAN HOECHST CORPORATION

Whenever a Delawarean, or any U.S. consumer, uses a major credit card; buys a package of luncheon meat; opens a blister-packaged pen, razor, or tablet; purchases an artificial Christmas tree; uses office supplies such as index tabs and file folders; or buys a floppy diskette, chances are American Hoechst Corporation was involved.

With sales and engineering offices in Newark and a production facility in Delaware City, American Hoechst manufactures rigid polyvinyl chloride film and sheet that is used to produce all of these consumer products plus many more.

American Hoechst is the U.S. unit of the Hoechst Group of 487 companies headquartered in Frankfurt, West Germany. American Hoechst manufactures products nationwide for use in agriculture and communications and also produces pharmaceuticals, chemicals, dyes and pigments, waxes, plastics, films, and fibers.

The 34-year-old American firm was founded in December 1951. However, the parent company's history dates back to 1863, when it was established as a manufacturer of synthetic dyes.

By the 1890s the firm had developed or reproduced over 10,000 different dyes. It also had started producing analgesics and other drugs in 1883. After the turn of the century the business became known as Hoechst Dyeworks.

The Delaware connection to American Hoechst began as a joint venture with Stauffer Chemical Company in 1964, when a multimillion-dollar polyvinyl chloride (PVC) film production facility was built in Delaware City. That partnership lasted until 1970, when Stauffer decided to concentrate on other ventures, and American Hoechst purchased Stauffer's half-interest in the business.

Today the American Hoechst PVC Film Products business group is the industry leader in the production and marketing of rigid PVC film and sheet. Its products are widely used in packaging for carded blister packages for food, such as luncheon meats; portion packs of cheese, crackers, jams, and jellies; and for pharmaceuticals, medical devices, and other items. The district sales offices are located in New Jersey, Georgia, Illinois, and California.

The Delaware sites are part of a worldwide Hoechst work force of 178,000 in 149 countries. American Hoechst employs more than 8,000 and has helped to create $1.7 billion dollars in sales annually while still adhering to its objectives of providing quality products that meet the ever-changing needs of the American marketplace.

In recent years the Hoechst World Group has turned its attention increasingly beyond traditional chemistry to the point where several scientific and technical disciplines join together—specifically chemistry, engineering, physics, medicine, and biology. This is Hoechst High Chem®—Hoechst's capability to produce new materials and to adapt existing materials for new applications.

The American Hoechst Corporation's polyvinyl chloride rigid film and sheet facility at Delaware City.

A master roll of film at the winder area being inspected by foreman Bruce Sturgeon and calender operators, Kenneth Ashley and Jim Gill.

CHRYSLER CORPORATION

The history of the Chrysler Corporation assembly plant in Newark began on a military note. In 1951, when the government-owned plant opened, the American military was participating in the Korean War and needed the Patton tanks that were built in Newark under contract with the U.S. government.

By 1956 the demand for tanks had abated, and the contract expired. Chrysler subsequently enlarged the facility and converted its assembly line to production of a Plymouth car with a newly designed suspension system. At that time "Torsion-Aire," designed by Chrysler, was the first entirely new suspension system produced by an American automobile manufacturer in nearly a quarter-century.

The first Plymouth with Torsion-Aire rolled off the Newark assembly line in April 1957. By the end of the year 34,023 cars were produced. Auto production began with 850 employees. That number had grown to 1,300 by the end of the 1957 model year, and the plant had a payroll of $6.2 million.

The Wilmington newspaper, *The Morning News,* covered the story of the first car rolling off the assembly line. It was reported as "a snappy two-tone, four-door sedan, meadow green with sand dune white trim." This Plymouth Plaza Sedan was also being built at two other assembly plants in Indiana and California.

Automobile assembly plants measure time periods in model years, the period of time in which a certain model is produced before the fall showing of new cars. A model year runs slightly longer than a calendar year. In 1957 at the Newark plant, 4,300 Plymouths were assembled by the end of the model year. But by the end of the calendar year the totals also included 1958 Plymouths (23,727 cars) and 1958 Dodges (5,996).

While the Newark plant recently celebrated its twenty-ninth year of auto production, it is part of a national industry that began in 1925. The Chrysler Corporation, headquartered in Detroit, Michigan, cele-

Chrysler Corporation's assembly plant, covering 246 acres along Route 896 in Newark, was opened in 1951 to produce Patton tanks for the U.S. military.

brated its sixtieth anniversary in 1985.

The firm's founder, Walter P. Chrysler, was already a legend in the auto industry when he founded his business. He was a machinist by trade, who began work in 1912 with the Buick Motor Car Company. Five years later he was its president and general manager.

In the early 1920s Chrysler was sought out to revitalize the Maxwell Motor Car Company. He and a team of engineers created the Chrysler Six for Maxwell, America's first medium-priced car with a high-compression engine. In 1924 Maxwell dealers sold nearly 32,000 Chrysler Six cars. A year later the Maxwell Motor Car Company became the Chrysler Corporation.

In 1981 the Chrysler Corporation hovered on the brink of bankruptcy. Today it is in the best financial shape of its sixty-year history. The firm's current return to economic health was spurred by the creation of new products, starting with the K-cars—Dodge Aries and Plymouth Reliant—introduced in model year 1981. The K-cars remain the best-selling automobiles in Chrysler's history.

Newark's production has been pivotal to Chrysler's success. It produces the Aries and the Reliant in four-door sedan and station wagon models. It is also the only one of the firm's plants that produces the popular station wagons. The facility also assembles one of Chrysler's newest lines—the LeBaron station wagon and sedan.

The LeBaron sport sedan, introduced in model year 1984, was designed to appeal to the fastest-growing segment in the auto industry—the "new middle" or "young professional" age group. The LeBaron and K-cars made at Newark were instrumental in Chrysler's successful 1984 financial turnaround, when the firm posted earnings of $2.4 billion.

In 1984 Newark employees numbered 4,500, with a payroll of $175 million. That payroll has a considerable impact, especially in Delaware, where 63 percent of Chrysler's employees live.

The year 1984 was a banner one in many ways for the Newark facility. It set a new record for production with 253,678 units assembled. The 1984 model year production was also a record with 262,175 cars assembled.

The plant site on Route 896 near the University of Delaware Field House covers 246 acres. Over ten miles of production lines wind through the 2.3-million-square-foot facility. In setting the new production records in 1984, employees worked two daily nine-hour shifts, assembling 1,080 units in a two-shift day.

The plant's physical and financial presence is significant to both Newark and the state. Chrysler paid seven million dollars in state and local taxes in 1984 and twelve million dollars to local vendors for products and services.

The plant is located entirely within the city of Newark. Its administrators are proud of the good working relationship Chrysler maintains with both the city and state governments.

The company is frequently called upon for its engineering expertise.

In addition to the 4,500 hourly and salaried employees at the Newark plant, Chrysler also employs 336 people in its fourteen Delaware dealerships.

Chrysler's Newark facility is part of the spectacular rejuvenation of a major automobile producer. It is proud of its role in the record-setting year that chairman Lee A. Iacocca reported to stockholders in February 1985. In its fourth year since a close brush with bankruptcy, Chrysler Corporation reported in 1984 that new records were set for sales, earnings, and productivity.

Today, with ten miles of production lines winding through the 2.3-million-square-foot facility, the plant now produces the K-car, Dodge Aries and Plymouth Reliant four-door sedan and station wagon models, and Chrysler's newest lines—the LeBaron station wagon and sedan.

BALTIMORE TRUST COMPANY

Baltimore Trust Company in Selbyville, named for the Sussex County
Hundred in which it is located, was
begun by one of Delaware's most illustrious and colorful public figures,
John G. Townsend, Jr.

In the first decade of the twentieth
century, Selbyville-area growers were
famed for their strawberry crops.
Townsend believed that a bank was
needed to aid the farmers. He had already been a private banker for some
years, loaning out money at interest
for short periods of time. Growers especially needed short-term financing
at the beginning of each season to
carry them until crops were har-
vested and sent to market.

In 1903, recognizing the need
among his neighbors for an institution that would lend money at reasonable rates of interest, Townsend
gathered a few of his colleagues to
invest in a bank. The new institution's charter was approved in March
by the general assembly. Townsend
was not inexperienced in commercial
banking either, having served on the
board of the Farmers Bank of the
State of Delaware.

Townsend became president of
Baltimore Trust. The vice-president
was Timothy E. Townsend, a mem-

John G. Townsend, Jr., founder.

ber of another branch of the family.
Isaiah W. Long, a Selbyville lumber-
man, merchant, and partner in the
new telephone company, served as
secretary/treasurer. Isaiah J. Brasure
and George H. Townsend, John
Townsend's political mentors and
business partners, were named as directors of the new institution.

The Baltimore Trust Company
opened for business in April 1903 in
a small wood-frame building in Selbyville, not far from its present location. On its first day of business,
capital stock totaled $5,000. At the
close of the first day the bank held
$6,150 in deposits; depositors earned

3 percent on their savings accounts.

In its first year of operation the
bank was so successful that Townsend opened branches in Bridgeville
and Camden, which later were sold
to Wilmington Trust Company. It
was unorthodox for the time, but he
organized the two branches by finding backers in each of the communities. Neither Camden nor Bridgeville
had a bank, and each was located in
an area of rapid agricultural growth.
Each institution had its own set of
backers, officers, and directors.
Townsend serving as president of
each and the bank's name, Baltimore
Trust Company, were the common
features. Today Baltimore Trust also
has branches in Bethany Beach and
Fenwick Island.

The stock market crash in 1929,
which precipitated the Depression of
the 1930s, did change the banking
picture in Selbyville. Baltimore
Trust Company survived with its de-
positors' monies intact, but the institution did absorb losses from the
purchase of another local bank. The
Selbyville National Bank, which had
opened only months before Townsend's institution, requested a take-
over to avoid having to close its

*The first office of Baltimore Trust Company
opened for business in 1903 in this small
wood-frame building in Selbyville.*

The present main office of Baltimore Trust Company at the corner of Main and Church streets in Selbyville.

doors. In taking over the reins, Baltimore Trust lost its only local rival. Delaware was the only state to weather the Depression without a single bank failure.

Throughout its history, many civic-minded and prominent citizens have contributed to the growth of Baltimore Trust, but until 1946 the bank was firmly guided by its founder.

Following Townsend Jr. as president and chairman of the board, was his son, John G. Townsend III, who served from 1946 to 1964. He was succeeded by his brother, Preston C. Townsend, who served from 1964 to 1984. Following the death of Preston C. Townsend in May 1984, the bank officers divided the duties that had been formerly combined in the offices of president and chairman of the board and for the first time appointed someone outside the family to run the institution. Robert E.

Dickerson is the current president, while J. Townsend Tubbs, grandson of the founder, is chairman of the board.

The bank's operating philosophy has always been conservative. The founder, writing to the community in 1930 in a handsome historical report, said: "Success in business is the result of confidence. . . . No legitimate banking house was ever organized unless its founders had a faith in the integrity and growth of the community. . . . Success . . . depends upon two things—first, whether the faith of the organizers is founded on good business judgment and foresight of a real need . . . second, whether those organizers hold or can, by their business dealings, inspire and win the confidence of the public."

Baltimore Trust Company has always been a commercial full-service

bank, and the intent of its founders to serve the community is as important today as it was in 1903.

Located in the center of the town's business district, Baltimore Trust has expanded four times, and today the red-brick bank building dominates the intersection of Main and Church streets. It stands only a few hundred feet from the original wood-frame building that housed the first bank.

As a financial institution characterized by conservative investment, the bank has grown steadily. In 1903 capital stock was $5,000; in 1984 the figure was $200,000. At year-end 1984, Baltimore Trust's balance had grown to $5 million, with assets of $118 million.

TOWNSEND'S, INC.

In 1935 U.S. Senator John G. Townsend, Jr., of Selbyville, in southern Sussex County, was sixty-four years old. He had just begun his second term in the U.S. Senate and had achieved notable success in half a dozen businesses after getting his start as a railroad telegrapher in his native Worcester County, Maryland, in 1890.

While still a telegrapher, he'd begun a lucrative sideline business cutting timber and supplying the railroad with cross ties. This had developed into a lumber business, followed soon after by Townsend's entry into the commercial strawberry business, then enjoying a boom in Worcester County, Maryland, and Sussex County, Delaware. In 1894 Townsend moved with his young family over the state line to Selbyville, Delaware, then the center of the strawberry business. He soon became a leading strawberry broker and established the first of what were to be many canneries.

During the first two decades of the twentieth century, Townsend became one of Delaware's most successful "agribusinessmen" in association with his brother, James Covington Townsend. A characteristic feature of his business style was his willingness to enter into partnership with men who he felt had good ideas and showed ability. Townsend would put up the money and some of the organizational talents. The partner would provide the "sweat equity" and they would share the profits. As his later political career was to demonstrate, Townsend was a rare judge of character and such partnerships did much to build the foundation of his far-flung enterprises.

His political career began in 1902 with his election to the Delaware House of Representatives. In 1916 he was elected governor of Delaware, building a four-year record of rare accomplishment. His election to the first of two terms in the U.S. Senate in 1928 led to achievements on the national level. The culmination of his public career came in 1946, when

In the mid-1930s Senator John G. Townsend, Jr. (center), and his youngest son, Preston Coleman (right), became deeply involved in the developing Delmarva poultry industry. The two are shown here in a photo that accompanied the November 1945 Country Gentleman article about the senator and his partners, one of whom stands at left.

he served as a member of the U.S. delegation to the first U.N. General Assembly in London.

During the 1920s Townsend was joined by members of a second generation in expanding his business enterprises. His older sons, Julian, John G. III, and Paul, and his son-in-law, John A. Tubbs, all became active associates. In 1921 the Highway Engineering and Construction Company was established. Until it was sold following the death of its manager, Paul Townsend, in 1940, the firm built highways throughout the East.

Senator Townsend and his family had observed with considerable interest the beginnings of Delmarva's commercial broiler industry in southeastern Sussex County in the early 1920s. They were not directly involved in what was to become the nation's modern commercial poultry industry until 1935, however.

Their entry into the poultry industry grew from one of the senator's now-legendary partnerships. By this time Senator Townsend's youngest

Senator Townsend driving one of his new Caterpillar tractors in the early 1930s. Courtesy, Delmarva Poultry Industry, Inc.

son, Preston Coleman Townsend, had completed his studies at the University of Delaware's College of Agriculture and had joined his father in running the family's far-flung orchard enterprises from their base at

Senator John G. Townsend, Jr. (right), and son Preston Coleman in the office at Townsend's, Inc.

Indian Swan Orchard on the Indian River just east of Millsboro. They were approached by a local farmer, Wilford Revel, who wanted to build some poultry houses but needed the senator's financial backing to do so. Townsend agreed to put up the money, but even he was surprised at the rapid and substantial return he realized on his investment.

Preston Townsend had been running orchards for his father since his college days and he'd grown up in the business. He was especially aware of the high degree of risk they possessed. Orchardists were constantly prey to late freezes or new blights that could ruin a year's crop or even an entire orchard.

He had also obtained some experience as a student in the newly emerging field of commercial poultry production and he knew that it was both less labor-intensive and less risky. On the basis of the Wilford Revel experience he talked his father into going into the poultry business directly. Within a few years they had a significant involvement in raising poultry. In 1938 Townsend's, Inc., was incorporated. Its base of operations remained the Indian Swan Orchard and the orchards were maintained until the early 1950s, when the land they'd once occupied was given over to the cultivation of corn and soybeans used in the pro-

duction of poultry feed.

Most pioneering poultry firms were involved in one or at the most two stages in the process of raising poultry, producing feed, and all the other steps required to get them to market. From the outset Townsend's, Inc., moved in more ambitious directions. The firm built its first hatchery in 1939 and quickly acquired several poultry-breeding farms in Maine and

New Hampshire to provide eggs. It built its first poultry houses in 1940 after several years of growing chickens in partnership arrangements, and hired growers directly, using innovative profit-sharing incentives.

By the end of World War II Townsend's, Inc., was the nation's leading producer of commercial poultry. Though the company enjoyed this status only temporarily, it achieved another first in the next few years that had great significance industry-wide. Townsend's, Inc., had begun the large-scale cultivation of grain on its own farmland and established its own feed mill and soybean-processing plant. In the early 1950s the firm added a major new poultry-processing plant and became the first poultry company in the nation to achieve "vertical integration." That is, it had direct control of the entire

process from the cultivation of grain for poultry feed and the manufacture of the feed to dressing poultry and delivering them to market in the company's own fleet of refrigerated trucks.

This record of accomplishment has continued throughout the fifty-year history of Townsend's, Inc. The senator remained active until his death in 1964. Preston Coleman Townsend

The Townsend's, Inc., facilities at Millsboro.

continued to head the company until he passed away in 1984. During his long career at the helm, the business grew steadily. A new state-of-the-art hatchery was built in the late 1970s. An equally sophisticated new feed mill was built in 1982. In the summer of 1985 Townsend's, Inc., added a new soybean oil-processing plant, which will enable the production of soybean salad oil, thus continuing the family's long tradition of finding new applications for products they've been turning out for years.

P. Coleman Townsend, Jr., is now guiding Townsend's, Inc., into its second half-century. Though only fifty years old, the firm is the innovative product of ninety years of agribusiness leadership in southern Delaware.

BLUE CROSS BLUE SHIELD OF DELAWARE

One Brandywine Gateway, the headquarters of Blue Cross Blue Shield of Delaware, was extensively remodeled in anticipation of the corporation's fiftieth anniversary in 1985.

In August 1935 the four Wilmington hospitals, business leaders, and physicians met and formed the nation's thirteenth Blue Cross corporation. From the signing of the first account—with the bank now known as Bank of Delaware—it was obvious that Blue Cross Blue Shield of Delaware was an idea whose time had come. By the end of 1935 thirty-one firms had joined. Six years later the organization had 42,000 customers and by 1945 over 100,000 Delawareans were customers.

Innovation has always been a guiding principle of the corporation. From its beginning it has distinguished itself by being a leader in the provision of highest-quality benefit plans. As needs changed, the corporation presented new programs to meet them. For its twentieth anniversary in 1955, the new concept of major medical/extended benefits was introduced to its 224,000 customers. That same year it assisted in the organization of the Blood Bank of Delaware.

In 1963 The Kiplinger Magazine featured the corporation and commended it for its surgical-medical plans, programs for persons over sixty-five, and its reputation for keeping costs down and coverage up.

When Medicare became law in 1965, the thirtieth year of the firm, Blue Cross Blue Shield was selected by the Social Security Administra-

tion and providers to administer the new program. By that year there were 250,000 customers.

Throughout its history the corporation has been locally and nationally recognized for its innovative coverages, such as outpatient care; benefits for prescription drugs, alcoholism, mental illness, and surgical-medical and dental care; and its cost-containment programs, including preadmission certification, second opinion, concurrent review, and ambulatory surgery.

To serve its customers using the growing number of benefit programs, the corporation has kept up to date with state-of-the-art computer technology and operations systems. Evidence of this continuing commit-

ment is the corporation's new data center in Christiana.

In 1983 The HMO of Delaware, Inc., the corporation's first subsidiary, was opened in Stanton and met with the same rapid growth rate as Blue Cross itself had experienced. Membership exceeded the most optimistic marketing projections. To meet the demand and to be the only company to offer its customers a full choice of products, documents were filed to begin the process for providing two new HMO choices for Delawareans in 1986.

Growth has been a hallmark of the corporation. Moves were made from several in-town offices to the Fourteenth and Orange location in 1965 as customers and the staff expanded. For the fiftieth-anniversary year in 1985, this headquarters building was extensively renovated and its address changed to One Brandywine Gateway.

Blue Cross Blue Shield's roots are firmly established in Delaware. Most of the 315,000 customers and nearly 700 employees are Delawareans. The board of directors has always included key Delawareans. Since 1971 Delaware customers have held a majority of seats on the board of directors. As Delawareans, the corporation is as committed to caring for the present and future needs of the customers of the First State who are its business as it was committed to caring for them during its first fifty years.

The HMO of Delaware, Inc., the corporation's first subsidiary, opened in Stanton in 1983.

PRICKETT, JONES, ELLIOTT, KRISTOL & SCHNEE

The law firm of Prickett, Jones, Elliott, Kristol & Schnee consists, in 1985, of approximately thirty-five lawyers as well as a support staff. The firm's practice includes litigation in state and federal courts, as well as corporate, business, tax, trust and estate, and real estate matters. The majority of the firm's attorneys practice in a complex built around the historic Starr House at 1310 King Street in Wilmington.

The Starr House was erected in 1804 by Michael Van Kirk, a prosperous marble worker who ornamented the building, including the fireplaces, with marble and stonework. In 1806 Van Kirk sold the house to Jacob Starr, a sea captain whose coastal vessels plied the Delaware River from wharfs along the nearby Brandywine Creek. The house was purchased in the mid-1950s by William Prickett, Sr. The Starr House is on the National Register of Historic Places.

The Starr House at 1310 King Street.

A student of history as well as an attorney, Prickett believed the purchase of the Starr House would provide a "pleasant office, handy to the courts, and preserve a structure worth saving." Since that time the firm has purchased adjoining properties and renovated them generally in the style and atmosphere of the original Starr House.

The firm's litigation section consists of approximately fourteen attorneys who handle personal injury,

compensation, domestic relations, and general litigation.

The corporate section handles corporate litigation and advises clients on Delaware corporate law. This section is also active in partnership law and acts as local counsel in patent and federal securities litigation matters.

The attorneys in the commercial and business section advise on real estate matters and substantial commercial transactions for individuals, banks, and businesses. In addition, the firm advises on environmental, labor, and tax matters and does a considerable amount of public sector work in the legislative, administrative, and regulatory areas.

In 1975 the firm established an office in Dover to conduct a general practice reflective of the practice in the Wilmington office and to provide a presence in the state capital.

Prickett, Jones, Elliott, Kristol & Schnee opened an office in nearby Kennett Square, Pennsylvania, in 1980. Again, this office provides a broad spectrum of services by the firm's group of lawyers admitted to practice in Pennsylvania.

The firm is also known for a substantial amount of pro bono work which its attorneys have always done and continue to do. Prickett, Jones, Elliott, Kristol & Schnee is proud of its reputation for aggressiveness, hard work, and integrity.

PRICKETT, JONES, ELLIOTT, KRISTOL & SCHNEE

WILLIAM PRICKETT	WILLIAM E. MANNING
RICHARD I. G. JONES	DAVID E. BRAND
WAYNE N. ELLIOTT	WILLIAM L. WITHAM, JR.
DANIEL M. KRISTOL	SUSAN C. DEL PESCO
CARL SCHNEE	DENNIS SPIVACK
RICHARD R. WIER, JR.	VERNON R. PROCTOR
WALTER P. McEVILLY, JR.	JOHN WILLIAMS
MYRON T. STEELE	JAMES P. DALLE PAZZE
MASON E. TURNER, JR.	TIMOTHY A. CASEY
DAVID S. SWAYZE	ELIZABETH M. McGEEVER
ROBERT W. RALSTON	WAYNE J. CAREY
JAMES L. HOLZMAN	MICHAEL F. BONKOWSKI
JOHN H. SMALL	WENDIE E. COHEN
RICHARD P. S. HANNUM	SAM GLASSCOCK, III
DAVID B. RIPSOM	MICHAEL P. KELLY
GEORGE H. SEITZ, III	BETH E. EVANS
GARY F. DALTON	DONNA LEE HARPSTER
MICHAEL HANRAHAN	NORMAN L. PERNICK

TRIAL AND APPELLATE LITIGATION
IN STATE AND FEDERAL COURTS,
COMMERCIAL LAW, BANKING LAW,
CORPORATION LAW, PARTNERSHIP LAW, BANKRUPTCY LAW,
REAL ESTATE LAW, ESTATE AND PROBATE LAW,
TAX LAW, WORKMAN'S COMPENSATION LAW, LABOR LAW

DELAWARE COUNSEL
IN FEDERAL SECURITIES, PATENT AND ADMIRALTY LITIGATION

135 EAST STATE STREET	26 THE GREEN
KENNETT SQUARE, PENNSYLVANIA 19348	DOVER, DELAWARE 19901
(215) 444-1573	(302) 674-3841

1310 KING STREET
WILMINGTON, DELAWARE 19899
(302) 658-5102

BENEFICIAL CORPORATION

Beneficial Corporation, with international headquarters in Wilmington, is the holding company of the largest independent finance company in the nation. Through its subsidiaries, it offers a wide variety of consumer financial services, including second mortgages, personal loans, and credit cards. Together with its mortgage and banking subsidiaries, it currently employs over 1,000 people in Delaware.

In 1924 the Beneficial Loan Society, already ten years old, opened a corporate office in Wilmington. The headquarters, located at Tenth and Market streets, made it possible for the society to efficiently handle all of its corporate affairs. Monthly rental in the downtown office was fifty dollars.

The Beneficial Loan Society was founded in 1914 by Colonel Clarence Hodson, a Maryland native and descendant of a prominent Eastern Shore family. He was a Baltimore lawyer who began his financial career as a banker in Crisfield, Maryland.

The international headquarters of Beneficial Corporation is located at 1100 Carr Road in Wilmington, Delaware.

Before chartering the society, he was director of more than forty banks, mortgage and trust companies, and public utilities. It was while working with the Russell Sage Foundation that Colonel Hodson brought to the attention of governmental leaders the urgent need for small loan legislation. His work resulted in the enactment in 1913 of the first uniform Small Loan Act in New Jersey.

The Beneficial Loan Society made the first loan in New Jersey in August 1914. The organization's expansion continued as other states enacted similar legislation. By 1919 Beneficial had seventeen offices in seven states.

By 1933, when Beneficial common stock was listed on the New York Stock Exchange, the firm had grown to more than 200 offices with over thirty million dollars in outstanding loans. Before its twenty-fifth anniversary in 1939, Beneficial had become the first American system of loan offices to pass the $50-million mark in outstanding loans. A decade later Beneficial's offices numbered more than 500.

In the mid-1950s the society and its subsidiaries underwent a system-wide name change to Beneficial Finance. The year 1956 marked the opening of the company's 1,000th office, and by the end of that decade the firm had diversified its services with the formation of Guaranty Life Insurance Company of America. Another landmark was the opening in 1959 of Beneficial's first office in London, England.

Beneficial had expanded into banking, merchandising, income tax preparation, consumer finance services, and various insurance programs by 1970. That same year the parent company assumed the name by which it is known today—Beneficial Corporation.

HERCULES
INCORPORATED

Hercules Incorporated, then known as Hercules Powder Company, began manufacturing smokeless powder in January 1913 with eight black powder mills and three dynamite plants. It had an issue of $6.5 million in 6-percent bonds and a mandate to compete vigorously in the manufacture and marketing of explosives.

Hercules' first annual report showed gross receipts of $7.6 million, with net earnings of $1.4 million. Since then, the firm has grown from a small, single-line manufacturer to a multibillion-dollar corporation, with hundreds of facilities and over 26,000 employees worldwide. Its 1984 sales were $2.6 billion with net income of $197 million.

The modern Hercules manufactures a broad line of natural and synthetic materials and products, including cellulose and natural gum thickeners, flavors and fragrances, natural and hydrocarbon rosins and resins, polypropylene fibers and films, smokeless powder for sportsmen, graphite fibers, and propellants and structures for military and aerospace use.

In 1983 it acquired Simmonds Precision Products, an aerospace company, and also formed HIMONT Incorporated, a firm jointly owned with Montedision of Milan, Italy. At its creation, HIMONT was the world's

Hercules Incorporated's $90-million corporate headquarters, Hercules Plaza, was completed in 1983. It is an important part of the revitalization of downtown Wilmington.

The north side of Hercules Plaza has the keystone representing the Brandywine Gateway to downtown Wilmington.

largest producer of polypropylene resins.

Under the leadership of its sixth president, A.F. Giacco, Hercules began a more aggressive, progressive management style, and the corporation is now structured along product lines into three separate entities: Hercules Specialty Chemicals Company, composed of major business groups that represent the core of many long-established product lines; Hercules Aerospace Company, a major supplier of systems to governments and the aerospace industry; and Hercules Engineered and Fabricated Products Company, which produces value-added polypropylene products.

When Hercules was incorporated, it maintained its headquarters at Tenth and Market streets in Wilmington for five years, and then moved some of its corporate offices to Philadelphia. Subsequently, Hercules moved its headquarters back to Wilmington, occupying space in the Delaware Trust Building at Ninth and Market. In 1930 the company began construction of its current re-

The atrium of Hercules Plaza offers springtime all year, shopping, and restaurants for employees and the community.

search center located off Lancaster Pike in suburban New Castle County. Since then the center has been joined by the country club and marketing center. Together they cover over 1,000 acres and employ approximately 1,500 people.

In 1959, to accommodate the corporation's growth, the 22-story Hercules Tower was added to the Delaware Trust Building. In 1983 Hercules moved into its new corporate headquarters, Hercules Plaza, which houses 1,350 employees. The $90-million complex was pivotal in the revitalization of downtown Wilmington and is the keystone of the Brandywine (River) Gateway.

WILMINGTON TRUST COMPANY

Wilmington Trust Company was founded in 1903, the same year pioneers settled the Alaska frontier and President Theodore Roosevelt signed the Panama Canal treaty. That year several Wilmingtonians joined together to start a commercial banking venture.

The doors opened July 8, 1903, at 915 Market Street in the dining room and parlor of a former private residence. Led by T. Coleman du Pont, president and chairman, directors included George A. Capelle, A.J. Moxham, James P. Winchester, Henry P. Scott, Pierre S. du Pont, William S. Hilles, and Harlan G. Scott.

The general assembly authorized capital of one million dollars for the new venture, made up of 10,000 shares with a par value of $100. On opening day $500,000 was subscribed.

By 1907 the bank had outgrown its quarters and relocated to the prestigious new DuPont Company building at Tenth and Market streets. The building was financed through the issuance of first mortgage bonds on a corporation known as Wilmington Trust Building Corporation, with the Trust Department taking its first step in corporate trust services by serving as trustee under the bond. The building remained Wilmington Trust's headquarters for seventy-six years.

The new location was advantageous in many ways, but it was some distance from the center of commerce near the harbor of the Christina River. In 1912 Wilmington Trust moved closer to the river by merging with two other banks: National Bank of Wilmington & Brandywine, located at Second and Market streets, and First National Bank of Wilmington, located at Fifth and Market streets. That year du Pont was succeeded by Capelle as chairman of the board, and Winchester became president.

Capelle served until 1921, when he became honorary chairman, and was succeeded by Winchester as chairman. The new president was Henry P. Scott, another of the original directors. Scott's success as a securities

This elegant, three-story McComb-Winchester Mansion once graced the land on Rodney Square that Wilmington Trust Company now occupies.

broker helped the bank to evolve from a relatively small institution to a large enterprise, enabling, in 1929, the sale of additional stock. Because of the bank's excellent earnings record, the growth of the Trust Department, and the public's confidence in its management, rights were issued to the holders of the bank's 40,000 shares for each to purchase one additional share at $250. The new issue was fully subscribed and produced ten million dollars in funds at a time when many financial institutions were failing. Wilmington Trust remained strong through both the 1929 stock market crash and the Great Depression.

The company continued to prosper and by 1971 the stock had split twice. In 1945 there was a two-for-one split, increasing the number of shares to 160,000. In 1954 a four-for-one split, as well as the addition of stock through mergers, increased the number of shares to 992,400. The stock split again in 1985.

As business and trade moved away from lower Market Street during the 1930s, the office at Second and Market streets was closed. In 1943 Wil-

mington Trust acquired the Union National Bank; however, the office was closed temporarily during the remaining years of World War II due to a shortage of manpower.

Following the war Wilmington Trust merged with three more banks—St. George's Trust in Newport (1946), Claymont Trust Company (1949), and Farmer's Trust in Newark (1952). In 1953 branches were opened in Greenville and in the DuPont Company's Louviers Building. Two years later it acquired Industrial Trust in Wilmington, New Castle Trust, and Delaware City National Bank.

Wilmington Trust celebrated its fiftieth-anniversary year in 1953 issuing a special publication in which it described itself as "plain, hardworking . . . having a sound start, a healthy growth, an active present, and a challenging future." At that time the institution was processing 40,000 checks daily and there were 1,684 stockholders, three-quarters of them Delawareans.

In those first fifty years the bank added only five branch offices: in Claymont, Greenville, Newark, Louviers, and Newport. In 1959 it made its first move downstate by merging with the First National Bank and Trust in Milford, the Seaford Trust Company, and Georgetown Trust

Company.

Wilmington Trust continued to expand, opening new branches in Dover and Camden, as well as in north Wilmington during the 1960s. It also acquired the Townsend Trust Company and Citizen's Acceptance Corporation in Georgetown.

The first five years of the 1970s saw branch offices opened at Tri-State Mall, Greenville Center, which subsequently took over operations of the smaller Greenville office, Stanton, Limestone Road, Branmar Plaza, and the DuPont Company Brandywine Building—all in New Castle County. Elsewhere in the state, branches were opened in West Seaford, Middletown, and Dover. By 1975 Wilmington Trust Company had grown to thirty-one offices statewide.

The bank entered the travel business in 1974 with the purchase of Holiday Travel in Wilmington. Known today as Holiday Travel Agency, it is one of nine Wilmington Trust subsidiaries.

Internal departments, as well as the number of branch offices, were expanding rapidly. By 1978 the trust department was one of the largest in the country, with clients throughout the United States and in many foreign countries. Today the Trust Department is ranked sixteenth in the nation. Wilmington Trust remains one of the top 300 commercial banks nationwide.

The 1980s have brought great changes to the banking industry in Delaware. Wilmington Trust saluted the new spirit of business and government cooperation in a special section of its 1984 annual report to stockholders. Bernard J. Taylor II, chairman, and A. Samuel Gray, president, wrote: "Nowhere in the nation have we heard of a better blending of conditions which lead to attracting new companies, starting new

The new thirteen-story Wilmington Trust tower rises far above the neoclassical frontage of the Old Post Office.

businesses, and developing new jobs. All branches of the state and local government work ... to preserve and nurture the advantages of doing business in Delaware."

Banking legislation enacted by the state legislature, as well as deregulation by federal agencies have created new fields for venture by commercial banks. The changes include interbank networks of automated teller machines, discount brokerage services, money market deposit accounts, and asset/cash management accounts. In 1982 Wilmington Trust became the first bank in Delaware to offer in-house asset/cash management and discount brokerage services.

If T. Coleman du Pont were to walk up Market Street today he would find no trace of that small bank that he helped to establish eighty-two years ago. Today Wilmington Trust Company occupies the entire north block of Rodney Square, a site which has special meaning for the institution. From 1865 to 1933 the land was occupied by an elegant three-story mansion, home of Colonel Henry S. McComb, a successful manufacturer and railroad pioneer. One of his heirs, Jane Elizabeth McComb, married James P. Winchester, one of the bank's founders and chairman from 1921 to 1942. The mansion was razed in the late 1930s to make way for a building to house the U.S. Post Office, Court House, and Custom House.

Wilmington Trust Center now incorporates the neoclassical frontage of this building. Rising far above and behind it is the thirteen-story tower that houses the bank's headquarters. A bit of the mansion remains, in the form of the mahogany entrance doors that now lead into the bank's board room.

The modern Wilmington Trust Company is still a "hardworking" bank. Its 1,500 employees work in thirty-two offices statewide. There are now 8.50 million shares of stock in the hands of more than 4,500 stockholders—and the future still looks challenging.

ICI AMERICAS INC.

Headquartered in Wilmington, ICI Americas is the U.S. operating subsidiary of Imperial Chemical Industries PLC of London, England, one of the largest chemical firms in the world. ICI Americas products serve almost every major industry, including pharmaceuticals, agricultural chemicals, specialty chemicals, dyes and textile chemicals, plastics, films, electronics, advanced composites, petrochemicals, security devices, and aerospace components.

The firm has manufacturing sites, research and development facilities, and sales and technical offices across the United States. With sales of $1.5 billion in 1984, ICI Americas employs over 6,000 men and women. About half of the employees are located in Delaware at two manufacturing facilities and at the company's Fairfax headquarters, located north of Wilmington.

ICI Americas and its predecessors have been a part of the Wilmington scene since incorporation in 1912. The business was formed as a result of President Theodore "Teddy" Roosevelt's "trustbusting" crusade. The U.S. District Court ordered E.I. du Pont de Nemours and Company to spin off two of its operations, giving birth to the Hercules Powder Company and Atlas Powder Company, the forerunner of ICI Americas.

Atlas Powder opened for business on January 2, 1913, in the old DuPont Building in Wilmington, where its explosives business and

Employees of Atlas Powder Company joined in the celebration parade in Wilmington following World War I.

The corporate headquarters of ICI Americas Inc. is located in Wilmington.

product line steadily expanded. In 1921 Atlas moved to the Delaware Trust Building in Wilmington, remaining there until 1955, when the corporate headquarters was relocated to a newly constructed site in Fairfax.

In 1936, as Atlas research activities intensified, the company opened a research/development/manufacturing facility, Atlas Point, on the Delaware River near New Castle. The plant produces a broad range of specialty chemicals. Standing behind these products is an industry-wide reputation for excellence in surfactant chemistry and the know-how to help customers develop formulations for existing and specialty applications.

During the 1950s Atlas production and sales climbed. In 1952, at the request of the federal government, the firm contracted to operate the Volunteer Ordnance Works in Chattanooga, Tennessee. Today the company operates the Tennessee facility

as well as one in Charlestown, Indiana, under government contract.

Over the years Atlas continued to grow and expand. Diversification was the course for the future, and the firm's product line now included activated carbons, plastics, and other products. In 1961 Atlas expanded into the pharmaceuticals industry by acquiring the Stuart Company of Pasadena, California. That same year the firm's name was changed to Atlas Chemical Industries, Inc.

Ten years later Atlas, with sales of approximately $225 million, was acquired by Imperial Chemical Industries, and the corporation set its sights on becoming a major competitor for a growing range of innovative products in the U.S. marketplace. The pharmaceuticals business, in par-

ticular, is one area where steady expansion has occurred, much to the benefit of Delaware.

In 1971 the firm opened a pharmaceutical manufacturing facility adjacent to I-95 near Newark. From modest beginnings of just 97 employees, the plant has grown rapidly and now employs over 400 men and women. In addition, the plant has undergone several modernization and expansion programs that vastly improved manufacturing and packaging capabilities. Stuart Newark has one of the most sophisticated, computer-automated warehouses in the industry.

Today ICI Americas is positioned for growth based on science and technology, employees dedicated to quality and excellence, and world-wide resources. A corporation with a spirit of community pride and a commitment to economic progress, ICI Americas looks to the future with confidence.

ALICO

The sun never sets on one of Delaware's best-kept business secrets. The American Life Insurance Company (ALICO) is headquartered in the state, and, through its branches, subsidiaries, and affiliates, writes insurance in more than sixty countries worldwide. Its new headquarters is in the $26-million Christina Gateway Financial Center, but ALICO remains unknown to many Delawareans because it writes no policies in the United States. While it may seem unusual, ALICO's low profile among its neighbors has a logical basis; it sells no policies in Delaware, or in any other state.

It all started in 1921 when Cornelius Vander Starr, a 27-year-old Californian, traveled to Shanghai where he opened an agency called American Asiatic Underwriters. For two years he tried to acquire general agency powers from an American life insurance company. Insurers on this side of the Pacific were reluctant to take risks in a country where actuarial statistics were unknown. As a result, Starr formed his own firm, Asia Life Insurance Company.

Within twenty years of Starr's opening his agency, Shanghai was the insurance mecca of the Far East, and Starr was famed as one of the city's most successful entrepreneurs. In 1926 he opened an office in New York City to write insurance on American-owned risks in foreign countries. He also opened branches in Central and South America. It was these operations that kept his company stable through World War II.

In 1951 Asia Life was renamed American Life Insurance Company and moved to headquarters in Bermuda. Prior to that, the firm had opened new markets by serving American occupation troops stationed in Japan and Germany.

Surviving in countries where political strife is common presents few problems for ALICO, according to company president Richard R. Collins. Respect for local customs and a preponderance of staff members native to the country in which

From 1969 to 1985 the acclaimed American International Building, designed by I.M. Pei, was the world headquarters for ALICO.

they serve keeps problems at a minimum. Additionally, ALICO has found that people buy insurance regardless of their country's economic stability.

Occasionally, as in Iran, political turmoil does threaten business. ALICO's operations in that country were seized in 1979 by the revolutionary government, and for a short time it held Collins under house arrest. Collins was in charge of the Iran office in Tehran. Although he was held for only twenty-four hours of interrogation, the remaining three months in Iran were tense and un-

pleasant. He was able to leave in June 1979 after convincing the revolutionaries that he was not a spy. ALICO currently maintains its Middle East headquarters in Cyprus where there have been no problems.

A life insurance company serving a global community has to be unique. The same policy that sells in Guyana may hold no appeal to the citizens of Argentina. As a result, ALICO fash-

ions its policies in a multitude of shapes and sizes tailored to meet local needs. All are written in the local language, and the reserves of the policyholders are always invested in their own country and in their own currency.

It was Starr's amazing business acumen and leadership for forty years that resulted in the firm's phenomenal growth. He began in a two-room office in Shanghai, selling twenty-year endowment policies. At the time of his death in 1968, the old American Asiatic Underwriters had gone through several name changes and acquisitions. It became ALICO in 1951 after Starr radically reorganized Asia Life and turned its corporate sights on writing policies in the Caribbean, Middle East, and emerging African nations.

Beginning in 1948 the firm's business was managed from world headquarters in Bermuda. In 1969 the favorable corporate climate in Delaware attracted ALICO. Its move to the acclaimed American International

Building, designed by I.M. Pei, was accomplished when thirty-five employees and 87.5 tons of paper were installed in the distinctive tower building at Twelfth and Market streets. In 1985 ALICO's 500 employees moved to the company's new ten-story building in the Christina Gateway. This move was the culmination of a successful four-way partnership that involved state and local governments, as well as ALICO's parent company, AIG.

The City of Wilmington assisted ALICO in financing the $26-million project by authorizing a $10-million Industrial Revenue Bond, securing a $1.5-million Urban Development Action Grant from the U.S. Department of Housing and Urban Development, and guaranteeing revenue bonds for the parking garage. In addition, the Delaware General Assembly appropriated funds through the state capital bond bill to purchase land and improve the public amenities surrounding ALICO Plaza.

The building, at One ALICO Pla-

An artist's rendering of the firm's new headquarters, occupied in 1985, in the Christina Gateway Financial Center.

za, features a distinctive illuminated semicircular driveway by which the main entrance lobby and granite-paved forecourt are approached. There are nine floors of offices and a tenth-floor penthouse training center. Beneath the building is a 500-car parking garage.

ALICO's 1984 year-end report reflected the company's energy and commitment to excellence. The new home office in Wilmington was only one of its construction projects. Buildings were completed in Kenya and Greece and will soon be finished in the Dominican Republic and Japan.

ALICO is moving into the 1980s with a giant step forward—its new corporate headquarters and a growth in excess of 25 percent. Both reflect the firm's commitment to the kind of flexibility that encourages creativity and expansion.

GEORGE D. HANBY CO., INC.

America was still in the throes of the Great Depression when George Dewey Hanby opened the doors of his office stationery store in 1932. Young Hanby moved into a small store at 825 Market Street in Wilmington, where he and three employees shared a cramped four- by ten-foot office. The employees were his wife, Gertrude, his father, George, and a secretary, Maxine Barratt.

In those days it was largely a walk-in clientele who came to the store to select stationery needs. The biggest demand was for gallon bottles of ink, blotting paper, account books, and fountain pens. Orders to be delivered were packed into the family car and dispersed by Mrs. Hanby and her father-in-law.

George D. Hanby Co., Inc., is still a thriving business, but the supplies that were in the greatest demand fifty-two years ago have nearly vanished. Company vice-president Ray Thompson says 40 percent of today's sales volume hadn't even been invented fifteen years ago. Current customers buy felt-tip pens, pocket calculators, self-sticking labels and note pads, carbonless carbon paper, and liquid correction fluid. Hardly anyone asks for blotters anymore.

In 1937 George Hanby moved his firm to larger quarters at 919 Market Street and hired the company's first outside salesman, Joseph R. Truitt. Before his retirement in 1978, Truitt was a vice-president, managing the firm's office furniture division, which opened in 1943 at 805 Shipley Street.

Today Hanby has four operating divisions: 921 Market Street and Price's Corner Center, both retail stores; a furniture division, located at 805 Shipley Street; and commercial office supplies, located at 917 South Herald Street. The products of the last two divisions are sold by Hanby's eleven outside sales representatives.

However, it is still a family business. Mildred Hanby Thompson, her husband, Ray, and their son, George A., work from corporate offices at 921 Market Street.

Steady growth has characterized the firm's image, and the Thompsons are proud of the loyalty of many of their employees. Maxine Barratt retired in 1979 after forty "odd" years with Hanby. At the time of her retirement, she was treasurer of the company. Ed Keeling still works for Hanby, having been associated with the firm almost steadily since 1940.

George Hanby died in 1957, and Ray Thompson joined the firm the following year. Mrs. Thompson has served the company in several capacities. She worked during the mid-1940s selling in Hanby's greeting card department. Until 1983, when the department was abolished, Hanby had one of the city's largest greeting card selections.

This office supply company that used to deliver six quarts of ink weekly to Wilmington Trust has grown and changed as the needs of its customers have changed. Gone are the stacks of mimeograph paper and bins of fountain pens. Today's buyers want felt-tip and ball-point pens, and supplies for data-processing and word-processing equipment.

During the 1960s and 1970s Hanby found itself needing a general contractor's license in order to fully service its customers. It filled a vacuum for several years before there were many interior designers and before most architects in the area became involved in interior design by planning the floor space, then installing the furniture.

Because of one of its customers, the DuPont Company, Hanby became one of the first in the United States to install systems furniture. In 1967 the concept of "office landscaping" was imported to Wilmington by DuPont executives who had traveled in Europe. Representatives of DuPont had admired systems furniture in European offices. Office landscaping, the forerunner of today's systems furniture, utilized modular furniture to design flexible work areas.

The firm has installed systems furniture in several New Castle County offices, including DuPont's Centre Road and Barley Mill Plaza sites, and several of the new banks. During the period when the firm held a general contractor's license it also supervised the interior work for the Delaware Trust Plaza on Delaware Avenue in Wilmington.

In 1963 Hanby opened its Prices Corner store in Elsmere to serve the many small business owners in suburban New Castle County who preferred shopping center facilities. The office furniture division, at 805 Shipley Street, is still the hub for all sales of business furniture. Hanby also maintains three warehouses.

Many customers still stream through the doors, continuing George D. Hanby Co.'s high volume of walk-in business. But today there are also nearly a dozen sales representatives who call on customers throughout New Castle County.

The opening of the 921 Market Street Mall store took place in September 1967. Pictured (from left to right) are Ray Thompson, Wilmington Mayor John Babiarz, Gertrude Hanby, and George Thompson.

PATRONS

The following individuals, companies, and organizations have made a valuable commitment to the quality of this publication. Windsor Publications and the Delaware State Chamber of Commerce gratefully acknowledge their participation in *The First State: An Illustrated History of Delaware.*

ALICO*
All American Engineering Company*
American Hoechst Corporation*
Artesian Water Company, Inc.*
Artisans' Savings Bank
Association of Delaware Hospitals, Inc.*
Baltimore Trust Company*
Bank of Delaware*
Barratt's Chapel Museum
the BARTLEY group
Beneficial Corporation*
Blue Cross Blue Shield of Delaware*
George H. Burns, Inc.
Caldwell Temporary Services
Chemical Bank (Delaware)
CHIORINO, Inc.
Chrysler Corporation*
Citibank (Delaware)*
The Clayton Bank & Trust Company
Commonwealth Trust Company/Commonwealth
    Management Corporation*
Computer Communications of America
Corporation Service Company
The Delaware Heritage Commission
Delaware Humanities Council, Inc.
Delle Donne & Associates*
Delmarva Power and Light Company*
Diamond State Telephone*
Ernest DiSabatino & Sons, Inc.
E.I. du Pont de Nemours and Company*
First National Bank of Wilmington
Fort Delaware Society
Franklin Fibre - Lamitex Corp.
Friends of the Smyrna Public Library
Ed & Betty Furjanic
General Motors*
George & Lynch, Inc.*
Mr. & Mrs. N.R. Gianoulis
Gilpin, Van Trump & Montgomery, Inc.*
Goldey Beacom College*
W.L. Gore and Associates, Inc.*
Grand Opera House*
Charles S. Haas
George D. Hanby Co., Inc.*

Hercules Incorporated*
Hotel Du Pont*
George H. Huber Coatings, Inc.
ICI Americas Inc.*
Kirkwood Tires, Inc.
Mr. and Mrs. Ellice McDonald, Jr.
Marine Midland Bank (Delaware), N.A.
Maryland Bank, N.A.
Megee Plumbing & Heating Co.
Mellon Bank Delaware*
METL-PRES, Inc.
Milford Historical Society
Mitchell Associates, Inc.*
Morris, Nichols, Arsht & Tunnell
Nanticoke Homes, Inc.*
Newark Newsstand
The News-Journal Company*
Jan Nibblett-Accountant
R.C. Nibblett Builders
Ralph G. Degli Obizzi, Inc.
Old Dinner Bell Inn, Inc.
Pepsi-Cola Bottling Co. of Wilmington
R.W. Peters, Rickel & Co., Inc.
Porter Sand & Gravel, Inc.
Potter Anderson & Corroon
Prickett, Jones, Elliott, Kristol & Schnee*
RLC Corp.*
Rollins Environmental Services, Inc.*
Sears Roebuck Acceptance Corp.
The Seasons
Joseph J. Sheeran, Inc.
Sheraton Inn - Dover
The Sussex Trust Company
Thornley Company, Inc.
Townsend's, Inc.*
Tull Brothers, Inc.
United Electric Supply
University of Delaware*
Wassam's, Inc.
William M. Young Company
WILM NEWSRADIO*
Wilmington Trust Company*

*Partners in Progress of *The First State: An Illustrated History of Delaware.* The histories of these companies and organizations appear in Chapter 8, beginning on page 158.

BIBLIOGRAPHY

The best modern comprehensive histories of Delaware are John A. Munroe's *History of Delaware* (1984), which is a chronological treatment, and Carol E. Hoffecker's *Delaware: A Bicentennial History* (1977), which has a topical format. Also of interest is Roger A. Martin's, *A History of Delaware Through Its Governors, 1776-1984* (1984). A two-volume, collaborative work edited by H. Clay Reed, *Delaware: A History of the First State* (1947) focuses on a number of topics important to understanding Delaware's past. J. Thomas Scharf's two-volume *History of Delaware, 1609-1888*, is crammed full of facts, but they are not always accurate.

A History of Kent County, Delaware (1976) and *The History of Sussex County, Delaware* (1976), both written by Harold Hancock, give a brief look at downstate Delaware. A detailed analytical treatment of Wilmington's past is found in Carol E. Hoffecker's *Wilmington, Delaware: Portrait of an Industrial City* (1974) and in *Corporate Capital: Wilmington in the Twentieth Century* (1983).

For the history of Delaware during the colonial period, see John A. Munroe, *Colonial Delaware* (1978). Studies of the Delaware and Nanticoke Indians may be found among the assorted works of C. A. Weslager. John A. Munroe's *Federalist Delaware* (1954), Harold Hancock's *The Loyalists of Revolutionary Delaware* (1977), and William H. Williams' *The Garden of American Methodism: The Delmarva Peninsula, 1769-1820* (1984), all deal with the post-colonial era. John A. Munroe's *Louis McLane: Federalist and Jacksonian* (1973) and Harold Hancock's *Delaware During the Civil War* (1962) focus on the nineteenth century. A thorough study of the emerging Du Pont Company in the early twentieth century is *Pierre S. du Pont and the Making of the Modern Corporation* (1971) written by Alfred D. Chandler and Stephen Salsbury. For a look at downstate Delaware and Governor John G. Townsend during the same period, readers are advised to examine Richard Carter's *Clearing New Ground* (1984). A recent

treatment of public school integration in New Castle County can be found in Part Four of Raymond Wolters' *The Burden of Brown: Thirty Years of School Desegregation* (1984). For a comprehensive history of the University of Delaware see John A. Munroe, *History of the University of Delaware* (1985).

A detailed bibliography of Delaware history can be found in the back of John A. Munroe's *History of Delaware*.

The New Castle and Frenchtown Railroad began operations in 1831. The railroad at first used horses to pull its fancy coaches. The company imported an engine from England in 1832 and assembled it in its New Castle shops. Courtesy, Historical Society of Delaware

INDEX